Parents and Children

1.0.2

This edition published 2017
By Living Book Press
147 Durren Rd, Jilliby, 2259

Copyright © Living Book Press, 2017

National Library of Australia Cataloguing-in-Publication entry:

Creator: Mason, Charlotte, author.
Title: Parents and Children / Charlotte Mason.
ISBN: 9780648063384 (paperback)
Series: Home education series : bk 2.
Subjects: Home schooling.
           Education--Parent participation.

'Home Education' Series

VOLUME II.

Parents and Children

By

Charlotte M. Mason

LIVING BOOK PRESS

'Home Education' Series
By Charlotte M. Mason

Available from Living Book Press
—
www.LivingBookPress.com

The role of the parent in the education of a child

Preface to the 'Home Education' Series

THE educational outlook is rather misty and depressing both at home and abroad. That science should be a staple of education, that the teaching of Latin, of modern languages, of mathematics, must be reformed, that nature and handicrafts should be pressed into service for the training of the eye and hand, that boys and girls must learn to write English and therefore must know something of history and literature; and, on the other hand, that education must be made more technical and utilitarian—these, and such as these, are the cries of expedience with which we take the field. But we have no unifying principle, no definite aim; in fact, no philosophy of education. As a stream can rise no higher than its source, so it is probable that no educational effort can rise above the whole scheme of thought which gives it birth; and perhaps this is the reason of all the 'fallings from us, vanishings,' failures, and disappointments which mark our educational records.

Those of us, who have spent many years in pursuing the benign and elusive vision of Education, perceive that her approaches are regulated by a law, and that this law has yet to be evoked. We can discern its outlines, but no more. We know that it is pervasive; there is no part of a child's home-life or school-work which the law does not penetrate. It is illuminating, too, showing the value, or lack of value, of a thousand systems and expedients. It is not only a light, but a measure, providing a standard whereby all things, small and great, belonging to educational work must be tested. The law is liberal, taking in whatsoever things are true, honest, and of good report, and offering no limitation or hindrance save where excess should injure. And the path indicated by the law is continuous and progressive, with no transition stage from the cradle to the grave, except that maturity takes up the regular self-direction to which immaturity has been trained. We shall doubtless find, when we apprehend the law, that certain German thinkers— Kant, Herbart, Lotze, Froebel—are justified; that, as they say, it is 'necessary' to believe in God; that, therefore, the knowledge of God is the principal know- ledge, and the chief end of education. By one more character shall we be able to recognise this perfect law of educational liberty when it shall be made evident. It has been said that 'The best idea which we can form of absolute truth is that it is able to meet every condition by which it can be tested.' This we shall expect of our law—that it shall meet every test of experiment and every test of rational investigation.

Not having received the tables of our law, we fall back upon Froebel or upon Herbart; or, if we belong to another School, upon Locke or Spencer; but we are not satisfied. A discontent, is it a divine discontent? is upon us; and assuredly we should hail a workable, effectual philosophy of education as a deliverance from much perplexity. Before this great deliverance comes to us it is probable that many tentative efforts will be put forth, having more or less of the characters of a philosophy; notably, having a central idea, a body of thought with various members working in vital harmony.

Such a theory of education, which need not be careful to call itself a system of psychology, must be in harmony with the thought movements of the age; must regard education, not as a shut-off compartment, but as being as much a part of life as birth or growth, marriage or work; and it must leave the pupil attached to the world at many points of contact. It is true that educationalists are already eager to establish such contact in several directions, but their efforts rest upon an axiom here and an idea there, and there is no broad unifying basis of thought to support the whole.

Fools rush in where angels fear to tread; and the hope that there may be many tentative efforts towards a philosophy of education, and that all of them will bring us nearer to the *magnum opus,* encourages me to launch one such attempt. The central thought, or rather body of thought, upon which I found, is the somewhat obvious fact that the child is a *person* with all the possibilities and powers included in personality. Some of the members which develop from this nucleus have been exploited from time to time by educational thinkers, and exist vaguely in the general common sense, a notion here, another there. One thesis, which is, perhaps, new, that *Education is the Science of Relations*, appears to me to solve the question of a curriculum, as showing that the object of education is to put a child in living touch with as much as may be of the life of Nature and of thought. Add to this one or two keys to self-knowledge, and the educated youth goes forth with some idea of self-management, with some pursuits, and many vital interests. My excuse for venturing to offer a solution, however tentative and passing, to the problem of education is twofold. For between thirty and forty years I have laboured without pause to establish a working and philosophic theory of education; and in the next place, each article of the educational faith I offer has been arrived at by inductive processes; and has, I think, been verified by a long and wide series of experiments. It is, however, with sincere diffidence that I venture to offer the results of this long labour; because I know that in this field there are many labourers far more able and expert than I—the 'angels' who fear to tread, so precarious is the footing!

But, if only *pour encourager les autres*, I append a short synopsis of the educational theory advanced in the volumes of the 'Home Education Series.' The treatment is not methodic, but incidental; here a little, there a little, as seemed to me most likely to meet the occasions of parents and teachers. I should add that in the course of a number of years the various essays have been prepared for the use of the Parents' Educational Union in the hope that that Society might witness for a more or less coherent body of educational thought.

> "The consequence of truth is great; therefore the judgment of it must not be negligent."
>
> WHICHCOTE.

1. Children are born *persons*.

2. They are not born either good or bad, but with possibilities for good and evil.

3. The principles of authority on the one hand and obedience on the other, are natural, necessary and fundamental; but—

4. These principles are limited by the respect due to the personality of children, which must not be encroached upon, whether by fear or love, suggestion or influence, or undue play upon any one natural desire.

5. Therefore we are limited to three educational instruments—the atmosphere of environment, the discipline of habit, and the presentation of living ideas.

6. By the saying, EDUCATION IS AN ATMO-SPHERE, it is not meant that a child should be isolated in what may be called a 'child environment,'

especially adapted and prepared; but that we should take into account the educational value of his natural home atmosphere, both as regards persons and things, and should let him live freely among his proper conditions. It stultifies a child to bring down his world to the 'child's' level.

7. By EDUCATION IS A DISCIPLINE, is meant the discipline of habits formed definitely and thoughtfully, whether habits of mind or body. Physiologists tell us of the adaptation of brain structure to habitual lines of thought—*i.e.*, to our habits.

8. In the saying that EDUCATION IS A LIFE, the need of intellectual and moral as well as of physical sustenance is implied. The mind feeds on ideas, and therefore children should have a generous curriculum.

9. But the mind is not a receptacle into which ideas must be dropped, each idea adding to an 'apperception mass' of its like, the theory upon which the Herbartian doctrine of interest rests.

10. On the contrary, a child's mind is no mere *sac* to hold ideas; but is rather, if the figure may be allowed, a spiritual *organism*, with an appetite for all knowledge. This is its proper diet, with which it is prepared to deal, and which it can digest and assimilate as the body does foodstuffs.

11. This difference is not a verbal quibble. The Herbartian doctrine lays the stress of education— the preparation of knowledge in enticing morsels, presented in due order—upon the teacher. Children

taught upon this principle are in danger of receiving much teaching with little knowledge; and the teacher's axiom is, 'What a child learns matters less than how he learns it.'

12. But, believing that the normal child has powers of mind that fit him to deal with all knowledge proper to him, we must give him a full and generous curriculum; taking care, only, that the knowledge offered to him is vital—that is, that facts are not presented without their informing ideas. Out of this conception comes the principle that,—

13. EDUCATION IS THE SCIENCE OF RELATIONS; that is, that a child has natural relations with a vast number of things and thoughts: so we must train him upon physical exercises, nature, handicrafts, science and art, and upon *many living* books; for we know that our business is, not to teach him all about anything, but to help him to make valid as many as may be of—

'Those first-born affinities,

That fit our new existence to existing things.'

14. There are also two secrets of moral and intellectual self-management which should be offered to children; these we may call the Way of the Will and the Way of the Reason.

15. *The Way of the Will*—Children should be taught—

(*a*) To distinguish between 'I want' and 'I will.'

(*b*) That the way to will effectively is to turn our

thoughts from that which we desire but do not will.

(c) That the best way to turn our thoughts is to think of or do some quite different thing, entertaining or interesting.

(d) That, after a little rest in this way, the will returns to its work with new vigour. (This adjunct of the will is familiar to us as *diversion*, whose office it is to ease us for a time from will effort, that we may 'will' again with added power. The use of suggestion— even self-suggestion—as an aid to the will, is to be deprecated, as tending to stultify and stereotype character. It would seem that spontaneity is a condition of development, and that human nature needs the discipline of failure as well as of success).

16. *The Way of the Reason.*—We should teach children, too, not to 'lean' (too confidently) 'unto their own understanding.' because the function of reason is, to give logical demonstration (a) of mathematical truth; and (b) of an initial idea, accepted by the will. In the former case reason is, perhaps, an infallible guide, but in the second it is not always a safe one; for whether that initial idea be right or wrong, reason will confirm it by irrefragable proofs.

17. Therefore children should be taught, as they become mature enough to understand such teaching, that the chief responsibility which rests on them as persons is the acceptance or rejection of initial ideas.

To help them in this choice we should give them principles of conduct and a wide range of the knowledge fitted for them.

These three principles (15, 16 and 17) should save children from some of the loose thinking and heedless action which cause most of us to live at a lower level than we need.

18. We should allow no separation to grow up between the intellectual and 'spiritual' life of children; but should teach them that the divine Spirit has constant access to their spirits, and is their continual helper in all the interests, duties and joys of life.

The 'Home Education' Series is so called from the title of the first volume, and not as dealing, wholly or principally, with 'Home' as opposed to 'School' education.

Preface to the Third Edition

OUR conduct is the outcome of our principles, even if these be only such as—'It does not matter'; 'What's the good?'

Every office implies the observance of certain fundamental principles in its discharge.

These two considerations lead me to think that a careful examination of the principles which naturally and necessarily underlie the office of parents may be of some little use to those who take their great work seriously.

Believing that the individuality of parents is a great possession for their children, and knowing that when an idea possesses the mind, ways of applying it suggest themselves, I have tried not to weight these pages with many directions, practical suggestions, and other such crutches, likely to interfere with the free relations of parent and child. Our greatness as a nation depends upon how far parents take liberal and enlightened views of their high office and of the means to discharge it which are placed in their hands.

The following essays have appeared in the *Parents' Review,* and were addressed, from time to time, to a body of parents who are making a practical study of the principles of education—the 'Parents' National Educational Union. 'The Parents' Union exists to advance, with more or less method and with more or less steadfastness, a definite school of educational thought of which the two main principles are—the recognition of the physical basis of habit, *i.e.*, of the material side of education; and of the inspiring and formative power of ideas, *i.e.*, of the immaterial, or spiritual, side of education. These two guiding principles, covering as they do the whole field of human nature, should enable us to deal rationally with all the complex problems of education; and the object of the following essays is, not to give an exhaustive application of these principles—the British Museum itself would hardly contain all the volumes needful for such an undertaking—but to give an example or a suggestion, here and there, as to how such and such a habit may be formed, such and such a formative idea be implanted and fostered. The intention of the volume will account to the reader for the iteration of the same principles in various connections. The author ventures to hope that the following hints and suggestions will not prove the less practically useful to busy parents, because they rest on profound educational principles; and also, that they may prove in some degree, suggestive and inspiring to teachers.

AMBLESIDE,

May 1904.

Contents

CHAPTER I

THE FAMILY

Rousseau succeeded in arousing parents—The family a commune—The family must be social—The family must serve poorer neighbours—The family must serve the nation —The Divine order for the family as regards other nations- The family should (*a*) learn languages; (*b*) show courtesy abroad—The restoration of the family

CHAPTER II

PARENTS AS RULERS

The family government an absolute monarchy—The rule of parents cannot be deputed—Causes which lead to the abdication of parents—The majesty of parenthood—Children a public trust and a divine trust—The limitations and scope of parental authority

CHAPTER III

PARENTS AS INSPIRERS

Children must be born again into the Life of Intelligence

Parents owe a second birth to their children—Science supports this contention—Processes and methods of this second birth —Dr Maudsley on heredity—Disposition and character- Dr Maudsley on the structural effects of 'particular life experiences'—Our age has acquired a great educational charter—Some articles of this charter

CHAPTER IV

PARENTS AS INSPIRERS

The Life of the Mind grows upon Ideas

CHAPTER V

PARENTS AS INSPIRERS

The Things of the Spirit

CHAPTER VI

PARENTS AS INSPIRERS

Primal Ideas derived from Parents

CHAPTER VII

THE PARENT AS SCHOOLMASTER

CHAPTER VIII

THE CULTURE OF CHARACTER

Parents as Trainers

CHAPTER IX

The Culture of Character

The Treatment of Defects

CHAPTER X

Bible Lessons

Parents as Instructors in Religion

CHAPTER XI

Faith and Duty (Review)

Parents as Teachers of Morals

CHAPTER XII

FAITH AND DUTY (*Review*)

Claims of Philosophy as an Instrument of Education

CHAPTER XIII

FAITH AND DUTY (*Review*)

Man lives by Faith, Godward and Manward

CHAPTER XIV

THE HEROIC IMPULSE (*Review*)

Parents are concerned to give this Impulse

CHAPTER XV

IS IT POSSIBLE? (*Review*)

The Attitude of Parents towards Social Questions

CHAPTER XVI

DISCIPLINE

A Consideration for Parents

CHAPTER XVII

SENSATIONS AND FEELINGS

Sensations educable by Parents

CHAPTER XVIII

SENSATIONS AND FELLINGS

Feelings educable by Parents

CHAPTER XIX

' What is Truth?'

Moral Discrimination required by Parents

CHAPTER XX

Show Cause Why

Parents Responsible for Competitive Examinations

CHAPTER XXI

A Theory of Education Proposed to Parents

CHAPTER XXII

A CATECHISM OF EDUCATIONAL THEORY

CHAPTER XXIII

WHENCE AND WHITHER

A Question for Parents. Whence

CHAPTER XXIV

WHENCE AND WHITHER

Whither

CHAPTER XXV

THE GREAT RECOGNITION REQUIRED OF PARENTS

CHAPTER XXVI

THE ETERNAL CHILD

The Highest Counsel of Perfection for Parents

Parents and Children

CHAPTER I

THE FAMILY

'The family is the unit of the nation.'—F. D. MAURICE.

Rousseau succeeded in awaking Parents.—It is probable that no other educational thinker has succeeded in affecting parents so profoundly as did Rousseau. *Emile* is little read now, but how many current theories of the regimen proper for children have there their unsuspected source? Everybody knows—and his contemporaries knew it better than we—that Jean Jacques Rousseau had not enough sterling character to warrant him to pose as an authority on any subject, least of all on that of education. He sets himself down a poor thing, and we see no cause to reject the evidence of his *Confessions*. We are not carried away by the charm of his style; his 'forcible feebleness' does not dazzle us. No man can say beyond that which he *is*, and there is a want of grit in his philosophic theories that removes most of them from the category of available thought.

But Rousseau had the insight to perceive one of
those patent truths which, somehow, it takes a genius
to discover; and, because truth is indeed prized above
rubies, the perception of that truth gave him rank
as a great teacher. Is *Jean Jacques* also among the
prophets? People asked, and ask still; and that he
had thousands of fervent disciples amongst the educated parents of Europe, together with the fact that
his teaching has filtered into many a secluded home
of our own day, is answer enough. Indeed, no other
educationalist has had a tithe of the influence exercised by Rousseau. Under the spell of his teaching,
people in the fashionable world, like that Russian
Princess Galitzin, forsook society, and went off with
their children to some quiet corner where they could
devote every hour of the day, and every power they
had, to the fulfilment of the duties which devolve
upon parents. Courtly mothers retired from the
world, sometimes even left their husbands, to work
hard at the classics, mathematics, sciences, that they
might with their own lips instruct their children.
'What else am I for?' they asked; and the feeling
spread that the bringing-up of their children was
the one work of primary importance for men and
women.

Whatever extravagance he had seen fit to advance,
Rousseau would still have found a following, because
he had chanced to touch a spring that opened many
hearts. He was one of the few educationalists who
made his appeal to the parental instincts. He did not
say, 'We have no hope of the parents, let us work
for the children!' Such are the faint-hearted and
pessimistic things we say to-day. What he said was,
in effect, 'Fathers and mothers, this is your work,

and you only can do it. It rests with you, parents of young children, to be the saviours of society unto a thousand generations. Nothing else matters. The avocations about which people weary themselves are as foolish child's play compared with this one serious business of bringing up our children in advance of ourselves.'

People listened, as we have seen; the response to his teaching was such a letting-out of the waters of parental enthusiasm as has never been known before nor since. And Rousseau, weak and little worthy, was a preacher of righteousness in this, that he turned the hearts of the fathers to the children, and so far made ready a people prepared for the Lord. But alas! having secured the foundation, he had little better than wood, hay, and stubble to offer to the builders.

Rousseau succeeded, as he deserved to succeed, in awaking many parents to the binding character, the vast range, the profound seriousness of parental obligations. He failed, and deserved to fail, as he offered his own crude conceits by way of an educational code. But his success is very cheering. He perceived that God placed the training of every child in the hands of two, a father and a mother; and the response to his teaching proved that, as the waters answer to the drawing of the moon, so do the hearts of parents rise to the idea of the great work committed to them.

Though it is true, no doubt, that every parent is conscious of unwritten laws, more or less definite and noble according to his own status, yet an attempt, however slight, to codify these laws may be interesting to parents.

The Family a Commune.—'The family is the unit of the nation.' This pregnant saying suggests some aspects of the parents' calling. From time to time, in all ages of the world, communistic societies have arisen, sometimes for the sake of co-operation in a great work, social or religious, more recently by way of protest against inequalities of condition; but, in every case, the fundamental rule of such societies is, that the members shall have all things in common. We are apt to think, in our careless way, that such attempts at communistic association are foredoomed to failure. But that is not the case. In the United States, perhaps because hired labour is less easy to obtain than it is with us, they appear to have found a congenial soil, and there many well-regulated communistic bodies flourish. There are failures, too, many and disastrous, and it appears that these may usually be traced to one cause, a government enfeebled by the attempt to combine democratic and communistic principles; that is, to dwell together in a common life, while each does what is right in his own eyes. A communistic body can thrive only under a vigorous and absolute rule.

A favourite dream of socialism is—or was until the idea of collectivism obtained—that each State of Europe should be divided into an infinite number of small self-contained communes. Now, it sometimes happens that the thing we desire is already realised had we eyes to see. The family is, practically, a commune. In the family the undivided property is enjoyed by all the members in common, and in the family there is equality of social condition, with diversity of duties. In lands where patriarchal practices still obtain, the family merges into the tribe, and the head of the family is the chief of the tribe—a very absolute sovereign indeed. In our own country, families are usually small, parents and their immediate offspring; with the attendants and belongings which naturally gather to a household, and, let it not be forgotten, *form part of the family.* The smallness of the family tends to obscure its character, and we see no force in the phrase at the head of this chapter; we do not perceive that, if the unit of the nation is the natural commune, the family; then, is the family pledged to carry on within itself all the functions of the State, with the delicacy, precision, and fulness of detail proper to work done on a small scale.

The Family must be Social.—It by no means follows from this communistic view of the family that the domestic policy should be a policy of isolation; on the contrary, it is not too much to say that a nation is civilised in proportion as it is able to establish close and friendly relations with other nations; and that, not with one or two, but with many; and, conversely, that a nation is barbarous in proportion to its isolation; and does not a family decline in intelligence and virtue when from generation to generation it 'keeps itself to itself'?

The Family must serve Neighbours.—Again, it is probable that a nation is healthy in proportion as it has its own proper outlets, its colonies and dependencies, which it is ever solicitous to include in the national life. So of the nation in miniature, the family: the struggling families at 'the back,' the orphanage, the mission, the necessitous of our acquaintance, are they not for the sustenance of the family in the higher life?

The Family must serve the Nation.—But it is not enough that the family commune maintain neighbourly relations with other such communes, and towards the stranger within the gates. The family is the unit of the nation; and the nation is an organic whole, a living body, built up, like the natural body, of an infinite number of living organisms. It is only as it contributes its quota towards the national life that the life of the family is complete. Public interests must be shared, public work taken up, the public welfare cherished—in a word, its integrity with the nation must be preserved, or the family ceases to be part of a living whole, and becomes positively injurious, as decayed tissue in the animal organism.

The Divine Order for the Family as regards other Nations.—Nor are the interests of the family limited to those of the nation. As it is the part of the nation to maintain wider relations, to be in touch with all the world, to be ever in advance in the great march of human progress, so is this the attitude which is incumbent on each unit of the nation, each family, as an integral part of the whole. Here is the simple and natural realisation of the noble dream of *Fraternity*: each individual attached to a family by ties of love where not of blood; the families united in a federal bond to form the nation; the nations confederate in love and emulous in virtue, and all, nations and their families, playing their several parts as little children about the feet and under the smile of the Almighty Father. Here is the divine order which every family is called upon to fulfil: a little leaven leaveneth the whole lump, and, therefore, it matters infinitely that every family should realise the nature and the obligations of the family bond, for as water cannot rise above its source, neither can we live at a higher level than that of the conception we form of our place and use in life.

The Family should (*a*) learn Languages; (*b*) show Courtesy abroad.—Let us ask the question: Has this, of regarding all education and all civil and social relations from the standpoint of the *family*, any practical outcome? So much so, that perhaps there is hardly a problem of life for which it does not contain the solution. For example: What shall we teach our children? Is there one subject that claims our attention more than another? Yes, there is a subject or class of subjects which has an imperative *moral* claim upon us. It is the duty of the nation to maintain relations of brotherly kindness with other nations; therefore it is the duty of every family, as an integral part of the nation, to be able to hold brotherly speech with the families of other nations as opportunities arise; therefore to acquire the speech of neighbouring nations is not only to secure an inlet of knowledge and a means of culture, but is a duty of that higher morality (the morality of the family) which aims at universal brotherhood; therefore every family would do well to cultivate two languages besides the mother tongue, even in the nursery.

Again; a fair young Englishwoman was staying with her mother at a German *Kurhaus*. They were the only English people present, and probably forgot that the Germans are better linguists than we. The young lady sat through the long meals with her book, hardly interrupting her reading to eat, and addressing no more than one or two remarks to her mother, as

—'I wonder what that mess is!' or, 'How much longer shall we have to sit with these tiresome people?' Had she remembered that no family can live to itself, that she and her mother represented England, *were* England for that little German community, she would have imitated the courteous greetings which the German ladies bestowed on their neighbours.

The Restoration of the Family.—But we must leave further consideration of this great subject, and conclude with a striking passage from Mr Morley's Appreciation of *Emile*. "Education slowly came to be thought of in connection with the family. The improvement of ideas upon education was only one phase of the great general movement towards the restoration of the family, which was so striking a spectacle in France after the middle of the century. Education now came to comprehend the whole system of the relations between parents and their children, from earliest infancy to maturity. The direction of such wider feeling about those relations tended strongly towards an increased closeness in them, more intimacy, and a more continuous suffusion of tenderness and long attachment."

His labours in this great cause, 'the restoration of the family,' give Rousseau a claim upon the gratitude and respect of mankind. It has proved a lasting, solid work. To this day, family relations in France are more gracious, more tender, more close and more inclusive, than they are with us. They are more expansive too, leading to generally benign and friendly behaviour; and so strong and satisfying is the family bond, that the young people find little necessity to' fall in love.' The mother lays herself out for the friendship of her young daughters, who respond with entire loyalty and devotion; and, Zola notwithstanding, French maidens are wonderfully pure, simple, and sweet, because their affections are abundantly satisfied.

Possibly 'the restoration of the family' is a labour that invites us here in England, each within the radius of our own hearth; for there is little doubt that the family bond is more lax amongst us than it was two or three generations ago. Perhaps nowhere is family life of more idyllic loveliness than where we see it at its best in English homes. But the wise ever find some new thing to learn. Though a nation, as an individual, must act on the lines of its own character, and we are, on the whole, well content with our English homes, yet we might learn something from the inclusiveness of the French family, where mother-in-law and father-in-law, aunt and cousins, widow and spinster, are cherished; and a hundred small offices devised for dependants who would be in the way in an English home. The result is that the children have a wider range for the practice of the thousand sweet attentions and self-restraints which make home life lovely. No doubt the medal has its obverse; there is probably much in French home life which we should shrink from; nevertheless, it offers object-lessons which we should do well to study. Again, where family life is most beauteous with us, is not the family a little apt to become self-centred and self-sufficient, rather than to cultivate that expansiveness towards other families which is part of the family code of our neighbours?

CHAPTER II

PARENTS AS RULERS

The Family Government an Absolute Monarchy.—Let us continue our consideration of the family as the nation in miniature, with the responsibilities, the rights, and the requirements of the nation. The parents represent the 'Government'; but, here, the government is ever an absolute monarchy, conditioned very loosely by the law of the land, but very closely by that law more or less of which every parent bears engraved on his conscience. Some attain the levels of high thinking, and come down from the Mount with beaming countenance and the tables of the law intact; others fail to reach the difficult heights, and are content with such fragments of the broken tables as they pick up below. But be his knowledge of the law little or much, no parent escapes the call to rule.

The Rule of Parents cannot be Deputed.—Now, the first thing we ask for in a ruler is, 'Is he able to rule? Does he know how to maintain his authority?' A ruler who fails to govern is like an unjust judge, an impious priest, an ignorant teacher; that is, he fails in the essential attribute of his office. This is even more true in the family than in the State;

the king may rule by deputy; but, here we see the exigeant nature of the parent's functions; he can have no deputy. Helpers he may have, but the moment he makes over his functions and authority to another, the rights of parenthood belong to that other, and not to him. Who does not know of the heart-burnings that arise when Anglo-Indian parents come home, to find their children's affections given to others, their duty owing to others; and they, the parents, sources of pleasure like the godmother of the fairy tale, but having no authority over their children? And all this, nobody's fault, for the guardians at home have done their best to keep the children loyal to the parents abroad.

Causes which lead to the Abdication of Parents.—Here is indicated a rock upon which the heads of families sometimes make shipwreck. They regard parental authority as inherent in them, a property which may lie dormant, but is not to be separated from the state of parenthood. They may allow their children from infancy upwards to do what is right in their own eyes; and then, Lear turns and makes his plaint to the winds, and cries—

> 'Sharper than a serpent's tooth it is
> To have a thankless child!'

But Lear has been all the time divesting himself of the honour and authority that belong to him, and giving his rights to his children. Here he tells us why; the biting anguish is the '*thankless*' child. He has been laying himself out for the thanks of his children. That they should think him a fond father has been more to him than the duty he owes them; and in proportion as he omits his duty are they oblivious of theirs. Possibly the unregulated love of approbation in devoted parents has more share in the undoing of families than any other single cause. A writer of to-day represents a mother as saying—

"'But you are not afraid of me, Bessie?'

"'No indeed; who could be afraid of a dear, sweet, soft, little mother like you?'"

And such praise is sweet in the ears of many a fond mother hungering for the love and liking of her children, and not perceiving that words like these in the mouth of a child are as treasonable as words of defiance.

Authority is laid down at other shrines than that of popularity. Prospero describes himself as,

'all dedicate
To study, and the bettering of my mind.'

And, meantime, the exercise of authority devolves upon Antonio; is it any wonder that the habit of authority fits the usurper like a glove, and that Prospero finds himself ousted from the office he failed to fill? Even so, the busy parent, occupied with many cares, awakes to find the authority he has failed to wield has dropped out of his hands; perhaps has been picked up by others less fit, and a daughter is given over to the charge of a neighbouring family, while father and mother hunt for rare prints.

In other cases, the love of an easy life tempts parents to let things take their course; the children are good children, and won't go far wrong, we are told; and very likely it is true. But however good the children be, the parents owe it to society to make them better than they are, and to bless the world with people, not merely good-natured and well-disposed, but good of set purpose and endeavour.

The love of ease, the love of favour, the claims of other work, are only some of the causes which lead to a result disastrous to society—the *abdication of parents*. When we come to consider the nature and uses of the parents' authority, we shall see that such abdication is as immoral as it is mischievous. Meantime, it is well worth while to notice that the causes which lead parents to resign the position of domestic rulers are resolvable into one—the office is too troublesome, too laborious. The temptation which assails parents is the same which has led many a crowned head to seek ease in the cloister—

'Uneasy lies the head that wears a crown,'

even if it be the natural crown of parenthood.

The Majesty of Parenthood.—The apostolic counsel of 'diligence' in ruling throws light upon the nature and aim of authority; it is no longer a matter of personal honour and dignity; authority is for use and service, and the honour that goes with it is only for the better service of those under authority. The arbitrary parent, the exacting parent, who claims this and that of deference and duty because he is a parent, all for his own honour and glory, is more hopelessly in the wrong than the parent who practically abdicates; the majesty of parenthood is hedged round with observances only because it is good for the children to 'faithfully serve, honour, and humbly obey' their natural rulers. Only at home can children be trained in the chivalrous temper of 'proud submission and dignified obedience'; and if the parents do not inspire and foster deference, reverence, and loyalty, how shall these crowning graces of character thrive in a hard and emulous world?

It is perhaps a little difficult to maintain an attitude of authority in these democratic days, when even educationists counsel that children be treated on equal terms from the very beginning; but the children themselves come to our aid; the sweet humility and dependence natural to them fosters the gentle dignity, the *soupçon* of reserve, which is becoming in parents. It is not open to parents either to lay aside or to sink under the burden of the honour laid upon them; and, no doubt, we have all seen the fullest, freest flow of confidence, sympathy, and love between parent and child where the mother sits as a queen among her children and the father is honoured as a crowned head. The fact that there are two parents, each to lend honour to the other, yet free from restraint in each other's presence, makes it the easier to maintain the impalpable 'state' of parenthood. And the presence of the slight, sweet, undefined feeling of dignity in the household is the very first condition for the bringing-up of loyal, honourable men and women, capable of reverence and apt to win respect.

Children are a Public Trust and a Divine Trust. —The foundation of parental authority lies in the fact that parents hold office as deputies; and that in a twofold sense. In the first place, they are the immediate and personally appointed deputies of the Almighty King, the sole Ruler of men; they have not only to fulfil his counsels regarding the children, but to represent his Person; his parents are as God to the little child; and, yet more constraining thought, *God is to him what his parents are*; he has no power to conceive a greater and lovelier personality than that of the royal heads of his own home; he makes his first approach to the Infinite through them; they are his measure for the highest; if the measure be easily within his small compass, how shall he grow up with the reverent temper which is the condition of spiritual growth?

More; parents hold their children in trust for society. 'My own child' can only be true in a limited sense; the children are held as a public trust to be trained as is best for the welfare of the community; and in this sense also the parents are persons in authority with the dignity of their office to support; and are even liable to deposition. The one State whose name has passed into a proverb, standing for a group of virtues which we have no other word to describe, is a State which practically deprived parents of the functions which they failed to fulfil to the furtherance of public virtue. No doubt the State reserves to itself virtually the power to bring up its own children in its own way, with the least possible co-operation of parents. Even to-day, a neighbouring nation has elected to charge itself with the training of its infants. So soon as they can crawl, or sooner, before ever they run or speak, they are to be brought to the 'Maternal School,' and carefully nurtured, as with mother's milk, in the virtues proper for a citizen. The scheme is as yet but in the experimental stage, but will doubtless be carried through, because the nation in question has long ago discovered—and acted consistently upon the discovery—that what you would have the man become, that you must train the child to be.

Perhaps such public deposition of parents is the last calamity that can befall a nation. These poor little ones are to grow up in a world where the name of God is not to be named; to grow up, too, without the training in filial duty and brotherly love and neighbourly kindness which falls to the children of all but the few unnatural parents. They may be returned to their parents at certain hours or after certain years; but once alienation has been set up, once the strongest and sweetest tie has been loosened and the parents have been publicly delivered from their duty, the desecration of the home is complete, and we shall have the spectacle of a people growing up orphaned almost from their birth. This is a new thing in the world's history, for even Lycurgus left the children to the parents for the first half-dozen years of life. Certain newspapers commend the example for our imitation, but God forbid that we should ever lose faith in the blessedness of family life. Parents who hold their children as at the same time a public trust and a divine trust, and who recognise the authority they hold as *deputed* authority, not to be trifled with, laid aside, or abused—such parents preserve for the nation the immunities of home, and safeguard the privileges of their order.

The Limitations and Scope of Parental Authority.—Having seen that it does not rest with the parents to use, or to forego the use of, the authority they hold, let us examine the limitations and the scope of this authority. In the first place, it is to be maintained and exercised solely for the advantage of the children, whether in mind, body, or estate. And here is room for the nice discrimination, the delicate intuitions, with which parents are blessed. The mother who makes her growing-up daughter take the out-of-door exercise she needs, is acting within her powers. The father of quiet habits, who discourages society for his young people, is considering his own tastes, and not their needs, and is making unlawful use of his authority.

Again, the authority of parents, though the deference it begets remains to grace the relations of parents and child, is itself a provisional function, and is only successful as it encourages the *autonomy*, if we may call it so, of the child. A single decision made by the parents which the child is, or should be, capable of making for itself, is an encroachment on the rights of the child, and a transgression on the part of the parents.

Once more, the authority of parents rests on a secure foundation only as they keep well before the children that it is deputed authority; the child who knows that he is being brought up for the service of the nation, that his parents are acting under a Divine commission, will not turn out a rebellious son.

Further, though the emancipation of the children is gradual, they acquiring day by day more of the art and science of self-government, yet there comes a day when the parents' right to rule is over; there is nothing left for them but to abdicate gracefully, and leave their grown-up sons and daughters free agents, even though these still live at home; and although, in the eyes of their parents, they are not fit to be trusted with the ordering of themselves: if they fail in such self-ordering, whether as regards time, occupations, money, friends, most likely their parents are to blame for not having introduced them by degrees to the full liberty which is their right as men and women. Anyway, it is too late now to keep them in training; fit or unfit, they must hold the rudder for themselves.

As for the employment of authority, the highest

art lies in ruling without seeming to do so. The law is a terror to evil-doers, but for the praise of them that do well; and in the family, as in the State, the best government is that in which peace and happiness, truth and justice, religion and piety, are maintained without the intervention of the law. Happy is the household that has few rules, and where 'Mother does not like this,' and; 'Father wishes that,' are all-constraining.

CHAPTER III

PARENTS AS INSPIRERS

Children must be born again into the Life of Intelligence

Parents owe a Second Birth to their Children.
—M. Adolf Monod claims that the child must owe
to his mother a second birth—the first into the
natural, the second into the spiritual life of the intelligence and moral sense. Had he not been writing of
women and for women, no doubt he would have
affirmed that the long travail of this second birth must
be undergone equally by both parents. Do we ask
how he arrives at this rather startling theory? He
observes that great men have great mothers; mothers,
that is, blest with an infinite capacity of taking pains
with their work of bringing up children. He likens
this labour to a second bearing which launches the
child into a higher life; and as this higher life is
a more blessed life, he contends that every child
has a right to this birth into completer being *at
the hands of his parents*. Did his conclusions rest
solely upon the deductive methods he pursues, we
might afford to let them pass, and trouble ourselves
very little about this second birth, which parents
may, and ofttimes do, withhold from their natural
offspring. We, too, could bring forward our con-

trary instances of good parents with bad sons, and indifferent parents with earnest children; and, pat to our lips, would come the *Cui bono?* Which absolves us from endeavour.

Science supports this Contention.—Be a good mother to your son because great men have had good mothers, is inspiring, stimulating; but is not to be received as a final word. For an appeal of irresistible urgency, we look to natural science with her inductive methods; though we are still waiting her last word, what she has already said is law and gospel for the believing parent. The parable of Pandora's box is true to-day; and a woman may in her heedlessness let fly upon her offspring a thousand ills. But is there not also 'a glass of blessings standing by,' into which parents may dip, and bring forth for their children health and vigour, justice and mercy, truth and beauty?

'Surely,' it may be objected, 'every good and perfect gift comes from God above, and the human parent sins presumptuously who thinks to bestow gifts divine.' Now this lingering superstition has no part nor lot with true religion, but, on the contrary, brings upon it the scandal of many an ill-ordered home and ill regulated family. When we perceive that God uses men and women, parents above all others, as vehicles for the transmission of his gifts, and that it is in the keeping of his law He is honoured—rather than in the attitude of the courtier waiting for exceptional favours—then we shall take the trouble to comprehend the law written not only upon tables of stone and rolls of parchment, but upon the fleshly tablets of the living organisms of the children; and, understanding the law, we shall see with thanksgiving and enlargement of heart in what *natural* ways God does indeed show mercy unto thousands of them that love Him and keep his commandments.

But his commandment is exceeding broad; becomes broader year by year with every revelation of science; and we had need gird up the loins of our mind to keep pace with this current revelation. We shall be at pains, too, to keep ourselves in that attitude of expectant attention wherein we shall be enabled to perceive the unity and continuity of this revelation with that of the written word of God. For perhaps it is only as we are able to receive the two, and harmonise the two in a willing and obedient heart, that we shall enter on the heritage of glad and holy living which is the will of God for us.

Processes and Methods of this Second Birth. —Let us, for example, consider, in the light of current scientific thought, the processes and the methods of this second birth, which the child claims at the hands of his parents. 'Train up a child in the way he should go, and when he is old he will not depart from it,' is not only a pledge, but is a statement of a result arrived at by deductive processes. The writer had great opportunities for collecting data; he had watched many children grow up, and his experience taught him to divide them into two classes—the well-brought-up who turned out well; and the ill-brought-up who turned out ill. No doubt, then, as now, there were startling exceptions, and—the exception proves the rule.

But, here as elsewhere, the promises and threatenings of the Bible will bear the searching light of inductive methods. We may ask, Why should this be so?

And not content ourselves with a general answer, that this is natural and right; we may search until we discover that this result is inevitable, and no other result conceivable (except for alien influences), and our obedience will be in exact proportion to our perception of the inevitableness of the law.

Dr Maudsley on Heredity.—The vast sum of what we understand by heredity is not to be taken into account in the consideration of this second birth; by the first natural birth it is, that "his father and mother, his grandfather and grandmother, are latent or declare themselves in the child; and it is on the lines thus laid down in his nature that his development will proceed. It is not by virtue of education so much as by virtue of inheritance that he is brave or timid, generous or selfish, prudent or reckless, boastful or modest, quick or placid in temper; the ground tone of his character is original in him, and it colours all the subsequently formed emotions and their sympathetic ideas. . . . The influence of systematic culture upon anyone is no doubt great, but that which determines the limit, and even in some degree the nature, of the effects of culture, that which forms the foundations upon which all the modifications of art must rest, is the inherited nature."

Disposition and Character.—If heredity means so much—if, as would seem at the first glance, the child comes into the world with his character ready-made— what remains for the parents to do but to enable him to work out his own salvation without let or hindrance of their making, upon the lines of his individuality? The strong naturalism, shall we call it, of our day, inclines us to take this view of the objects and limitations of education; and without doubt it is a gospel;

it is the truth; but it is not the whole truth. The child brings with him into the world, not character, but disposition. He has tendencies which may need only to be strengthened, or, again, to be diverted or even repressed. His character—the efflorescence of the man wherein the fruit of his life is a-preparing —is original disposition, modified, directed, expanded by education; by circumstances; later, by self-control and self-culture; above all, by the supreme agency of the Holy Ghost, even where that agency is little suspected, and as little solicited.

How is this great work of character-making, the single effectual labour possible to human beings, to be carried on? We shall rest our inquiries on a physiological basis; the lowest, doubtless, but therefore the foundation of the rest. The first-floor chambers of the psychologist are pleasant places, but who would begin to build with the first floor? What would he rear it upon? Surely the arbitrary distinction between the grey matter of the brain and the 'mind' which plays upon it—even as the song upon the vocal chords of the singer—is more truly materialistic than is the recognition of the pregnant truth that the brain is the mere organ of the spiritual part; registering and effecting every movement of thought and feeling, whether conscious or unconscious, by appreciable molecular movement; and sustaining the infinite activities of mind by corresponding enormous activity and enormous waste; that it is the organ of mind which, under present conditions, is absolutely inseparable from, and indispensable to, the quickening spirit. Once we recognise that in the thinking of a thought there is as distinct motion set up in some tract of the brain as there is in the muscles of the hand employed in writing a sentence, we shall see that the behaviour of the grey nerve-substance of the cerebrum should afford the one possible key to certitude and system in our attempts at education, using the word in the most worthy sense—as its concern is the formation of character.

Having heard Dr Maudsley on the subject of heredity, let us hear him again on this other subject, which practically enables us to define the possibilities of education.

Dr Maudsley on the Structural Effects of 'Particular Life Experiences.'—"That which has existed with any completeness in consciousness leaves behind it, after its disappearance therefrom, in the mind or brain, a functional disposition to its reproduction or reappearance in consciousness at some future time. Of no mental act can we say that it is 'writ in water'; something remains from it, whereby its recurrence is facilitated. Every impression of sense upon the brain, every current of molecular activity from one to another part of the brain, every cerebral action which passes into muscular movement, leaves behind it some modification of the nerve elements concerned in its function, some after-effect, or, so to speak, memory of itself in them which renders its reproduction an easier matter, the more easy the more often it has been repeated, and makes it impossible to say that, however trivial, it shall not under some circumstances recur. Let the excitation take place in one of two nerve cells lying side by side, and between which there was not any original specific difference, there will be ever afterwards a difference between them. This physiological process, whatever be its nature, is the physical basis of memory, and it is the foundation of the development of all our mental functions.

"That modification which persists, or is retained, in structure after functions, has been differently described as a residuum, or relic, or trace, or disposition, or vestige; or again as potential, latent, or dormant idea. Not only definite ideas, but all affections of the nervous system, feelings of pleasure and pain, desire, and even its outward reactions, thus leave behind them their structural effects, and lay the foundation of modes of thought, feeling, and action. Particular talents are sometimes formed quite, or almost quite, involuntarily; and complex actions, which were first consciously performed by dint of great application, become automatic by repetition; ideas which were at first consciously associated, ultimately coalesce and call one another up without any consciousness, as we see in the quick perception or intuition of the man of large worldly experience; and feelings, once active, leave behind them their large unconscious residua, thus affecting the generation of the character, so that, apart from the original or inborn nature of the individual, contentment, melancholy, cowardice, bravery, and even moral feeling, are generated as the results of particular life-experiences."

Our Age has acquired a great Educational Charter.—Here we have sketched out a magnificent educational charter. It is as well, perhaps, that we do not realise the extent of our liberties; if we did, it may be, such a fervour of educational enthusiasm would seize us that we should behave as did those early Christians who every day expected the coming of

the Lord. How should a man have patience to buy
and sell and get gain had it been revealed to him
that he was able to paint the greatest picture ever
painted? And we, with the enthralling vision of
what our little child might become under our hands,
how should we have patience for common toils?
That science should have revealed the *rationale* of
education in our day is possibly the Divine recognition that we have become more fit for the task,
because we have come to an increasing sense of
moral responsibility. What would it be for an
immoral people to discern fully the possibilities of
education? But how slow we are! how—

> 'Custom lies upon us with a weight,
> Heavy as frost, and deep almost as life!'

A generation has passed away since these words
of Dr Maudsley, and many of like force by other
physiologists, were published to the world. We have
purposely chosen words that have stood the test of
time; for to-day a hundred eminent scientific men, at
home and abroad, are proclaiming the same truths.
Every scientist believes them! And we? We go on
after our use and wont, as if nothing had been said;
dropping, hour by hour, out of careless hands, seeds
of corn and hemlock, of bramble and rose.

Let us run over the charter of our liberties, as
Dr Maudsley has summed them up in the passage
quoted above.

Some Articles of this Charter.—We may lay
the physical basis of memory: while the wide-eyed
babe stretches his little person with aimless kickings
on his rug, he is receiving unconsciously those first
impressions which form his earliest memories; and

we can order those memories for him: we can see that the earliest sights he sees are sights of order, neatness, beauty; that the sounds his ear drinks in are musical and soft, tender and joyous; that the baby's nostrils sniff only delicate purity and sweetness. These memories remain through life, engraved on the unthinking brain. As we shall see later, memories have a certain power of accretion—where there are some, others of a like kind gather, and all the life is ordered on the lines of these first pure and tender memories.

We may lay the foundation for the development of all the mental functions. Are there children who do not wonder, or revere, or care for fairy tales, or think wise child-thoughts? Perhaps there are not; but if there are, it is because the fertilising pollen grain has never been conveyed to the ovule waiting for it in the child's soul.

These are some of the things that—according to the citations we have given from Dr Maudsley's *Physiology of Mind*—his parents may settle for the future man, even in his early childhood:—

His definite ideas upon particular subjects, as, for example, his relations with other people.

His habits, of neatness or disorder, of punctuality, of moderation.

His general modes of thought, as affected by altruism or egoism.

His consequent modes of feeling and action.

His objects of thought—the small affairs of daily life, the natural world, the operations or the productions of the human mind, the ways of God with men.

His distinguishing talent—music, eloquence, invention.

His disposition or tone of character, as it shows itself in and affects his family and other close relations in life—reserved or frank, morose or genial, melancholy or cheerful, cowardly or brave.

CHAPTER IV

PARENTS AS INSPIRERS

The Life of the Mind grows upon Ideas

'Sow an act, reap a habit; sow a habit, reap a character; sow a character, reap a destiny.'

Summary of the Preceding Chapter.—The last chapter closed with an imperfect summary of what we may call the educational functions of parents. We found that it rests with the parents of the child to settle for the future man his ways of thinking, behaving, feeling, acting; his disposition, his particular talent; the manner of things upon which his thoughts shall run. Who shall fix limitations to the power of parents? The destiny of the child is ruled by his parents, because they have the virgin soil all to themselves. The first sowing must be at their hands, or at the hands of such as they choose to depute.

Educational Conceptions of the Past.—What do parents sow? *Ideas.* We cannot too soon recognise what is the sole educational seed in our hands, or how this seed is to be distributed. But how radically wrong is all our thought upon education! We cannot use the fit words because we do not think the right thing. We have perhaps got over the educational misconception of the *tabula rasa*. No one now looks on the child's white soul as a tablet prepared for the exercise of the educator's supreme art. But the conception which has succeeded this time-honoured heresy rests on the same false bases of the august office and the infallible wisdom of the educator. Here it is in its cruder form:

Pestalozzi's Theory.—'Pestalozzi aimed more at harmoniously developing the faculties than at making use of them for the acquirement of knowledge; he sought to prepare the vase rather than to fill it.'

Froebel's Theory.—In the hands of Froebel the figure gains in boldness and beauty; it is no longer a mere vase to be shaped under the potter's fingers; but a flower, say, a perfect rose, to be delicately and consciously and methodically moulded, petal by petal, curve and curl; for the perfume and living glory of the flower, why, these will come; do you your part and mould the several petals; wait, too, upon sunshine and shower, give space and place for your blossom to expand. And so we go to work with a touch to 'imagination' here, and to 'judgment' there; now, to the 'perceptive faculties,' now, to the 'conceptive'; in this, aiming at the moral, and in this, at the intellectual nature of the child; touching into being, petal by petal, the flower of a perfect life under the genial influences of sunny looks and happy moods.

The Kindergarten a Vital Conception.—This reading of the meaning of education and of the work of the educator is very fascinating, and it calls forth singular zeal and self-devotion on the part of those gardeners whose plants are the children. Perhaps, indeed, this of the Kindergarten is the one vital conception of education we have had hitherto.

But Science is changing Front.—But in these days of revolutionary thought, when all along the line—in geology and anthropology, chemistry, philology, and biology—science is changing front, it is necessary that we should reconsider our conception of Education.

As to Heredity.—We are taught, for example, that 'heredity' is by no means the simple and direct transmission, from parent or remote ancestor, to child of power and proclivity, virtue and defect; and we breathe freer, because we had begun to suspect that if this were so, it would mean to most of us an inheritance of exaggerated defects: imbecility, insanity, congenital disease—are they utterly removed from any one of us?

Is Education Formative?—So of education, we begin to ask, Is its work so purely formative as we thought? Is it directly formative at all? How much is there in this pleasing and easy doctrine, that the drawing forth and strengthening and directing of the several 'faculties' is education? Parents are very jealous over the individuality of their children; they mistrust the tendency to develop all on the same plan; and this instinctive jealousy is right; for, supposing that education really did consist in systematised efforts to draw out every power that is in us, why, we should all develop on the same lines, be as like as 'two peas,' and (should we not?) die of weariness of one another! Some of us have an uneasy sense that things are tending towards this deadly sameness; but, indeed, the fear is groundless.

We may believe that the personality, the individuality, of each of us, is too dear to God, and too necessary to a complete humanity, to be left at the mercy of empirics. We are absolutely safe, and the tenderest child is fortified against a battering-ram of educational forces.

'Education' an Inadequate Word.—The problem of education is more complex than it seems at first sight, and well for us and the world that it is so. 'Education is a life'; you may stunt and starve and kill, or you may cherish and sustain; but the beating of the heart, the movement of the lungs, and the development of the faculties (are there any 'faculties'?) are only indirectly our care. The poverty of our thought on the subject of education is shown by the fact that we have no word which at all implies the sustaining of a *life*: education (*e*, out, and *ducere*, to lead, to draw) is very inadequate; it covers no more than those occasional gymnastics of the mind which correspond with those by which the limbs are trained: training (*trahere*) is almost synonymous, and upon these two words rests the misconception that the development and the exercise of the 'faculties' is the object of education (we must needs use the word for want of a better).

'Bringing-up'?—Our homely Saxon 'bringing-up' is nearer the truth, perhaps because of its very vagueness; any way, 'up' implies an aim, and 'bringing' an *effort*.

The happy phrase of Mr Matthew Arnold[1].— Education is an atmosphere, a discipline, a life'—is perhaps the most complete and adequate definition of education we possess. It is a great thing to have said it; and our wiser posterity may see in that

[1] The writer has not been able to trace the phrase in question, but this attribution persists in her memory.

'profound and exquisite remark' the fruition of a lifetime of critical effort.

An Adequate Definition.—Observe how it covers the question from the three conceivable points of view. Subjectively, in the child, education is a life; objectively, as affecting the child, education is a discipline; relatively, if we may introduce a third term, as regards the environment of the child, education is an atmosphere.

We shall examine each of these postulates later; at present we shall attempt no more than to clear the ground a little, with a view to the subject of this chapter, 'Parents as Inspirers'—not 'modellers,' but 'inspirers.'

Method, a Way to an End.—It is only as we recognise our limitations that our work becomes effective: when we see definitely what we are to do, what we can do, and what we cannot do, we set to work with confidence and courage; we have an end in view, and we make our way intelligently towards that end, and a *way to an end* is *method*. It rests with parents not only to give their children birth into the life of intelligence and moral power, but to sustain the higher life which they have borne.

The Life of the Mind grows upon Ideas.— Now that life, which we call education, receives only one kind of sustenance; it grows upon *ideas*. You may go through years of so-called 'education' without getting a single vital idea; and that is why many a well-fed body carries about a feeble, starved intelligence; and no society for the prevention of cruelty to children cries shame on the parents. Some years ago I heard of a girl of fifteen who had spent two years at a school without taking part in a single lesson, and this by the express desire of her mother, who wished all her time and all her pains to be given to 'fancy needlework.' This, no doubt, is a survival (not of the fittest), but it is possible to pass even the Universities Local Examinations with credit, without ever having experienced that vital stir which marks the inception of an idea; and, if we have succeeded in escaping this disturbing influence, why, we have 'finished our education' when we leave school; we shut up our books and our minds, and remain pigmies in the dark forest of our own dim world of thought and feeling.

What is an Idea?—A live thing of the mind, according to the older philosophers, from Plato to Bacon, from Bacon to Coleridge. We say of an idea that it strikes us, impresses us, seizes us, takes possessionof us, rules us; and our common speech is, as usual, truer to fact than the conscious thought which it expresses. We do not in the least exaggerate in ascribing this sort of action and power to an idea. We form an *ideal*—a, so to speak, embodied idea— and our ideal exercises the very strongest formative influence upon us. Why do you devote yourself to this pursuit, that cause? 'Because twenty years ago such and such an idea *struck* me,' is the sort of history which might be given of every purposeful life—every life devoted to the working out of an idea. Now is it not marvellous that, recognising as we do the potency of ideas, both the word and the conception it covers enter so little into our thought of education?

Coleridge brings the conception of an 'idea' within the sphere of the scientific thought of to-day; not as that thought is expressed in *Psychology*—a term which he himself launched upon the world with an apology for it as an *insolens verbum*,[1] but in that science of the correlation and interaction of mind and brain, which is at present rather clumsily expressed in such terms as 'mental physiology' and 'psycho-physiology.'

In his *Method* Coleridge gives us the following illustration of the rise and progress of an idea:—

Rise and Progress of an Idea.—"We can recall no incident of human history that impresses the imagination more deeply than the moment when Columbus, on an unknown ocean, first perceived that startling fact, the change of the magnetic needle. How many such instances occur in history when the ideas of Nature (presented to chosen minds by a Higher Power than Nature herself) suddenly unfold, as it were, in prophetic succession, systematic views destined to produce the most important revolutions in the state of man! The clear spirit of Columbus was doubtless eminently *methodical*. He saw distinctly that great leading *idea* which authorised the poor pilot to become a 'promiser of kingdoms.'"

Genesis of an Idea.—Notice the genesis of such ideas—'presented to chosen minds by a Higher Power than Nature'; notice how accurately this history of an idea fits in with what we know of the history of great inventions and discoveries, with that of the *ideas* which rule our own lives; and how well does it correspond with that key to the origin of 'practical' ideas which we find elsewhere:—

"Doth the plowman plow continually to. . . . open and break the clods of his ground? When he hath made plain the face thereof, doth he not cast abroad

[1] 'We beg pardon for the use of this insolms verbum, but it is one of which our language stands in great need' (Method-S. T. Coleridge).

the fitches, and scatter the cummin, and put in the wheat in rows, and the barley in the appointed place, and the spelt in the border thereof? For his God doth instruct him aright, and doth teach him. . . .

"Bread corn is ground; for he will not ever be threshing it. . . . This also cometh forth from the Lord of hosts, which is wonderful in counsel and excellent in wisdom."[1]

An Idea may exist as an 'Appetency.'— Ideas may invest as an atmosphere, rather than strike as a weapon. 'The idea may exist in a clear, distinct, definite form, as that of a circle in the mind of a geometrician; or it may be a mere instinct, a vague appetency towards something, . . . like the impulse which fills the young poet's eyes with tears, he knows not why: To excite this 'appetency towards something'—towards things lovely, honest, and of good report, is the earliest and most important ministry of the educator. How shall these indefinite ideas which manifest themselves in appetency be imparted? They are not to be given of set purpose, nor taken at set times. They are held in that thought-environment which surrounds the child as an atmosphere, which he breathes as his breath of life; and this atmosphere in which the child inspires his unconscious ideas of right living emanates from his parents. Every look of gentleness and tone of reverence, every word of kindness and act of help, passes into the thought-environment, the very atmosphere which the child breathes; he does not think of these things, may never think of them, but all his life long they excite that 'vague appetency towards something' out of which most of his actions spring. Oh,

[1] Isaiah xxviii.

The wonderful and dreadful presence of the little child in the midst!

A Child draws Inspiration from the Casual Life around him.—That he should take direction and inspiration from all the casual life about him, should make our poor words and ways the starting-point from which, and in the direction of which, he develops—this is a thought which makes the best of us hold our breath. There is no way of escape for parents; they must needs be as 'inspirers' to their children, because about them hangs, as its atmosphere about a planet, the thought-environment of the child, from which he derives those enduring ideas which express themselves as a life-long 'appetency' towards things sordid or things lovely, things earthly or divine.

Order and Progress of Definite Ideas.—Let us now hear Coleridge on the subject of those *definite* ideas which are not inhaled as air, but conveyed as meat to the mind:—[1]

"From the first, or initiative idea, as from a seed, successive ideas germinate."

"Events and images, the lively and spirit-stirring machinery of the external world, are like light and air and moisture to the seed of the mind, which would else rot and perish."

"The paths in which we may pursue a methodical course are manifold, and at the head of each stands its peculiar and guiding idea."

"Those ideas are as regularly subordinate in dignity as the paths to which they point are various and eccentric in direction. The world has suffered much, in modern times, from a subversion of the natural

[1] *Method*—S. T. Coleridge.

and necessary order of Science. . . . from summoning reason and faith to the bar of that limited physical experience to which, by the true laws of method, they owe no obedience."

"Progress follows the path of the idea from which it sets out; requiring, however, a constant wakefulness of mind to keep it within the due limits of its course. Hence the orbits of thought, so to speak, must differ among themselves as the initiative ideas differ."

Platonic Doctrine of Ideas.—Have we not here the corollary to, and the explanation of, that law of unconscious cerebration which results in our 'ways of thinking,' which shapes our character, rules our destiny? Thoughtful minds consider that the new light which biology is throwing upon the laws of mind is bringing to the front once more the Platonic doctrine, that "An idea is a distinguishable power, self-affirmed, and seen in its unity with the Eternal Essence."

Ideas alone matter in Education.—The whole subject is profound, but as practical as it is profound. We must disabuse our minds of the theory that the functions of education are, in the main, gymnastic. In the early years of the child's life it makes, perhaps, little apparent difference whether his parents start with the notion that to educate is to fill a receptacle, inscribe a tablet, mould plastic matter, or nourish a life; but in the end we shall find that only those ideas which have fed his life are taken into the being of the child; all the rest is thrown away, or worse, is like sawdust in the system, an impediment and an injury to the vital processes.

How the Educational Formula should run.— This is, perhaps, how the educational formula should run: Education is a life; that life is sustained on ideas; ideas are of spiritual origin; and,

'God has made us so'

that we get them chiefly as we convey them to one another. The duty of parents is to sustain a child's inner life with ideas as they sustain his body with food. The child is an eclectic; he may choose this or that; therefore, in the morning sow thy seed, and in the evening withhold not thy hand, for thou knowest not which shall prosper, whether this or that, or whether they both shall be alike good.

The child has affinities with evil as well as with good; therefore, hedge him about from any chance lodgment of evil ideas.

The initial idea begets subsequent ideas; therefore, take care that children get right primary ideas on the great relations and duties of life.

Every study, every line of thought, has its 'guiding idea'; therefore, the study of a child makes for living education in proportion as it is quickened by the guiding idea 'which stands at the head.'

'Infallible Reason'; what is it?—In a word, our much boasted 'infallible reason'—is it not the involuntary thought which follows the initial idea upon necessary logical lines? Given, the starting idea, and the conclusion may be predicated almost to a certainty. We get into the *way* of thinking such and such manner of thoughts, and of coming to such and such conclusions, ever further and further removed from the starting-point, but on the same lines. There is structural adaptation in the brain tissue to the manner of thoughts we think—a place and a way for them to run in. Thus we see how the destiny of a life is shaped in the nursery, by the reverent naming of the Divine Name; by the light scoff at holy things; by the thought of duty the little child gets who is made to finish conscientiously his little task; by the hardness of heart that comes to the child who hears the faults or sorrows of others spoken of lightly.

CHAPTER V

PARENTS AS INSPIRERS

The Things of the Spirit

Parents, Revealers of God to their Children.—
It is probable that parents as a class feel more than
ever before the responsibility of their prophetic office.
It is as revealers of God to their children that parents
touch their highest limitations; perhaps it is only as
they succeed in this part of their work that they fulfil
the Divine intention in giving them children to bring
up—in the nurture and admonition of the Lord.

How to Fortify them against Doubt.—How
to fortify the children against the doubts of which
the air is full, is an anxious question. Three courses
are open: to teach as we of an older generation have been taught, and to let them bide their
time and their chance; to attempt to deal with the
doubts and difficulties which have turned up, or are
likely to turn up; or, to give children such hold upon
vital truth, and at the same time such an outlook
upon current thought, that they shall be landed on
the safe side of the controversies of their day, open to
truth, in however new a light presented, and safeguarded against mortal error.

Three Ways: the First Unfair.—The first

course is unfair to the young: when the attack comes, they find themselves at a disadvantage; they have nothing to reply; their pride is in arms; they jump to the conclusion that there is no defence possible of that which they have received as truth; had there been, would they not have been instructed to make it? They resent being made out in the wrong, being on the weaker side—so it seems to them,—being behind their times; and they go over without a struggle to the side of the most aggressive thinkers of their day.

'Evidences' are not Proofs.—Let us suppose that, on the other hand, they have been fortified with 'Christian evidences,' defended by bulwarks of sound dogmatic teaching. Religion without definite dogmatic teaching degenerates into sentiment, but dogma, as dogma, offers no defence against the assaults of unbelief. As for 'evidences,' the *role* of the Christian apologist is open to the imputation conveyed in the keen proverb, *qui s'excuse, s'accuse*; the truth by which we live must needs be self-evidenced, admitting of neither proof nor disproof. Children should be taught Bible history with every elucidation which modern research makes possible. But they should not be taught to think of the inscriptions on Assyrian monuments, for example, as *proofs* of the truth of the Bible records, but rather as illustrations of those records; though they are, and cannot but be, subsidiary proofs.

The Outlook upon Current Thought.—Let us look at the third course: and first, as regards the outlook upon current thought. Contemporary opinion is the fetish of the young mind. Young people are eager to know what to think on all the serious questions of religion and life. They ask what is the opinion of this and that leading thinker of their day. They by no means confine themselves to such leaders of thought as their parents have elected to follow; on the contrary, the 'other side' of every question is the attractive side for them, and they do not choose to be behind the foremost in the race of thought.

Free-will in Thought.—Now, that their young people should thus take to the water need not come upon parents as a surprise. The whole training from babyhood upward should be in view of this plunge. When the time comes, there is nothing to be done; openly, it may be, secretly if the home rule is rigid, the young folk think their own thoughts, that is, they follow the leader they have elected; for they are truly modest and humble at heart, and do not yet venture to think for themselves; only they have transferred their allegiance. Nor is this transfer of allegiance to be resented by parents; we all claim this kind of 'suffrage' in our turn when we feel ourselves included in larger interests than those of the family.

Preparation.—But there is much to be done beforehand, though nothing when the time comes. The notion that any contemporary authority is in-fallible may be steadily undermined from infancy onwards, though at some sacrifice of ease and glory to the parents. 'I don't know' must take the place of the vague wise-sounding answer, the random shot which children's pertinacious questionings too often provoke. And 'I don't know' should be followed by the effort to know, the research necessary to find out. Even then, the possibility of error in a 'printed book' must occasionally be faced. The results of this kind of training in the way of mental balance and repose are invaluable.

Reservation as regards Science.—Another safeguard is in the attitude of reservation, shall we say? Which it may be well to preserve towards 'Science.' It is well that the enthusiasm of children should be kindled, that they should see how glorious it is to devote a lifetime to patient research, how great to find out a single secret of Nature, a key to many riddles. The heroes of science should be their heroes; the great names, especially of those who are amongst us, should be household words. But here, again, nice discrimination should be exercised; two points should be kept well to the front—the absolute silence of the oracle on all ultimate questions of origin and life, and the fact that, all along the line, scientific truth comes in like the tide, with steady advance, but with ebb and flow of every wavelet of truth; so much so, that, at the present moment, the teaching of the last twenty years is discredited in at least a dozen departments of science. Indeed, it would seem to be the part of wisdom to wait half a century before fitting the discovery of to-day into the general scheme of things. And this, not because the latest discovery is not absolutely true, but because we are not yet able so to adjust it—according to the 'science of the proportion of things'—that it shall be relatively true.

Knowledge is Progressive.—But all this is surely beyond children? By no means; every walk should quicken their enthusiasm for the things of Nature, and their reverence for the priests of that temple; but occasion should be taken to mark the progressive advances of science, and the fact that the teaching of to-day may be the error of to-morrow, because new light may lead to new conclusions even from the facts already known. 'Until quite lately, geologists thought. . . . they now think. . . . but they may find reason to think otherwise in the future.' To perceive that knowledge is *progressive*, and that the next 'find' may always alter the bearings of what went before; that we are waiting, and may have very long to wait, for the last word; that science also is 'revelation,' though we are not yet able fully to interpret what we know; and that 'science' herself contains the promise of great impetus to the spiritual life—to perceive these things is to be able to rejoice in all truth and to wait for final certainty.

Children should learn some Laws of Thought. —In another way we may endeavour to secure for the children that stability of mind which comes of self-knowledge. It is well that they should know, so early that they will seem to themselves always to have known, some of the laws of thought which govern their own minds. Let them know that, once an idea takes possession of them, it will pursue, so to speak, its own course, will establish its own place in the very substance of the brain, will draw its own train of ideas after it. One of the most fertile sources of youthful infidelity is the fact that thoughtful boys and girls are infinitely surprised when they come to notice the course of their own thoughts. They read a book or listen to talk with a tendency to what is to them 'free-thought.' And then, the 'fearful joy' of finding that their own thoughts begin with the thought they have heard, and go on and on to new and startling conclusions on the same lines! The mental stir of all this gives a delightful sense of power, and a sense of inevitableness and certainty too; for they do not intend or try to think this or that. It comes of itself; their reason, they believe, is acting independently of them, and how can they help assuming that what comes to them of itself, with an air of absolute certainty, must of necessity be right?

To look at Thoughts as they come.—But what if from childhood they had been warned, 'Take care of your thoughts, and the rest will take care of itself; let a thought in, and it will stay; will come again to-morrow and the next day, will make a place for itself in your brain, and will bring many other thoughts like itself. Your business is to look at the thoughts as they come, to keep out the wrong thoughts, and let in the right. See that ye *enter not* into temptation.' This sort of teaching is not so hard to understand as the rules for the English nominative, and is of infinitely more profit in the conduct of life. It is a great safeguard to know that your 'reason' is capable of proving any theory you allow yourself to entertain.

The Appeal of the Children.—We have touched here only on the negative side of the parent's work as prophet, inspirer. There are perhaps few parents to whom the innocence of the babe in its mother's arms does not appeal with pathetic force. 'Open me the gates of righteousness, that I may go in unto them,' is the voice of the little unworldly child; and a wish, anyway, that he may be kept unspotted from the world, is breathed in every kiss of his mother, in the light of his father's eyes. But how ready we are to conclude that children cannot be expected to understand spiritual things. Our own grasp of the things of the Spirit is all too lax, and how can we expect that the child's feeble intelligence can apprehend the highest mysteries of our being? But here we are altogether wrong. It is with the advance of years that a materialistic temper settles upon us. But the children live in the light of the morning-land. The spirit-world has no mysteries for them; that parable and travesty of the spirit-world, the fairy-world, where all things are possible, is it not their favourite dwelling-place? And fairy-tales are so dear to children because their spirits fret against the hard and narrow limitations of time and place and substance; they cannot breathe freely in a material world. Think what the vision of God should be to the little child already peering wistfully through the bars of his prison-house. Not a far-off God, a cold abstraction, but a warm, breathing, spiritual Presence about his path and about his bed—a Presence in which he recognises protection and tenderness in darkness and danger, towards which he rushes as the timid child to hide his face in his mother's skirts.

'My Hiding-place.'—A friend tells me the following story of her girlhood. It so happened that extra lessons detained her at school until dark every day during the winter. She was extremely timid, but, with the unconscious reserve of youth, never thought of mentioning her fear of 'something.' Her way home lay by a river-side, a solitary path under trees—big trees, with masses of shadow. The black shadows, in which 'something' might lie hid—the *swsh-sh, swsh-sh,* of the river, which might be whisperings or the rustle of garments—filled her night by night with unabated terror. She fled along that river-side path with beating heart; but, quick as flying steps and beating heart, these words beat in her brain, over, and over, and over, the whole length of the way, evening by evening, winter after winter: 'Thou art my hiding-place; Thou shalt preserve me from trouble; Thou shalt compass me about with songs of deliverance.' Years after, when the woman might be supposed to have outgrown girlish terrors, she found herself again walking alone in the early darkness of a winter's evening under trees by the *swsh-sh* of another river. The old terror returned, and with it the old words came to her, and kept time the whole length of the way with her hasty steps. Such a place to hide him in should be the thought of God to every child.

The Mind of the Child is 'Good Ground.' —Their keen sensitiveness to spiritual influences is not due to ignorance on the part of the children. It is we, not they, who are in error. The whole tendency of modern biological thought is to confirm the teaching of the Bible: the ideas which quicken come from above; the mind of the little child is an open field, surely 'good ground,' where, morning by morning, the sower goes forth to sow, and the seed is the Word. All our teaching of children should be given reverently, with the humble sense that we are invited in this matter to co-operate with the Holy Spirit; but it should be given dutifully and diligently, with the awful sense that our co-operation would appear to be made a condition of the Divine action; that the Saviour of the world pleads with us to 'Suffer the little children to come unto Me,' as if we had the power to hinder, as we know that we have.

Children suffer from a deep-seated Discontent.—This thought of the Saviour of the world implies another conception which we sometimes leave out of sight in dealing with children. Young faces are not always sunny and lovely; even the brightest children in the happiest circumstances have their clouded hours. We rightly put the cloud down to some little disorder, or to the weather, but these are the secondary causes which reveal a deep-seated discontent Children have a sense of sin, acute in proportion to their sensitiveness. We are in danger of trusting too much to a rose-water treatment; we do not take children seriously enough; brought face to face with a child, we find he is a very real person, but in our educational theories we take him as 'something between a wax doll and an angel.' He sins; he is guilty of greediness, falsehood, malice, cruelty, a hundred faults that would be hateful in a grown-up person; we say he will know better by-and-by. He will never know better; he is keenly aware of his own odiousness. How many of us would say about our childhood, if we told the whole truth, 'Oh, I was an odious little thing!' and that, not because we recollect our faults, but because we recollect our childish estimate of ourselves. Many a bright and merry child is odious in his own eyes; and the 'peace, peace, where there is no peace,' of fond parents and friends is little comfort It is well that we 'ask for the old paths, where is the good way'; it is not well that, in the name of the old paths, we lead our children into blind alleys; nor that we let them follow the new into bewildering mazes.

CHAPTER VI

PARENTS AS INSPIRERS

Primal Ideas derived from Parents

'One of the little boys gazing upon the terrible desolation of the scene, so unlike in its savage and inhuman aspects anything he had ever seen at home, nestled close to his mother, and asked with bated breath, "Mither, is there a God here?"'-*John Burroughs.*

The Chief Thing we have to do.—The last chapter introduced the thought of parents in their highest function—as revealers of God to their children. To bring the human race, family by family, child by child, out of the savage and inhuman desolation where He is not, into the light and warmth and comfort of the presence of God, is, no doubt, the chief thing we have to do in the world. And this individual work with each child, being the most momentous work in the world, is put into the hands of the wisest, most loving, disciplined, and divinely instructed of human beings. Be ye perfect *as your Father* is perfect, is the perfection of parenthood, perhaps to be attained in its fulness only through parenthood. There are mistaken parents, ignorant parents, a few indifferent parents; even, as one in a thousand, callous parents; but the good that is done upon the earth is done, under God, by parents, whether directly or indirectly.

Ideas of God fitting for Children.—Parents who recognise that their great work is to be done by the instrumentality of the ideas they are able to introduce into the minds of their children, will take anxious thought as to those ideas of God which are most fitting for children, and as to how those ideas may best be conveyed. Let us consider an idea which is just now causing some stir in people's thoughts.

'We ought to work slowly up through the Human Side'—why not?—'We read some of the Old Testament history as "history of the Jews," and Job and Isaiah and the Psalms as poetry—and I am glad to say he is very fond of them; and parts of the Gospels in Greek, as the life and character of a hero. It is the greatest mistake to impose them upon children as authoritative and divine all at once. It at once diminishes their interest: we ought to work slowly up through the human side.'[1]

Here is a theory which commends itself to many persons because it is 'so reasonable.' But it goes upon the assumption that we are ruled by Reason, an infallible entity, which is certain, give it fair play, to bring us to just conclusions. Now the exercise of that function of the mind which we call reasoning—we must decline to speak of 'the Reason'—does indeed bring us to inevitable conclusions; the process is definite, the result convincing; but whether that result be right or wrong depends altogether upon the initial idea which, when we wish to discredit it, we call a prejudice; when we wish to exalt, we call an

[1] *Memoirs of Arthur Hamilton.* Messrs Kegan Paul & Co.

intuition, even an inspiration. It would be idle to illustrate this position; the whole history of Error is the history of the logical outcome of what we happily call misconceptions. The history of Persecution is the tale of how the inevitable conclusions arrived at by reasoning pass themselves off for truth. The Event of Calvary was due to no hasty, mad outburst of popular feeling. It was a triumph of reasoning: the inevitable issue of more than one logical sequence; the Crucifixion was not criminal, but altogether laudable, *if* that is right which is reasonable. And this is why the hearts of religious Jews were hardened and their understanding darkened; they were truly doing what was *right* in their own eyes. It is a marvellous thing to perceive the thoughts within us driving us forward to an inevitable conclusion, even against our will. How can that conclusion which presents itself to us in spite of ourselves fail to be right?

Logical Certainty and Moral Right—the Conscientious Jew and the Crucifixion.—Let us place ourselves for one instant in the position of the logical and conscientious Jew. "Jehovah" is a name of awe, unapproachable in thought or act except in ways Himself has specified. To attempt unlawful approach is to blaspheme. As Jehovah is infinitely great, presumptuous offence is infinitely heinous, is criminal, is the last crime as committed against Him who is the First. The blasphemer is worthy of death. This man makes himself equal with God, the unapproachable. He is a blasphemer, arrogant as Beelzebub. He is doubly worthy of death. To the people of the Jews is committed in trust the honoured Name; upon them it is incumbent

to exterminate the blasphemer. The man must die.'
Here is the secret of the virulent hatred which dogged
the steps of the blameless Life. These men were
following the dictates of reason, and *knew*, so they
would say, that they were doing right. Here we have
the invincible ignorance which the Light of the world
failed to illumine; and He,

> 'Who knows us as we are,
> Yet loves us better than He knows,'

offers for them the true plea, 'They know not what
they do.' The steps of the argument are incontro-
vertible; the error lies in the initial idea—such a conception of Jehovah as made the conception of Christ
inadmissible, impossible.

The Patriotic Jew and the Crucifixion.—Thus
reasoned the Jew upon whom his religion had the first
claim. The patriotic Jew, to whom religion itself was
subservient to the hopes of his nation, arrived by quite
another chain of *spontaneous* arguments at the same
inevitable conclusion:—'The Jews are the chosen
people. The first duty of a Jew is towards his nation.
These are critical times. A great hope is before us,
but we are in the grip of the Romans; they may
crush out the national life before our hope is realised.
Nothing must be done to alarm their suspicions. This
Man? By all accounts He is harmless, perhaps
righteous. But He stirs up the people. It is rumoured
that they call Him King of the Jews. He must not
be permitted to ruin the hopes of the nation. He must
die. It is expedient that one man die for the people,
and that the whole nation perish not.' Thus the
consummate crime that has been done upon the earth
was done probably without any consciousness of

criminality; on the contrary, with the acquittal of that spurious moral sense which supports with its approval all *reasonable* action. The Crucifixion was the logical and necessary outcome of ideas imbibed from their cradles by the persecuting Jews. So of every persecution; none is born of the occasion and the hour, but comes out of the habit of thought of a lifetime.

Primal Ideas derived from Parents.—It is the primal impulse to habits of thought which children must owe to their parents; and, as a man's thought and action Godward, is

'The very pulse of the machine,'

the introduction of such primal ideas as shall impel the soul to God is the first duty and the highest privilege of parents. Whatever sin of unbelief a man is guilty of, are his parents wholly without blame?

First Approaches to God.—Let us consider what is commonly done in the nursery in this respect. No sooner can the little being lisp than he is taught to kneel up in his mother's lap, and say 'God bless. . . .' and then follows a list of the near and dear, and 'God bless. . . . and make him a good boy, for Jesus' sake. Amen.' It is very touching and beautiful. I once peeped in at an open cottage door in a moorland village, and saw a little child in its nightgown kneeling in its mother's lap and saying its evening prayer. The spot has ever since remained to me a sort of shrine. There is no sight more touching and tender. By-and-by, so soon as he can speak the words,

'Gentle Jesus, meek and mild,'

is added to the little one's prayer, and later, 'Our Father.' Nothing could be more suitable and more beautiful than these morning and evening approaches to God, the little children brought to Him by their mothers. And most of us can 'think back' to the hallowing influence of these early prayers. But might not more be done? How many times a day does a mother lift up her heart to God as she goes in and out amongst her children, and they never know! 'To-day I talked to them' (a boy and girl of four and five) 'about Rebekah at the well. They were very much interested, especially about Eliezer praying in his heart and the answer coming at once. They said, "How did he pray?" I said, "I often pray in my heart when you know nothing about it. Sometimes you begin to show a naughty spirit, and I pray for you in my heart, and almost directly I find the good spirit comes, and your faces show my prayer is answered." O. stroked my hand and said, "Dear mother, I shall think of that!" Boy looked thoughtful, but didn't speak; but when they were in bed I knelt down to pray for them before leaving them, and when I got up, Boy said, "Mother, God filled my heart with goodness while you prayed for us; and, mother, I *will* try to-morrow."'

Communing out loud before the Children.— Is it possible that the mother could, when alone with her children, occasionally hold this communing out loud, so that the children might grow up in the sense of the presence of God? It would probably be difficult for many mothers to break down the barrier of spiritual reserve in the presence of even their own children. But, could it be done, would it not lead to glad and natural living in the recognised presence of God?

A Child's Gratitude.—A mother, who remembered a little penny scent-bottle as an early joy of her own, took three such small bottles home to her three little girls. They got them next morning at the family breakfast, and enjoyed them all through the meal. Before it ended the mother was called away, and little M. was sitting rather solitary with her scent-bottle and the remains of her breakfast. And out of the pure well of the little girl's heart came this, intended for nobody's ear, 'Dear mother, you are too good!' Think of the joy of the mother who should overhear her little child murmuring over the first primrose of the year, 'Dear God, you are too good!' Children are so imitative, that if they hear their parents speak out continually their joys and fears, their thanks and wishes, they, too, will have many things to say.

Another point in this connection; the little German child hears and speaks many times a day of der liebe Gott; to be sure he addresses Him as 'Du,' but du is part of his every-day speech; the circle of the very dear and intimate is hedged in by the magic du. So with the little French child, whose thought and word are ever of le bon Dieu; he also says Tu, but that is how he speaks to those most endeared to him.

Archaic Forms in Children's Prayers.—But the little English child is thrust out in the cold by an archaic mode of address, reverent in the ears of us older people, but forbidding, we may be sure, to the child. Then, for the Lord's Prayer, what a boon would be a truly reverent translation of it into the English of to-day! To us, who have learned to spell it out, the present form is dear, almost sacred; but we must not forget that it is after all only a translation, and is, perhaps, the most archaic piece of English in modern use: 'which art,'[1] commonly rendered

[1] Catholics say 'who art.'

'chart,' means nothing for a child. 'Hallowed' is the speech of a strange tongue to him—not much more to us; 'trespasses' is a semi-legal term, never likely to come into his every-day talk; and no explanation will make 'Thy' have the same force for him as 'your.' To make a child utter his prayers in a strange speech is to put up a barrier between him and his 'Almighty Lover.' Again, might we not venture to teach our children to say 'Dear God'? A parent, surely, can believe that no austerely reverential style can be so sweet in the Divine Father's ears as the appeal to 'dear God' for sympathy in joy and help in trouble, which flows naturally from the little child who is 'used to God.' Let children grow up aware of the constant, immediate, joy-giving, joy-taking Presence in the midst of them, and you may laugh at all assaults of 'infidelity,' which is foolishness to him who knows his God as—only far better than—he knows father or mother, wife or child.

'The Shout of a King.'—Let them grow up, too, with the shout of a King in their midst. There are, in this poor stuff we call human nature, founts of loyalty, worship, passionate devotion, glad service, which have, alas! To be unsealed in the earth-laden older heart, but only ask place to flow from the child's. There is no safeguard and no joy like that of being under orders, being possessed, controlled, continually in the service of One whom it is gladness to obey. We lose sight of the fact in our modern civilisation, but a king, a leader, implies warfare, a foe, victory— possible defeat and disgrace. And this is the conception of life which cannot too soon be brought before children.

The Fight of Christ against the Devil.—
After thinking the matter over with some care, I
resolved that I cannot do better than give you my
view of what it was that the average boy carried away
from our Rugby of half a century ago which stood
him in the best stead—was of the highest value to
him—in after life. . . . I have been in some doubt as
to what to put first, and am by no means sure that
the few who are left of my old schoolfellows would
agree with me; but, speaking for myself, I think
this was our most marked characteristic, the feeling
that in school and close we were in training for a big
fight—were, in fact, already engaged in it—a fight
which would last all our lives, and try all our powers,
physical, intellectual, and moral, to the utmost. I
need not say that this fight was the world-old one of
good with evil, of light and truth against darkness
and sin, of Christ against the devil."

So said the author of *Tom Brown* in an address
to Rugby School delivered on a recent Quinquagesima
Sunday. This is plain speaking; education is only
worthy of the name as it teaches this lesson; and it is
a lesson which should be learnt in the home or ever
the child sets foot in any other school of life. It is
an insult to children to say they are too young to
understand this for which we are sent into the world.

'Oh dear, it's very hard to do God's Work!'—
A boy of five, a great-grandson of Dr Arnold, was
sitting at the piano with his mother, choosing his
Sunday hymn; he chose 'Thy will be done,' and,
as his special favourite, the verse beginning 'Renew
my will from day to day.' The choice of hymn and
verse rather puzzled his mother, who had a further
glimpse into the world of child-thought when the

little fellow said wistfully, 'Oh, dear, it's very hard to do God's work!' The difference between doing and bearing was not plain to him, but the battle and struggle and strain of life already pressed on the spirit of the 'careless, happy child.' That an evil spiritual personality can get at their thoughts, and incite them to 'be naughty,' children learn all too soon and understand, perhaps, better than we do. Then, they are cross, 'naughty,' separate, sinful, needing to be healed as truly as the hoary sinner, and much more aware of their need, because the tender soul of the child, like an infant's skin, is fretted by spiritual soreness. 'It's very good of God to forgive me so often; I've been naughty so many times to-day,' said a sad little sinner of six, not at all because any one else had been at the pains to convince her of naughtiness. Even 'Pet Marjorie's' buoyancy is not proof against this sad sense of shortcoming:—

'Yesterday I behaved extremely ill in God's most holy church, for I would never attend myself nor let Isabella attend, . . . and it was the very same *Devil* that tempted Job that tempted me, I am sure; but he resisted Satan, though he had boils and many other misfortunes which I have escaped.'—(At six!)

We must needs smile at the little 'crimes,' but we must not smile too much, and let children be depressed with much 'naughtiness' when they should live in the instant healing, in the dear Name, of the Saviour of the world.

CHAPTER VII

THE PARENT AS SCHOOLMASTER

'The Schoolmaster will make him sit up!'—
'Sit up,' that is, 'come when he's called,' apparently, for
the remark concerned a young person who went on
spinning his top with nonchalance, ignoring an inter-
mittent stream of objurgations from his mother, whose
view was that bedtime had arrived. Circumstances
alter cases, but is it unheard of in higher ranks of
life to trust to the schoolmaster to make a child 'sit
up,' after a good deal of mental and moral sprawling
about at home?

**Reasons why this Task is left to the School-
master.**— 'Oh, he's a little fellow yet; he will know
better by-and-by.'

'My view is, let children have a delightful childhood.
Time enough for restraint and contradiction
when they go to school.'

'We do not hold with punishing children; love
your children, and let them alone, is our principle.'

'They will meet with hardness enough in the world.
Childhood shall have no harsh memories for them.'

'School will break them in. Let them grow like
young colts till the time comes to break them. All
young things should be free to kick about.'

'What's bred in the bone must come out in the

flesh. I do not care much for all this clipping and shaping of children. Destroys individuality.'

'When he's older, he will know better. Time cures many faults.'

And so on; we might fill pages with the wise things people say, who, for one excellent reason or another, prefer to leave it to the schoolmaster to make a child 'sit up.' And does the schoolmaster live up to his reputation? How far does he succeed with the child who comes to him with no self-management? His real and proud successes are with the children who have been trained to 'sit up' at home. His pleasure in such children is unbounded; the pains he takes with them unlimited; the successful careers he is able to launch them upon exceed the ambition of those most wildly ambitious of human beings (dare we say it?)—parents, quiet, sensible, matter-of-fact parents. But the schoolmaster takes little credit to himself for these happy results. Schoolmasters and schoolmistresses are modest people, though they are not always credited with their virtues.

His Successes are with Children who have been Trained at Home.—'You can do anything with So-and-so; his parents have turned him out so well.' Observe, the master takes little credit to himself (by no means so much as he deserves); and why? Experience makes fools wise; and what then of those who add experience to wisdom? 'People send us their cubs to lick into shape, and what can we do?' Now the answer to this query concerns parents rather closely: what and how much can the schoolmaster do to make the boy 'sit up' who has not been to the manner bred?

No suasion will make you 'sit up' if you are an

oyster; no, nor even if you are a cod. You must have a backbone, and your backbone must have learned its work before sitting up is possible to you. No doubt the human oyster may grow a backbone, and the human cod may get into the way of sitting up, and some day, perhaps, we shall know of the heroic endeavours made by schoolmaster and mistress to prop up, and haul up, and draw up, and anyhow keep alert and sitting up, creatures whose way it is to sprawl. Sometimes the result is surprising; they sit up in a row with the rest and look all right; even when the props are removed they keep to the trick of sitting up for a while. The schoolmaster begins to rub his hands, and the parents say, 'I told you so. Didn't I always say Jack would come right in the end?' Wait a bit. The end is not yet.

The Habits of School Life are Mechanical.— The habits of school, as of military life, are more or less mechanical. The early habits are vital; reversion to these takes place, and Jack sprawls as a man just as he sprawled as a child, only more so. Various social props keep him up; he has the wit to seem to 'sit up'; he is lovable and his life is respectable; and no one suspects that this easy-going Mr John Brown is a failure: a man who had the elements of greatness in him, and might have been of use in the world had he been put under discipline from his infancy.

Mental 'Sprawling' exemplified in 'Edward Waverley.'— Sprawling is an ugly word, but the attitude we are thinking of is by no means always inelegant. Scott gives a delightful illustration of one kind of mental sprawling in *Waverley*:—

"Edward Waverley's powers of apprehension were

so quick as almost to resemble intuition, and the chief care of his preceptor was to prevent him, as a sportsman would phrase it, from overrunning his game; that is, from acquiring his knowledge in a slight, flimsy, and inadequate manner. And here the instructor had to combat another propensity too often united with brilliancy of fancy and vivacity of talent— the indolence, namely, which can only be stirred by some strong motive of gratification, and which renounces study as soon as curiosity is gratified, the pleasure of conquering the first difficulties exhausted, and the novelty of pursuit at an end." And the story goes on to show, without laborious pointing of the moral, how *Waverley* by name was *wavering* by nature, was ever the sport of circumstances because he had not learned in youth to direct his course. He blunders into many (most interesting) misadventures because he had failed to get, through his studies, the alertness of mind and the self-restraint which should make a man of him. Many pleasant things befall him, but not one of them, unless we except Rose Bradwardine's love—and when did woman study justice in the bestowal of her favours?—not one did he earn by his own wit or prowess; each advantage and success which came to him was the earnings of another man. The elder Waverley had not only fortune but force of character to make friends, so we are not made sad for the amiable young man for whom we must needs feel affection; he does nothing to carve out a way for himself, and he does everything to his own hindrance out of pure want of the power of self-direction, but his uncle has fortune and friends, and all ends well. For the sake, no doubt, of young persons less happily situated, and of parents who are not able to play the part of bountiful Providence to sons and daughters whom they have failed to fit for the conduct of their own lives, the great novelist takes care to point out that Edward Waverley's personal failure in life was the fault of his education. His abilities were even brilliant, but 'I ought' had waited upon 'I like' from his earliest days, and he had never learned to make himself do the thing he would.

Parents are apt to leave training in Self-compelling Power to the Schoolmaster.—Now it is this sort of 'bringing under' that parents are apt to leave to the schoolmaster. They do not give their children the discipline which results in self-compelling power; and by-and-by, when they make over the task to another, the time for training in the art of self-mastery has gone by, and a fine character is spoiled through indolence and wilfulness.

'But why will it not do to leave it to the schoolmaster to make a child "sit up"? It is natural for a child to be left free as a bird in matters of no moral significance. We would not let him tell lies, but if he hate his lessons, that may be Nature's way of showing he had better let them alone.'

We are not meant to grow up in a state of Nature.—We must face the facts. We are not meant to grow up in a state of nature. There is something simple, conclusive, even idyllic, in the statement that So-and-so is 'natural.' What more would you have? Jean Jacques Rousseau preached the doctrine of natural education, and no reformer has had a greater following. 'It's human nature,' we say, when stormy Harry snatches his drum from Jack; when baby Marjorie, who is not two, screams for Susie's doll. So it is, and for that very reason it must be dealt with early. Even Marjorie must be taught better. 'I always finish teaching my children obedience before they are one year old,' said a wise mother; and any who know the nature of children, and the possibilities open to the educator, will say, Why not? Obedience in the first year, and all the virtues of the good life as the years go on; every year with its own definite work to show in the training of character. Is Edward a selfish child when his fifth birthday comes? The fact is noted in his parents' year-book, with the resolve that by his sixth birthday he shall, please God, be a generous child. Here, the reader who has not realised that to exercise discipline is one of the chief functions of parenthood, smiles and talks about 'human nature' with all the air of an unanswerable argument

The First Function of the Parent is that of Discipline.—But we live in a redeemed world, and one of the meanings which that unfathomable phrase bears is, that it is the duty of those who have the care of childhood to eradicate each vulgar and hateful trait, to plant and foster the fruits of that kingdom in the children who have been delivered from the kingdom of nature into the kingdom of grace; that is to say, all children born into this redeemed world. The parent who believes that the possibilities of virtuous training are unlimited will set to work with cheerful confidence, will forego the twaddle about 'Nature,' whether as lovely in itself or as an irresistible force, and will perceive that the first function of the parent is that function of *discipline* which is so cheerfully made over to the schoolmaster.

Education is a Discipline.—Discipline does

not mean a birch-rod, nor a corner, nor a slipper, nor a bed, nor any such last resort of the feeble. The sooner we cease to believe in merely penal suffering as part of the divine plan, the sooner will a spasmodic resort to the birch-rod die out in families. We do not say the rod is never useful; we do say it should never be necessary. The fact is, many of us do not believe in education, except as it means the acquirement of a certain amount of knowledge; but education which shall deal curatively and methodically with every flaw in character does not enter into our scheme of things possible. No less than this is what we mean when we say, Education is a Discipline. Where his parents fail, the poor soul has one further chance in the discipline of life; but we must remember that, while it is the nature of the child to submit to discipline, it is the nature of the undisciplined man to run his head in passionate wilfulness against the circumstances that are for his training; so that the parent who wilfully chooses to leave his child to be 'broken in' by the schoolmaster or by life leaves him to a fight in which all the odds are against him. The physique, the temper, the disposition, the career, the affections, the aspirations of a man are all, more or less, the outcome of the discipline his parents have brought him under, or of the lawlessness they have allowed.

Discipline is not Punishment.—What is discipline? Look at the word; there is no hint of punishment in it. A disciple is a follower, and discipline is the state of the follower, the learner, imitator. Mothers and fathers do not well to forget that their children are, by the very order of Nature, their disciples. Now no man sets himself up for a following of disciples who does not wish to indoctrinate these with certain principles, or at the least, maxims, rules of life. So should the parent have at heart notions of life and duty which he labours without pause to instil into his children.

How Disciples are Lured.—He who would draw disciples does not trust to force; but to these three things—to the attraction of his doctrine, to the persuasion of his presentation, to the enthusiasm of his disciples; so the parent has teachings of the perfect life which he knows how to present continually with winning force until the children are quickened with such zeal for virtue and holiness as carries them forward with leaps and bounds.

Steady Progress on a Careful Plan.—Again, the teacher does not indoctrinate his pupils all at once, but here a little and there a little, steady progress on a careful plan; so the parent who would have his child a partaker of the Divine nature has a scheme, an ascending scale of virtues, in which he is diligent to practise his young disciple. He adds to the faith with which the child is so richly dowered, virtue; and to virtue, knowledge; and to knowledge, self-control. Having practised his child in self-control, he trains him in patience; and to patience he adds godliness; and to godliness, kindness; and to kindness, love. These, and such as these, wise parents cultivate as systematically and with as definite results as if they were teaching the 'three R's.'

But how? The answer covers so wide a field that we must leave it for another chapter. Only this here every quality has its defect, every defect has its quality. Examine your child; he has qualities, he is generous;

see to it that the lovable little fellow, who would give away his soul, is not also rash, impetuous, self-willed, passionate, 'nobody's enemy but his own.' It rests with parents to make low the high places and exalt the valleys, to make straight paths for the feet of their little son.

CHAPTER VIII

THE CULTURE OF CHARACTER

Parents as Trainers

"What get I from my father?
Lusty life and vigorous will:
What from my gentle mother?
Cheerful days and poet's skill," [1]

says Goethe; for poets, like the rest of us, are born, not made, and get the most of what they are from their parents. But it did not take poet or modern scientist to discover this; people have known it time out of mind. Like father, like child, they said, and were satisfied; for it was not the way in earlier days to thresh out the great facts of life.

How far does Heredity count?—Not so now; we talk about it and about it; call it *heredity*, and take it into count in our notions, at anyrate, if not in our practice. Nobody writes a biography now without attempting to produce progenitors and early surroundings that shall account for his man or his woman. This fact of heredity is very much before the public, and by-and-by will have its bearing on the loose

[1] "Vom Vater hab' ich die Statur,
Des Lebens ernstes Fuhren;
Vom Mutterchen die Frohnatur,
Und Lust zu fabuliren."

notions people hold about education. In this sort of way—'Harold is a bright little boy, but he hasn't the least power of attention.'

'Oh, I know he hasn't; but then, poor child, he can't help it! "What's bred in the bone," you know; and we are feather-brained on both sides of the house.'

Now the practical educational question of our day is just this, Can he help it? Or, Can his parents help it? or, Must the child sit down for life with whatever twist he has inherited? The fact is, many of us, professional teachers, have been taking aim rather beside the mark; we talk as if the development of certain faculties were the chief object of education; and we point to our results, intellectual, moral, aesthetic, physical, with a—'See there, what culture can effect!'

For their Education, Children want chiefly Opportunity.—But we forget that the child has inborn cravings after all we have given him. Just as the healthy child must have his dinner and his bed, so too does he crave for knowledge, perfection, beauty, power, society; and all he wants is opportunity. Give him opportunities of loving and learning, and he will love and learn, for "tis his nature to.' Whoever has taken note of the sweet reasonableness, the quick intelligence, the bright imaginings of a child, will think the fuss we make about the right studies for developing these is like asking, How shall we get a hungry man to eat his dinner?

Many a man got his turn for natural science because as a boy he lived in the country, and had a chance to observe living things and their ways. Nobody took pains to develop his faculty; all he had was opportunity. If the boy's mind is crammed with other matters, he has no opportunity; and you may meet men of culture who have lived most of their lives in the country, and don't know a thrush from a blackbird. I know of a woman who has developed both a metaphysical and a literary turn, because as a girl of ten she was allowed to browse on old volumes of the *Spectator*, the most telling part of her education, she thinks.

An Experiment in Art Education.—Again, I watched quite lately an extraordinary educational result of opportunity. A friend, interested in a Working Boys' Club, undertook to teach a class to model in clay. There was no selection made; the boys were mill-boys, taken as they came in, with no qualifications, except that, as their teacher said, they had not been spoilt—that is, they had not been taught to draw in the ordinary way. She gave them clay, a model, one or two modelling tools, and also, being an artist, the *feeling* of the object to be copied. After half a dozen lessons, the things they produced cannot be called less than works of art; and delightful it was to see the vigour and spirit they worked with, the artistic instinct which caught the sentiment of the object, as the creases made by a little foot which make a child's shoe a thing to kiss. This lady maintains that she only *let out* what was in the boys; but she did more—her own art enthusiasm forced out artistic effort. Even taking into account the enthusiasm of the teacher—I wish we might always count on that factor—this remains a fair case to prove our point, which is, give them opportunity and direction, and children will do the greater part of their own education, intellectual, aesthetic, even moral, by reason of the wonderfully balanced desires, powers, and affections which go to make up human nature.

A cheerful doctrine this, which should help to swell the ranks of the unemployed. Outlets for their energies, a little direction, a little control, and then we may sit by with folded hands and see them do it. But, in fact, there are two things to be done: powers to be developed—where a little of our help goes a long way; and character to be formed—and here children are as clay in the hands of the potter, absolutely dependent on their parents.

But Character is an Achievement.—Disposition, intellect, genius, come pretty much by nature; but character is an achievement, the one practical achievement possible to us for ourselves and for our children; and all real advance in family or individual is along the lines of character. Our great people are great simply by reason of their force of character. For this, more than for their literary successes, Carlyle and Johnson are great. Boswell's *Life* is, and perhaps deserves to be, more of a literary success than anything of his master's; but what figure does he make after all?

Two Ways of Preserving Sanity.—Greatness and littleness belong to character, and life would be dull were we all cast in one mould; but how come we to differ? Surely by reason of our inherited qualities. It is hereditary tendencies which result in character. The man who is generous, obstinate, hot-tempered, devout, is so, on the whole, because that strain of character runs in his family. Some progenitor got a bent from his circumstances towards fault or virtue, and that bent will go on repeating itself to the end of the chapter. To save that single quality from the exaggeration which would destroy the balance of qualities we call sanity, two counter-forces are provided: marriage into alien families, and *education*.

The Development of Character the Main Work of Education.—We come round now to the point we started from. If the development of character rather than of faculty is the main work of education, and if people are born, so to speak, ready-made, with all the elements of their after-character in them, certain to be developed by time and circumstances, what is left for education to do?

Plausible Reasons for Doing Nothing.—Very commonly, the vote is, do nothing; though there are three or four ways of arriving at that conclusion.

As, What's the good? The fathers have eaten sour grapes; the children's teeth *must* be set on edge. Tommy is obstinate as a little mule—but what would you have? So is his father. So have been all the Joneses, time out of mind; and Tommy's obstinacy is taken as a fact, not to be helped nor hindered.

Or, Mary is a butterfly of a child, never constant for five minutes to anything she has in hand. 'That child is just like me!' says her mother; 'but time will steady her.' Fanny, again, sings herself to sleep with the Sicilian Vesper Hymn (her nurse's lullaby) before she is able to speak. 'It's strange how an ear for music runs in our family!' is the comment, but no particular pains are taken to develop the talent.

Another child asks odd questions, is inclined to make little jokes about sacred things, to call his father 'Tom,' and, generally, to show a want of reverence. His parents are earnest-minded people—think with pain of the loose opinions of Uncle Harry, and decide on a policy of repression. 'Do as you're bid, and make no remarks,' becomes the child's rule of life, until he finds outlets little suspected at home.

In another case, common thought is much more on a level with the science of the day; there is a tendency to lung-trouble: the doctors undertake to deal with the tendency so long as the *habit* of delicacy is not set up. The necessary precautions are taken, and there is no reason why the child should not die at a good old age.

Once more—there are parents who are aware of the advances science has made in education, but doubt the lawfulness of looking to science for aid in the making of character. They see hereditary defects in their children, but set them down as of 'the natural fault and corruption of the nature of every man which naturally is engendered of the offspring of Adam.' This, they believe, it is not their part to remedy; that is, unless the boy's fault be of a disturbing kind— a violent temper, for example—when the mother thinks no harm to whip the offending Adam out of him.

But the Laws by which Body, Mind, and Moral Nature flourish have been Revealed by Science.—But so surely as we believe the laws of the spiritual life to have been revealed to us, so, not less surely, though without the same sanctity, have been revealed the laws by which body, mind and moral nature flourish or decay. These it behoves us to make ourselves acquainted with; and the Christian parent who is shy of science, and prefers to bring up his children by the light of Nature when that of authoritative revelation fails, does so to his children's irreparable loss.

The Race is Advancing.—If the race is advancing, it is along the lines of character, for each new generation inherits and adds to the best that has gone before it. We should have to-day the very flower and fruit that has been a-preparing through long lines of progenitors. Children have always been lovely, so far back as that day when a little child in the streets of Jerusalem was picked up and set in the midst to show of what sort are the princes in the Kingdom to come:

'In the Kingdom are the children—
You may read it in their eyes;
All the freedom of the Kingdom
In their careless humour lies.'

And what mother has not bowed before the princely heart of innocence in her own little child? But apart from this, of their glad living in the sunshine of the Divine countenance, surely our children are 'more so' than those of earlier days. Never before was a 'Jackanapes' written, or the 'Story of a Short Life.' Shakespeare never made a child, nor Scott, hardly Dickens, often as he tried; either we are waking up to what is in them, or the children are indeed advancing in the van of the times, holding in light grasp the gains of the past, the possibilities of the future. It is the age of child-worship; and very lovely are the well-brought-up children of Christian and cultured parents. But alas, how many of us degrade the thing we love! Think of the multitude of innocents to be launched on the world, already mutilated, spiritually and morally, at the hands of doting parents.

The duty of cherishing certain Family Traits.—The duteous father and mother, on the contrary, who discern any lovely family trait in one of their children, set themselves to nourish and cherish it as a gardener the peaches he means to show. We know how 'that kiss made me a painter,' that is, warmed into life whatever art faculty the child had. The choicer the plant, the gardener tells us, the greater the pains must he take with the rearing of it: and here is the secret of the loss and waste of some of the most beauteous and lovable natures the world has seen; they have not had the pains taken with their rearing that their delicate, sensitive organisations demanded. Think how Shelley was left to himself! We live in embarrassing days. It is well to cry, 'Give us light—more light and fuller'; but what if the new light discover to us a maze of obligations, intricate and tedious?

Distinctive Qualities ask for Culture.—It is, at first sight, bewildering to perceive that for whatever distinctive quality, moral or intellectual, we discern in the children, special culture is demanded; but, after all, our obligation towards each such quality resolves itself into providing for it these four things: nourishment, exercise, change, and rest.

Four Conditions of Culture—Exercise.—A child has a great turn for languages (his grandfather was the master of nine); the little fellow 'lisps in Latin,' learns his '*mensa*' from his nurse, knows his declensions before he is five. What line is open to the mother who sees such an endowment in her child? First, let him use it; let him learn his declensions, and whatever else he takes to without the least sign of effort. Probably the Latin case-endings come as easily and pleasantly to his ear as does 'See-saw, Margery Daw,' to the ordinary child, though no doubt 'Margery Daw' is the wholesomer kind of thing.

Nourishment.—Let him do just so much as he takes to of his own accord; but never urge, never applaud, never show him off. Next, let words convey ideas as he is able to bear them. Buttercup, primrose, dandelion, magpie, each tells its own tale; daisy is day's-eye, opening with the sun, and closing when he sets—

> 'That well by reason it men callen may
> The daisie, or else the eye of day.'

Let him feel that the common words we use without a thought are beautiful, full of story and interest. It is a great thing that the child should get the *ideas* proper to the qualities inherent in him. An idea fitly put is taken in without effort, and, once in, ideas behave like living creatures—they feed, grow, and multiply.

Change.—Next, provide him with some one delightful change of thought, that is, with work and ideas altogether apart from his bent for languages. Let him know, with friendly intimacy, the out-of-door objects that come in his way—the redstart, the rosechaffer, the ways of the caddis-worm, forest trees, field flowers—all natural objects, common and curious, near his home. No other knowledge is so delightful as this common acquaintance with natural objects.

Or, again, some one remarks that all our great inventors have in their youth handled material— clay, wood, iron, brass, pigments. Let him work in material. To provide a child with delightful resources on lines opposed to his natural bent is the one way of keeping a quite sane mind in the presence of an absorbing pursuit.

Rest.—At the same time, change of occupation is not rest: if a man ply a machine, now with his foot, and now with his hand, the foot or the hand rests, but the man does not. A game of romps (better, so far as mere rest goes, than games with laws and competitions), nonsense talk, a fairy tale, or to lie on his back in the sunshine, should rest the child, and of such as these he should have his fill.

Work and Waste of Brain Tissue Necessary.— This, speaking broadly, is the *rationale* of the matter: just as actually as we sew or write through the instrumentality of the hand, so the child learns, thinks, feels, by means of a material organ—the very delicate nervous tissue of the cerebrum. Now this tissue is constantly and rapidly wearing away. The more it is used, whether in the way of mental effort or emotional excitement, the more it wears away. Happily, rapid new growth replaces the waste, wherefore work and consequent waste of tissue are necessary. But let the waste get ahead of the gain, and lasting mischief happens. Therefore never let the child's brain-work exceed his chances of reparation, whether such work come in the way of too hard lessons, or of the excitement attending childish dissipations. Another plea for abundant rest is that one thing at a time, and that done well, appears to be Nature's rule; and his hours of rest and play are the hours of the child's physical growth; witness the stunted appearance of children who are allowed to live in a whirl of small excitements.

A word more as to the necessity of *change of thought* for the child who has a distinct bent. The brain tissue not only wastes with work, but, so to speak, wastes locally. We all know how done up we are after giving our minds for a few hours or days to any one subject, whether anxious or joyous: we are glad at last to escape from the engrossing thought, and find it a weariness when it returns upon us. It would appear that, set up the continuous working of certain ideas, and a certain tract of the brain substance is, as it were, worn out and weakened with the constant traffic in these ideas. And this is of more consequence when the ideas are moral than when they are merely intellectual. Hamlet's thoughts play continuously round a few distressing facts; he becomes morbid, not entirely sane; in a word, he is *eccentric*.

Danger of Eccentricity.—Possibly, eccentricity is a danger against which the parents of well-descended children must be on the watch. These are born with strong tendencies to certain qualities and ways of thinking. Their bringing-up tends to accentuate their qualities; the balance between these and other qualities is lost, and their become eccentric persons. Mr Matthew Arnold writes down the life and the work of a great poet as *ineffectual*; and this is, often enough, the verdict passed upon the eccentric. Whatever force of genius and of character, whatever lovely moral traits they may have, the world will not take them as guides for good unless they do as others do in things lawful and expedient; and truly there is a broad margin for originality in declining to hunt with the hounds in things neither lawful nor expedient.

Causes of Oddity in Children.—What is the mother's course who notices in her most promising child little traits of oddity? He does not care much for games, does not get on well with the rest, has some little den of his own where he ruminates. Poor little fellow! he wants a confidante badly; most likely he has tried nurse and brothers and sisters, to no purpose. If this go on, he will grow up with the idea that nobody wants him, nobody understands him, will take his slice of life and eat it (with a snarl) all by himself. But if his mother have tact enough to get at him, she will preserve for the world one of its saving characters. Depend upon it, there is something at work in the child—genius, humanity, poetry, ambition, pride of family; it is that he wants outlet and exercise for an inherited trait almost too big for his childish soul. Rosa Bonheur was observed to be a restless child whose little shoes of life were a misfit: lessons did not please her, and play did not please her; and her *artist* father hit on the notion of soothing the child's divine discontent by—apprenticing her to a needlewoman! Happily she broke her bonds, and we have her pictures. In the case of pride of birth, it is well that the child should be brought face to face and heart to heart with the 'great humility' of our Pattern. But that being done, this sense of family distinction is a wonderful lever to raise the little world of the child's nature. *Noblesse oblige*. He must needs add honour and not dishonour to a distinguished family. I know of a little boy who bears two distinguished family names—Browning-Newton, let us say. He goes to a preparatory school, where it is the custom to put the names of defaulters on the blackboard. By-and-by, his little brother went to school too, and the bigger boy's exordium was: 'We'll *never* let two such names as ours be stuck up on the blackboard!'

The   Dreariness   of   a   Motiveless   Life.—
Amongst the immediate causes of eccentricity is the
dreariness of daily living, the sense of which falls
upon us all at times, and often with deadly weight
upon the more finely strung and highly gifted. 'Oh,
dear, I wish I was in Jupiter!' sighed a small urchin
who had already used up this planet. It rests with
the parents to see that the dreariness of a motiveless
life does not settle, sooner or later, on any one of
their children. We are made with a yearning for the
'fearful joy' of passion; and if this do not come to
us in lawful ways, we look for it in eccentric, or worse,
in illegitimate courses. The mother, to whom her
child is as an open book, must find a vent for the
restless workings of his nature, the more apt to be
troubled by—

> 'The burden of the mystery,
> The heavy and the weary weight
> Of all this unintelligible world'

the more finely he is himself organised. Fill him
with the enthusiasm of humanity. Whatever gifts he
has, let them be cultivated as 'gifts for men.' "The
thing best worth living for is *to be of use*," was well
said lately by a thinker who has left us; and the child
into whose notion of life that idea is fitted will not
grow up to find time heavy on his hands. The life
blessed with an enthusiasm will not be dull; but a
weight must go into the opposite scale to balance
even the noblest enthusiasm. As we have said,
open for him some door of natural science, some way
of mechanical skill; in a word, give the child an
absorbing pursuit and a fascinating hobby, and you
need not fear eccentric or unworthy developments.

We must Save our 'Splendid Failures.'—
It seems well to dwell at length on this subject of
eccentricity, because the world loses a great deal by
its splendid failures, the beautiful human beings who,
through one sort of eccentricity or another, become
ineffectual for the raising of the rest of us.

CHAPTER IX

THE CULTURE OF CHARACTER

The Treatment of Defects

The Ultimate Object of Education.—Suppose the parent see that the formation of character is the ultimate object of education; see, too, that character is, in the rough, the inherited tendencies of the child, modified by his surroundings, but that character may be debased or ennobled by education; that it is the parents' part to distinguish the first faint budding of family traits; to greet every fine trait as the highest sort of family possession to be nourished and tended with care; to keep up at the same time the balance of qualities by bringing forward that which is of little account—the more so when they must deliver their child from eccentricity, pitfall to the original and forceful nature;—suppose they have taken all this into the *role* of their duties, there yet remains much for parents to do.

The Defects of our Qualities.—We are open to what the French call the defects of our qualities; and as ill weeds grow apace, the defects of a fine character may well choke out the graces. A little maiden loves with the passion and devotion of a woman, but she is exacting of return, and jealous of intrusion, even with her mother. A boy is ambitious; he will be leader in the nursery, and his lead is wholesome for the rest; but there is the pugnacious little brother who will not 'follow my leader,' and the two can hardly live in the same rooms; the able boy is a tyrant when his will is crossed. There is the timid, affectionate little maid who will even tell a fib to shield her sister; and there is the high-spirited girl who never lies, but who does, now and then, bully; and so on without end. What is the parents' part here? To magnify the quality; make the child feel that he or she has a virtue to guard—a *family* possession, and, at the same time, a gift from above. A little simple reasonable teaching may help; but let us beware of much talk. 'Have you *quite* finished, mother?' said a bright little girl of five in the most polite way in the world. She had listened long to her mother's sermonising, and had many things on hand. A wise word here and there may be of use, but much more may be done by carefully hindering each 'defect of its quality' from coming into play. Give the ill weeds no room to grow. Then, again, the defect may often be reclaimed and turned back to feed the quality itself. The ambitious boy's love of power may be worked into a desire to win by love his restive little brother. The passion of the loving girl may be made to include all whom her mother loves.

Children with Defects.—There is another aspect of the subject of heredity and the duties it entails. As the child of long lineage may well inherit much of what was best in his ancestors—fine physique, clear intellect, high moral worth—so also he has his risks. As some one puts it, not all the women have been brave, nor all the men chaste. We know how the tendency to certain forms of disease runs in families; temper and temperament, moral and physical nature alike, may come down with a taint. An unhappy child may, by some odd freak of nature, appear to have left out the good and taken into him only the unworthy. What can the parents do in such a case? They may, not *re*form him—perhaps that is beyond human skill and care, once he has become all that is possible to his nature— but *transform* him, so that the being he was calculated to become never develops at all; but another being comes to light blest with every grace of which he had only the defect. This brings us to a beneficent law of Nature, which underlies the whole subject of early training, and especially so this case of the child whose mother must bring him forth a second time into a life of beauty and harmony. To put it in an old form of words—the words of Thomas a Kempis—what seems to me the fundamental law of education is no more than this: 'Habit is driven out by habit.' People have always known that 'Use is second nature,' but the reason why, and the scope of the saying, these are discoveries of recent days.

A Malicious Child.—A child has an odious custom, so constant, that it is his quality, will be his *character*, if you let him alone; he is spiteful, he is sly, he is sullen. No one is to blame for it; it was born in him. What are you to do with such inveterate habit of nature? Just this; treat it as a bad *habit*, and set up the opposite good habit. Henry is more than mischievous; he is a malicious little boy. There are always tears in the nursery, because, with 'pinches, nips, and bobs,' he is making some child wretched. Even his pets are not safe; he has done his canary to death by poking at it with a stick through the bars of its cage; howls from his dog, screeches from his cat, betray him in some vicious trick. He makes fearful faces at his timid little sister; sets traps with string for the housemaid with her water-cans to fall over; there is no end to the malicious tricks, beyond the mere savagery of untrained boyhood, which come to his mother's ear. What is to be done? 'Oh, he will grow out of it!' say the more hopeful who pin their faith to time. But many an experienced mother will say, 'You can't cure him; what is in will out, and he will be a pest to society all his life.' Yet the child may be cured in a month if the mother will set herself to the task with both hands and of set purpose; at any rate, the cure may be well begun, and that is half done.

Special Treatment.—Let the month of treatment be a deliciously happy month to him, he living all the time in the sunshine of his mother's smile. Let him not be left to himself to meditate or carry out ugly pranks. Let him feel himself always under a watchful, loving, and *approving* eye. Keep him happily occupied, well amused. All this, to break the old custom which is assuredly broken when a certain length of time goes by without its repetition. But one habit drives out another. Lay new lines in the old place. Open avenues of kindness for him. Let him enjoy, daily, hourly, the pleasure of pleasing. Get him into the way of making little plots for the pleasure of the rest—a plaything of his contriving, a dish of strawberries of his gathering, shadow rabbits to amuse the baby; take him on kind errands to poor neighbours, carrying and giving of his own. For a whole month the child's whole heart is flowing out in deeds and schemes and thoughts of lovingkindness, and the ingenuity which spent itself in malicious tricks becomes an acquisition to his family when his devices are benevolent. Yes; but where is his mother to get time in these encroaching days to put Henry under special treatment? She has other children and other duties, and simply cannot give herself up for a month or a week to one child. If the boy were ill, in danger, would she find time for him then? Would not other duties go to the wall, and leave her little son, for the time, her chief object in life?

Moral Ailments need Prompt Attention.— Now here is a point all parents are not enough awake to—that serious mental and moral ailments require prompt, purposeful, curative treatment, to which the parents must devote themselves for a short time, just as they would to a sick child. Neither punishing him nor letting him alone—the two lines of treatment most in favour—ever cured a child of any moral evil. If parents recognised the efficacy and the immediate effect of treatment, they would never allow the spread of ill weeds. For let this be borne in mind, whatever ugly quality disfigures the child, he is but as a garden overgrown with weeds: the more prolific the weeds, the more fertile the soil; he has within him every possibility of beauty of life and character. Get rid of the weeds and foster the flowers. It is hardly too much to say that most of the failures in life or character made by man or woman are due to the happy-go-lucky philosophy of the parents. They say, 'The child is so young; he does not know any better; but all that will come right as he grows up.' Now, a fault of character left to itself can do no other than strengthen.

An objection may be raised to this counsel of short and determined curative treatment. The good results do not last, it is said; a week or two of neglect, and you lose the ground gained: Henry is as likely as ever to grow up of the 'tiger' order, a Steerforth or a Grandcourt. But here science comes to help us to cheerful certainty.

There is no more interesting subject of inquiry open just now than that of the interaction between the thoughts of the mind and the configuration of the brain. The fair conclusion appears to be that each is greatly the cause of the other; that the character of the persistent thoughts actually shapes the cerebrum, while on the configuration of this organ depends in turn the manner of thoughts we think.

Automatic Brain Action.—Thought is, for the most part, automatic. We think, without intention or effort, as we have been accustomed to think, just as we walk or write without any conscious arrangement of muscles. Mozart could write an overture, laughing all the time at the little jokes his wife made to keep him awake; to be sure he had thought it out before, and there it was, ready to be written; but he did not consciously try for these musical thoughts, they simply came to him in proper succession. Coleridge thought 'Kubla Khan' in his sleep, and wrote it when he awoke; and, indeed, he might as well have been asleep all the time for all he had to do with the production of most of his thoughts.

> 'Over the buttons she falls asleep,
> And stitches them on in a dream'—

is very possible and likely. For one thing which we consciously set ourselves to think about, a thousand words and acts come from us every day of their own accord; we don't think of them at all. But all the same, only a poet or a musician could thus give forth poetry or music, and it is the words and acts which come from us without *conscious* thought which afford the true measure of what we are. Perhaps this is why such serious weight is attached to our every 'idle word'—words spoken without intention or volition.

We are getting, by degrees, to Henry and his bad habits. Somehow or other, the nervous tissue of the cerebrum 'grows to' the thoughts that are allowed free course in the mind. *How*, science hardly ventures to guess as yet; but, for the sake of illustration, let us imagine that certain thoughts of the mind run to and fro in the nervous substance of the cerebrum until they have made a way there: busy traffic in the same order of thoughts will always be kept up, for there is the easy way for them to run in. Take the child with an inherited tendency to a resentful temper: he has begun to think resentful thoughts; finds them easy and gratifying; he goes on; evermore the ugly traffic becomes more easy and natural, and resentfulness is rapidly becoming *himself*, that trait in his character which people couple with his name.

One Custom Overcomes Another.—But one custom overcomes another. The watchful mother sets up new tracks in other directions; and she sees to it, that while she is leading new thoughts through the new way, the old, deeply worn '*way* of thinking' is quite disused. Now, the cerebrum is in a state of rapid waste and rapid growth. The new growth takes shape from the new thought: the old is lost in the steady waste, and the child is reformed, physically as well as morally and mentally. That the nervous tissue of the cerebrum should be thus the *instrument* of the mind need not surprise us when we think how the muscles and joints of the tumbler, the vocal organs of the singer, the finger-ends of the watchmaker, the palate of the tea-taster, grow to the uses they are steadily put to; and, much more, both in the case of the brain and all other organs, grow to the uses they are *earliest* put to.

This meets in a wonderful way the case of the parent who sets himself to cure a moral failing. He sets up the course of new thoughts, and hinders those of the past, until the *new* thoughts shall have become automatic and run of their own accord. All the time a sort of disintegration is going on in the place that held the disused thoughts; and here is the parent's advantage. If the boy return (as, from inherited tendency, he still may do) to his old habits of thought, behold, there is no more place for them in his physical being; to make a new place is a work of time, and in this work the parent can overtake and hinder him without much effort.

A Material Register of Educational Efforts. —Here, indeed, more than anywhere, 'Except the Lord build the house, they labour but in vain that build it'; but surely intelligent co-operation in this divine work is our bounden duty and service. The training of the will, the instruction of the conscience, and, so far as it lies with us, the development of the divine life in the child, are carried on simultaneously with this training in the habits of a good life; and these last will carry the child safely over the season of infirm will, immature conscience, until he is able to take, under direction from above, the conduct of his life, the moulding of his character, into his own hands.

and that the Sunday School may be allowed to drop, the clergyman undertaking instead to ascertain, by means of catechising, that certain work is done month by month.

The scheme seems full of promise. Nothing should do more to strengthen the bonds of family life than that the children should learn religion at the lips of their parents; and to grow up in a Church which takes constant heed of you from baptism or infancy, until, we will not say confirmation, but through manhood and womanhood, until the end, should give the right tone to corporate life.

Parents are the Fit Instructors.—No doubt we have parishes, and even whole denominations, in which the young people are taken hold of from first to last; but then it is by the clergy, teachers, class leaders, and so on; and all parents do not regard it as an unmixed blessing that the most serious part of their children's training should be undertaken by outsiders. The thing that seems most worthy of imitation in this Australian movement is, that parents themselves are recognised as the fit instructors of their children in the best things, and that they are led to acknowledge some responsibility to the Church with regard to the instruction they give.

Report of a Committee on the Religious Education of the Upper and Middle Classes.—But do we manage these things so well 'at home' that we have no occasion to look about us for hints? It may be in the memories of some of us, that in May 1889 a Committee of the House of Laymen for the Province of Canterbury was appointed to examine into the religious education of the upper and middle

It is a comfort to believe that there is even a material register of our educational labours being made in the very substance of the child's brain; and, certainly, here we have a note of warning as to the danger of letting ill ways alone in the hope that all will come right by-and-by.

Mother-love is not Sufficient for Child-training.—Some parents may consider all this as heavy hearing; that even to 'think on these things' is enough to take the joy and spontaneousness out of their sweet relationship; and that, after all, parents' love and the grace of God should be sufficient for the bringing-up of children. No one can feel on this subject more sincere humility than those who have not the honour to be parents; the insight and love with which parents—mothers most so—are blest, is a divine gift which fills lookers-on with reverence, even in many a cottage home; but we have only to observe how many fond parents make foolish children to be assured that something more is wanted. There are appointed ways, not always the old paths, but new ones, opened up step by step as we go. The labour of the mother who sets herself to understand her work is not increased, but infinitely lightened; and as for life being made heavy with the thought of these things, once make them our own, and we act upon them as naturally as upon such knowledge—scientific also—as, loose your hold of a cup, and it falls. A little painstaking thought and effort in the first place, and all comes easy.

CHAPTER X

BIBLE LESSONS

Parents as Instructors in Religion

"The history of England is now reduced to a game at cards, —the problems of mathematics to puzzles and riddles. . . . There wants but one step further, and the Creed and Ten Commandments may be taught in the same manner, without the necessity of the grave face, deliberate tone of recital, and devout attention hitherto exacted from the well-governed childhood of this realm."—*Waverley*.

Sunday Schools are Necessary.—That parents should make over the religious education of their children to a Sunday School is, no doubt, as indefensible as if they sent them for their meals to a table maintained by the public bounty. We 'at home' plead not guilty to this particular count. Our Sunday Schools are used by those toil-worn and little-learned parents who are willing to accept at the hands of the more leisured classes this service of the religious teaching of their children. That is, the Sunday School is, at present, a necessary evil, an acknowledgment that there are parents so hard pressed that they are unable for their first duty. Here we have the theory of the Sunday School—the

parents who can, teach their childre Sunday, and substitutes step in to act f can not.

But Educated Parents should Ins Children in Religion—An Australian of the Parents' Union.—It is upon this theory of the Sunday School that a clerg the Antipodes has taken action. Never appear to occur to him that the members upper and middle classes do not need to be de and regularly instructed in religion—'from a His contention is, only that such children s not be taught at Sunday School, but at home, by their parents; and the main object of his paroc 'Parents' Union' is to help parents in this w These are some of the rules:—

1. The object of the Union shall be to unit strengthen, and assist fathers and mothers in th discharge of their parental duties.

2. Members shall be pledged, by the fact of their joining, to supervise the education of their own children, and to urge the responsibility of the parental relationship upon other parents.

3. Lesson sketches shall be furnished monthly to each family in connection with the Union.

4. Members shall bring their children to the monthly catechising, and sit with them, etc., etc. Probably the 'lesson-sketches' are to secure that the children do just such Bible-lessons at home with their parents on Sunday as they have hitherto done at the Sunday School with teachers.

It seems to be contemplated that parents of every class will undertake their proper duties in this matter,

[1] The Rev. E. Jackson, sometime of Sydney.

classes.[1] The Committee considered that they might obtain a good basis for their investigations by examining into the religious knowledge of boys entering school. They sent a paper of inquiries to sixty-two headmasters, most of whom sent replies; and from these replies the Committee were led to conclude that, "for the most part, the standard of religious education attained by boys before going to school is far below what might be hoped or expected; and that even this standard, thus ascertained to be far too low, is deteriorating; and further, that the chief cause of deterioration is considered to be the want of home-teaching and religion."

Why do Parents Neglect this Duty?—Here is matter of grave consideration for us all—for, though the investigation was conducted by Churchmen, it naturally covered boys of various denominations attending public and middle-class schools; the distinctive character of the religious education was the subject of separate inquiry. No doubt there are many beautiful exceptions; families brought up in quiet homes in the nurture and admonition of the Lord; but if it is, as some of us fear, a fact that there is a tendency among parents of the middle and upper classes to let the religious education of their children take care of itself, it is worth while to ask, What is the reason? and, What is the remedy? Many reasons are assigned for this alleged failure in parental duty—social claims, the restive temper of the young people and their impatience of religious

[1] See "Report of the Committee of the House of Laymen for the Province of Canterbury on the Duty of the Church with regard to the Religious Education of the Upper and Middle Classes."— *Nat. Soc. Depository, Westminster.*

teaching, and much else. But these reasons are inadequate. Parents are, on the whole, very much
alive to their responsibilities; perhaps there has never
been a generation more earnest and conscientious
than the young parents of these days. All the same,
these thoughtful young parents do not lay themselves
out to teach their children religion, before all things.

Discredit thrown upon the Bible.—The fact
is, our religious life has suffered, and by-and-by our
national character will suffer, through the discredit
thrown upon the Bible by adverse critics. We rightly
regard the Bible as the entire collection of our Sacred
Books. We have absolutely nothing to teach but what
we find written therein. But we no longer go to the
Bible with the old confidence: our religion is fading
into a sentiment, not easy to impart; we wait until the
young people shall conceive it for themselves. Mean
time, we give them such aesthetic culture as should
tend to develop those needs of the soul that find their
satisfaction in worship. The whole superstructure of
'liberal' religious thought is miserably shaky, and
no wonder there is some shrinking from exposing it
to the Ithuriel's spear of the definite and searching
young mind. For we love this flimsy habitation we
have builded. It bears a shadowy resemblance to
the old home of our souls, and we cling to it with a
tender sentiment which the younger generation might
not understand.

'Miracles do not Happen.'—Are we then un-
housed? Undoubtedly we are, upon one assumption
—that assumption which it takes a brilliant novelist
to put forth in its naked asperity—'Miracles do not
happen.' The educated mind is more essentially
logical than we are apt to suppose. Remove the

keystone of miracle and the arch tumbles about our ears. The ostentatious veneration for the Person of Christ, as separated from the 'mythical' miraculous element, is, alas, no more than a spurious sentiment toward a self-evolved conception. Eliminate the 'miraculous,' and the whole fabric of Christianity disappears; and not only so, what have we to do with that older revelation of 'the Lord, the Lord, a God full of compassion and gracious'? Do we say, Nay, we keep this; here is no miracle; and, of Christ, have we not the inimitable Sermon on the Mount—sufficient claim on our allegiance? No, we have not; therein we are taught to pray, to consider the lilies of the field, the fowls of the air, and to remember that the very hairs of our head are all numbered. Here we have the doctrine of the personal dealing, the particular providence of God, which is of the very essence of miracle. If 'miracles do not happen,' it is folly and presumption to expect in providence and invite in prayer the faintest disturbance of that course of events which is fixed by inevitable law. The educated mind is severely logical, though an effort of the will may keep us from following out our conclusions to the bitter end. What have we left? A God who, of necessity, can have no personal dealings with you or me, for such dealings would be of the nature of a miracle; a God, prayer to whom, in the face of such certainty, becomes blasphemous. How dare we approach the Highest with requests which, in the nature of things (as we conceive), it is impossible He should grant?

Our Conception of God depends upon Miracles. —We cannot pray, and we cannot trust, may be yet we are not utterly godless; we can admire, adore, worship, in uttermost humility. But how? What shall we adore? The Divine Being can be known to us only through His attributes; He is a God of love and a God of justice; full of compassion and gracious, slow to anger, and plenteous in mercy. But these are attributes which can only be conceived of as in action, from Person to person. How be gracious and merciful unless to a being in need of grace and mercy? Grant that grace and mercy may modify the slightest circumstance in a man's existence, spiritual or temporal, and you grant the whole question of 'miracles'; grant, that is, that it is possible to God to act otherwise than through such inevitable laws as we are able to recognise. Refuse to concede 'the miraculous element,' and the Shepherd of Israel has departed from our midst; we left are orphaned in a world undone.

Such and so great are the issues of that question of 'miracle' with which we are fond of dallying, with a smile here and a shrug there, and a special sneer for that story of the swine that ran violently down a steep place, because we know so much about the dim thoughts of the brute creation—living under our eyes indeed, but curiously out of our ken. Grant the possibility of miracles, that is, of the voluntary action of a Personal God, and who will venture to assign limits of less or more?

Natural Law and Miracles.—How long halt we betwixt two opinions?—to the law and to the testimony. Let us boldly accept the alternative which Hume proposes, however superciliously. Let it be that 'No testimony is sufficient to establish a miracle unless the testimony be of such a kind that its falsehood would be more miraculous than the fact which it endeavours to establish.' Even so. We believe that Christ rose again the third day and ascended into heaven; or we accept the far more incredible hypothesis that 'there is no God'; or, anyway, the God of revelation, in his adorable Personality, has ceased to be for us. There is no middle way. Natural law, as we understand it, has nothing to do with these issues; not that the Supreme abrogates his laws, but that our knowledge of 'natural law' is so agonisingly limited and superficial that we are incompetent to decide whether a break in the narrow circle within which our knowledge is hemmed, is or is not an opening into a wider circle, where what appears to us as an extraordinary exception does but exemplify the general rule.[1]

We would not undervalue the solid fruits of Biblical criticism, even the most adverse. This should be a great gain in the spiritual life; that henceforth a miracle is accredited, not merely by the fact that it is recorded in the sacred history, but by its essential fitness with the divine Character; just as, if we may reverently compare human things with divine, we say of a friend, 'Oh, he would never do that!' or, 'That is just like him.' Tried by this test, how unostentatious, simple, meekly serviceable are the miracles of Christ; how utterly divine it is

"To have all power, and be as having none!"

How Fit are the Miracles of Christ.—The mind which is saturated with the Gospel story in all

[1] "What are the laws of Nature? To me perhaps the rising of one from the dead were no violation of these laws, but a confirmation; even some far deeper law, now first penetrated into, and by spiritual force (even as the rest have been) brought to bear on us with its material force."—Carlyle.

its sweet reasonableness, which has absorbed the more confused and broken rays wherein the Light of the World is manifested in Old Testament story, will perhaps be the least tempted to the disloyalty of 'honest doubt'; for disloyalty to the most close and sacred of all relationships it is, though we must freely concede that such doubt is the infirmity of noble minds. Believing that faith comes by hearing, and hearing by the word of God, that the man is established in the Christian faith according as the child has been instructed, the question of questions for us, is, how to secure that the children shall be well grounded in the Scriptures by their parents, and shall pursue the study with intelligence, reverence, and delight.

CHAPTER XI

FAITH AND DUTY (REVIEWS)

Parents as Teachers of Morals

Laws of Nature and Ways of Men.—Education, properly understood, is the science of life, and every attempt to formulate this science is to be hailed with interest, and with a measure of gratitude in proportion to its success. Thinking minds everywhere are engaged in furnishing their quota towards this great work, in one or another of its aspects, physical, social, religious. We see at once the importance of every attempt to solve scientific and social problems, or problems of faith, as helping us to understand those 'laws of nature' and 'ways of men,' the love, and dutiful attitude of the will towards which, Mr Huxley considers to be the sole practical outcome of education. Let us consider three important works[1] on these lines. One deals with the problems of 'secular' morality from an American point of view; the second

[1] *The Moral Instruction of Children.* 6s. By Felix Adler. Published by Edward Arnuld.

Education from a National Standpoint. By Alfred Fouillée. Translated and edited by W. J. Greenstreet, M.A. Published by Edward Arnold.

Faith. Eleven Sermons, with a Preface, by Rev. H. C. Beeching. Published by Percival & Co.

with the whole problem of national education from a French and 'scientific' standpoint. The third is not professedly an educational work. It deals with 'the ways of men,' but with the ways of men as they are concerned with the ways and will of God. That is, it deals with the deep-seated springs out of which are the issues of life. As the true educationalist works from within outwards, he will probably find much aid in a work whose outlook on life is from the standpoint of 'faith.'

The Moral Instruction of Children.—Mr Felix Adler, in *The Moral Instruction of Children,* undertakes a by no means easy task in setting himself to solve the problem of unsectarian moral instruction. He brings unusual qualifications to the work—a wide outlook, philosophic training, and that catholic love of literature and knowledge of books which is essential to the teacher of morals. The work before us is one which should find a place on the educated parent's book-shelves, not perhaps to be swallowed whole as a 'complete guide,' but to be studied with careful attention and some freedom of choice as to which counsel of perfection is worthy to be acted upon, and which other counsel may be rejected as not fitting in with that scheme of educational thought which the parent has already made for himself. Mr Adler is most seriously handicaped at the outset. He writes for American schools, in which the first condition of moral instruction is that it must be unsectarian. This he, rightly or wrongly, interprets to exclude all theistic teaching whatever; that is to say, the child he writes for has no sanctions beyond those he finds in his own breast. For example: 'It is the business of the moral instructor in the school to deliver to his pupils the subject-matter of morality, but not to deal with the sanctions of it. He says to the pupil, "Thou shalt not lie." He takes it for granted that the pupil feels the force of this commandment, and acknowledges that he ought to yield obedience to it. For my part, I should suspect of quibbling and dishonest intention any boy or girl who would ask me, Why ought I not to lie? I should hold up before such a child the *ought* in all its awful majesty. The right to reason about these matters cannot be conceded until after the mind has attained a certain maturity.'

No Infallible Sense of 'Ought.'—Where does the *ought* get its awful majesty? That there is in the human breast an infallible sense of 'ought' is an error prolific of much evil. It is a common idea to-day that it is right to do that which the doer holds to be right; or, as it is popularly expressed, . . . man does all that can be expected of him when he acts according to his 'lights.' Now, a very slight acquaintance with history demonstrates that every persecution and most outrages, from the Inquisition to Thuggee, are the outcome of that same majesty of 'ought,' as it makes its voice heard in the breast of an individual or of a community. To attempt to treat of morals without dealing with the sanctions of morality is to work from the circumference instead of from the centre.

Moses, Moses, und immer Moses! says a German pedagogue of the modern school, who writes in hot disdain of the old-school system, in which ten or twelve, and, in some of the German States, fifteen or sixteen hours a week were devoted to Bible-teaching. We in England, and they in America, also rebel against the Bible as a class-book. Educationalists say there is so much else to be learned, that this prolonged study of sacred literature is a grievous waste of time; and many religious persons, on the other hand, object on the ground that it is not good to make the Bible common as a class-book.

The Bible a Classic Literature.—But it is singular that so few educationalists recognise that the Bible is not a single book, but a classic literature of wonderful beauty and interest; that, apart from its Divine sanctions and religious teaching, from all that we understand by 'Revelation,' the Bible, as a mere instrument of education, is, at the very least, as valuable as the classics of Greece or Rome. Here is poetry, the rhythm of which soothes even the jaded brain past taking pleasure in any other. Here is history, based on such broad, clear lines, such dealing of slow and sure and even-handed justice to the nations, such stories of national sins and national repentances, that the student realises, as from no other history, the solidarity of the race, the brotherhood, and, if we may call it so, the individuality of the nations. Here is philosophy which, of all the philosophies which have been propounded, is alone adequate to the interpretation of human life. We say not a word here of that which is the raison d'etre of the Bible, its teaching of religion, its revelation of God to man; but, to urge only one point more, all the literatures of the world put together utterly fail to give us a system of ethics, in precept and example, motive and sanction, complete as that to which we have been born as our common inheritance in the Bible.

The Bible Tabooed in Education.—For 1700 years, roughly speaking, the Bible has been the school-book of modern Europe; its teaching, con-

veyed directly or indirectly, more or less pure, has
been the basis upon which the whole superstructure
of not only religious but ethical and, to some extent,
literary training rested. Now, the Bible as a lesson-
book is tabooed; and educationalists are called
upon to produce what shall take its place in the
origination of ideas and the formation of character.
This is the task to which Mr Adler sets himself; and
that he is at all successful is obviously due to the fact
that his own mind is impregnated with the Bible lore
and the sacred law which he does not feel himself
at liberty to propound to his students. But this pre-
possession of the author's makes his work very helpful and suggestive to parents who desire to take the
Bible as the groundwork and the sanction of that
moral teaching which they are glad to supplement
from other sources.

May we recommend the following suggestion to
parents?—

A Mother's Diary.—"Parents and teachers should
endeavour to answer such questions as these: When
do the first stirrings of the moral sense appear in the
child? How do they manifest themselves? What
are the emotional and the intellectual equipments
of the child at different periods, and how do these
correspond with its moral outfit? At what time does
conscience enter on the scene? To what acts or
omissions does the child apply the terms right or
wrong? If observations of this kind were made
with care and duly recorded, the science of education
would have at its disposal a considerable quantity of
material from which, no doubt, valuable generalisa-
tions might be deduced. Every mother, especially,
should keep a diary in which to note the successive

phases of her child's physical, mental, and moral growth, with particular attention to the moral; so that parents may be enabled to make a timely forecast of their children's character, to foster in them every germ of good, and by prompt precautions to suppress, or at least restrain, what is bad."

Fairy Tales and how to Use them.—We are glad to find that Mr Adler reinstates fairy tales. He says, justly, that much of the selfishness of the world is due, not to actual hard-heartedness, but to a lack of imaginative power; and adds: 'I hold that something, nay, much, has been gained if a child has learned to take the wishes out of its heart, as it were, and to project them on the screen of fancy.' The German *Marchen* hold the first place in his regard. He says they represent the childhood of mankind, and it is for this reason that they never cease to appeal to children.

"But how shall we handle these *Marchen*? And what method shall we employ in putting them to account for our special purpose? My first counsel is, Tell the story. Do not give it to the child to read. The child, as it listens to the *Marchen*, looks up with wide-opened eyes to the face of the person who tells the story, and thrills responsive to the touch of the earlier life of the race, which thus falls upon its own." That is, our author feels, and rightly so, that traditions should be orally delivered. This is well worth noting. His second counsel is equally important. 'Do not,' he says, 'take the moral plum out of the fairy-tale pudding, but let the child enjoy it as a whole. . . . Treat the moral element as an incident, emphasise it indeed, but incidentally. Pluck it as a wayside flower.'

Mr Felix Adler's third counsel is, to eliminate from the stories whatever is merely superstitious, merely a relic of ancient animism, and, again, whatever is objectionable on moral grounds. In this connection he discusses the vexed question of how far we should acquaint children with the existence of evil in the world.

'My own view,' he says, 'is that we should speak in the child's hearing only of those lesser forms of evil, physical or moral, with which it is already acquainted.' On this ground he would rule out all the cruel stepmother stories, the unnatural father stories, and so on; though probably most of us would make an exception in favour of Cinderella, and its charming German rendering *Aschenbrodel*. I am inclined to think, too, that fairy tales suffer in vigour and charm when they are prepared for the children; and that Wordsworth is right in considering that the very knowledge of evil conveyed in fairy tales under a certain glamour, is of use in saving children from painful and injurious shocks in real life.

Fables.—*Fables*, according to our author, should form the basis of moral instruction at the second stage; probably when children emerge from the nursery. We have all grown up on 'Aesop's Fables'; and 'The Dog in the Manger,' 'King Log,' 'The Frog and the Stork,' have passed into the current coinage of our thought. But it is interesting to be reminded that the so-called Aesop's fables are in finitely older than the famous Greek story-teller, and are, for the most part, of Asiatic origin. We are reminded that it is important to keep this origin of the fable before us, and exercise discrimination in our choice of those which we use to convey moral ideas to our children.

Such fables as 'The Oak and the Reed,' 'The Brazen
and the Earthen Pot,' 'The Kite and the Wolf,' Mr
Adler would reject, as breathing of Eastern sub-
serviency and fear. But possibly for the very reason
that the British backbone is little disposed to bow
before man or circumstances, the lessons of life culled
by peoples of other habits and other thoughts may
be quite specially useful to the English child. Anyway, we should lose some of the most charming fables
if we cut out all that savours of the wisdom of the
East. The fables Mr Felix Adler specially commends are those which hold up virtue for our praise
or evil for our censure; such as *Cowardice*, the fable
of 'the Stag and the Fawn'; *Vanity*, 'The Peacock
and the Crane'; *Greediness*, 'The Dog and the
Shadow.'

"In the third part of our primary course," he says,
"we shall use selected stories from the classical literature of the Hebrews, and later on from that of Greece,
particularly the 'Odyssey' and the 'Iliad.'"

Bible Stories.—Here we begin to be at issue with
our author. We should not present Bible stories as
carrying only the same moral sanction as the myths
of ancient Greece; neither should we defer their introduction until the child has gone through a moral
course of fairy tales and a moral course of fables. He
should not be able to recall a time before the sweet
stories of old filled his imagination; he should have
heard the voice of the Lord God in the garden in the
cool of the evening; should have been an awed spectator where the angels ascended and descended upon
Jacob's stony pillow; should have followed Christ
through the cornfield on the Sabbath-day, and sat in
the rows of the hungry multitudes—so long ago that

such sacred scenes form the unconscious background of his thoughts. All things are possible to the little child, and the touch of the spiritual upon our material world, the difficult problems, the hard sayings, which are an offence, in the Bible sense of the word, to his elders, present no difficulties to the child's all-embracing faith. We should not say, far otherwise, that every Bible story is fit for children because it is a Bible story; neither would we analyse too carefully, nor draw hard and fast lines to distinguish what we should call history from that of which it may be said, 'Without a parable spake He not unto them.'

The child is not an exegetical student. The moral teaching, the spiritual revelations, the lovely imagery of the Bible, are the things with which he is concerned, and of these he cannot have too much. As Mr Adler says: 'The narrative of the Bible is saturated with the moral spirit, the moral issues are everywhere to the forefront. Duty, guilt and its punishment, the conflict of conscience with inclination, are the leading themes. The Hebrew people seem to have been endowed with what may be called a moral genius, and especially did they emphasise the filial and fraternal duties. Now, it is precisely these duties that must be impressed on young children.'

Let us see how our author would use the Bible narratives. We have only space for a fragmentary sentence here and there: 'Once upon a time there were two children, Adam and Eve. Adam was a fine and noble-looking lad.' . . . 'It was so warm that the children never needed to go indoors.' . . . 'And the snake kept on whispering, "Just take one bite of it; nobody sees you."'. . . 'You, Adam, must learn to labour, and you, Eve, to be patient and self-denying for others,' etc.

We leave it to our readers to decide whether 'treatment' improves the Bible narrative, or whether this is the sort of thing to lay hold of a child's imagination.

The Cadence of Biblical Phraseology Charming to a Child.—Mr Ruskin tells us that his incomparable style is due entirely to his early familiarity with the Bible classics. It is a mistake to translate Bible stories into slipshod English, even when the narrator keeps close to the facts of the narrative. The rhythm and cadence of Biblical phraseology is as charming to a child as to his elders, if not more so. Read your Bible story to the child, bit by bit; get him to tell you in his own words (keeping as close as he can to the Bible words) what you have read, and then, if you like, talk about it; but not much. Above all, do not let us attempt a 'practical commentary on every verse in Genesis,' to quote the title of a work lately published. Two points it seems worth while to dwell upon here.

Shall the stories of Miracles be used in Moral Instruction?—Is it advisable to tell children the stories of the Bible miracles in an age when the possibility of miracles is so hotly discussed? In the first place, all that the most advanced scientists have to urge against 'miracles' is that precisely such phenomena have not come under their personal notice; but they, before all people, are open to admit that nothing is impossible and that no experience is final. In the second place, as for the moral and spiritual instruction which the story of the miracle affords, it is immaterial whether, in the particular case in question, a historical fact is recorded; or whether, in this case also, it is true that 'without a parable spake He not unto them.' It is the essential, not the historical, truth of the story which matters to the child. As for the latter, he is a bold critic, and well in advance of the scientific knowledge of the day, who ventures to say, '*This* is possible; *that other* is impossible.'

Should the whole Bible be put into the hands of a Child?—The second point worthy of our attention in regard to Bible-teaching is, Is the Bible to be taken whole and undivided, or to be dealt out to children as they are able to bear it? There are recitals in the Bible which we certainly should not put into the hands of children in any other book. We should do well to ask ourselves gravely, if we have any warrant for supposing that our children will be shielded from the suggestions of evil which we deliberately lay before them; or if there is any Divine law requiring that the whole Bible—which is not only the Word of God, but is also a collection of the legal, literary, historical, poetical, philosophical, ethical, and polemical writings of a nation—should be placed altogether and all at once in the hands of a curious child, as soon as he is able to read? When will our superstitious reverence for the mere *letter* of the Scriptures allow us to break the Bible up, to be read, as all other literature is, in separate books; and, for the children anyway, those passages 'expunged' which are not fit for their reading; and even those which are perfectly uninteresting, as, for example, long genealogies? How delightful it would be that each birthday should bring with it a gift of a new book of the Bible, progressing in difficulty from year to year, beautifully bound and illustrated, and printed in clear, inviting type and on good paper. One can imagine the Christian child collecting his library of sacred books with great joy and interest, and making a diligent and delighted study of the volume for the year in its appointed time. The next best thing, perhaps, is to read bit by bit (of the Old Testament anyway) to the children, as beautifully as may be, requiring them to tell the story, after listening, as nearly in the Bible words as they can.

Moral Rules from the Pentateuch.—But to return to Mr Adler: here is a valuable suggestion: "Children should be taught to observe moral pictures before any attempt is made to deduce moral principles. But certain simple *rules* should be given to the very young —must, indeed, be given them—for their guidance. Now, in the legislation ascribed to Moses we find a number of rules fit for children, and a collection of these rules might be made for the use of schools, such as: Ye shall not lie; ye shall not deceive one another; ye shall take no bribe; thou shalt not go about as a tale-bearer among thy fellows;" and so on—a very useful collection of sixteen rules by way of specimen.

Further on we read: "The story of David's life is replete with dramatic interest. It may be arranged in a series of pictures. First picture, David and Goliath—i.e., skill pitted against brute strength, or the deserved punishment of a bully." Conceive the barren, common, self-complete and self-complacent product of 'moral' teaching on this level!

The 'Odyssey' and the 'Iliad.'—In his treatment of the 'Odyssey' and the 'Iliad,' Mr Adler makes some good points: 'My father, anxious that I should become a good man, made me learn all the poems of Homer,' Xenophon makes one of his characters say; and here we have suggestive lines as to how the great epics may be used for example of life and instruction in manners.

What so inspiring as the story of Ulysses to the boy in search of adventures? And what greater stimulus to courage, prudence, presence of mind, than in the escapes of the hero? 'Ulysses is the type of sagacity as well as of bravery; his mind teems with inventions.' The ethical elements of the 'Odyssey' are said to be conjugual affection, filial conduct (Telemachus), presence of mind, and veneration shown to grand parents (Laertes). Friendly relations with dependents might have been added, as illustrated by the lovely story of the nurse Eurycleia recognising Ulysses when his wife sat by with stony face. Friendship, again, in the story of Achilles' grief for Patroclus.

The Initial Weakness of 'Secular Morality.'— Mr Adler treats the Homeric stories with more grace and sympathy, and with less ruthless violation, than he metes out to those of the Bible; but here again we trace the initial weakness of 'secular' morality. The 'Odyssey' and the 'Iliad' are religious poems or they are nothing. The whole motive is religious; every incident is supernaturally directed. The heroic inspiration is entirely wanting if we fail to bear in mind that the characters do and suffer with super- lative courage and fortitude, only because they willed to do and suffer, in all things, the will of the gods. The acquiescence of the will with that which they guessed, however darkly, of the divine will, is the truly inspiring quality of the Homeric heroes; and here, as much as in the teaching of Bible morality, 'secular' ethics are at fault.

Lessons on Duty.—The third section of Mr Adler's work consists of lessons on duty. Here again we have excellent counsels and delightful illustrations. 'The teacher should always take the moral habit for granted. He should never give his pupils to understand that he and they are about to examine whether, for instance, it is wrong or not wrong to lie. The commandment against lying is assumed, and its obligation acknowledged at the outset.' This we heartily agree with, and especially we like the apparently inadvertent use of the word 'commandment,' which concedes the whole question at issue—that is, that the idea of duty is a relative one depending on an Authority supreme and intimate, which embraces the thoughts of the heart and the issues of the life.

A Child's Inducements to Learn.—The story of Hillel, as illustrating the duty of acquiring knowledge, is very charming, and is deeply interesting to the psychologist, as illustrating that a naturally implanted desire for knowledge is one of the springs of action in the human breast. The motives proposed for seeking knowledge are poor and inadequate: to succeed in life, to gain esteem, to satisfy yourself, and even to be able, possibly, to benefit others, are by no means soul-compelling motives. The child, who is encouraged to learn, because to learn is his particular duty in that state of life to which it has pleased God to call him, has the strongest of conceivable motives, in the sense that he is rendering that which is required of him by the Supreme Authority.

This one note of feebleness runs through the whole treatment of the subject. The drowning man is supposed to counsel himself to 'be brave, because as a human being you are superior to the forces of Nature, because there is something in you—your moral self— over which the forces of Nature have no power, be cause what happens to you in your private character is not important; but it is important that you assert the dignity of humanity to the last breath.' This reads rather well; but how much finer is the attitude of the man who struggles manfully to save the life that *God has given him*!

Moral Value of Manual Training.—The chapter on the influence of manual training is well worthy of consideration. The concluding sentence runs: 'It is a cheering and encouraging thought that technical labour, which is the source of our material aggrandisement, may also become, when employed in the education of the young, the means of enlarging their manhood, quickening their intellect, and strenthening their character.'

I have taken up Mr Adler's work so fully because it is one of the most serious and successful attempts with which I am acquainted to present a graduated course of ethics suitable for children of all ages. Though I am at issue with the author on the all-important point of moral sanctions, I commend the work to the perusal of parents. The Christian parent will assuredly present the thought of Law in connection with a Law-giver, and will supplement the thousand valuable suggestions he will find here with his own strong conviction that 'Ought' is of the Lord God.

Slipshod Moral Teaching.—But even the Christian child suffers from what may be called slipshod moral teaching. The failings of the good are a source of sorrow and surprise to the moralist as well as to the much-endeavouring and often-failing Christian soul. That temptation and sin are inseparable from our present condition may be allowed;

but that an earnest and sincere Christian should be habitually guilty of failing in candour, frankness, justice to the characters and opinions of others, should be intemperate in censure, and—dare we say it?— spiteful in criticism, is possibly to be traced, not to fallible human nature, but to defective education.

Importance of Ethical Instruction.—The ethical idea has never been fairly and fully presented to the mind on these vulnerable points. The man is unable to give due weight to the opinions of another, because the child has not been instructed in the duty of candour. There is little doubt that careful, methodical, ethical instruction, with abundant illustration—and, we need not add—inspired by the thought, 'God wills it,' should, if such instruction could be made general, have an appreciable effect in elevating the national character. Therefore we hail with gratitude such a contribution to the practical ethics of the nursery and school-room as Mr Adler's work on the moral instruction of children.

CHAPTER XII

FAITH AND DUTY

Claims of Philosophy as an Instrument of Education

English Educational Thought tends towards Naturalism.—Since Locke established a school of English educational thought, based on English philosophy, our tendency has been exclusively towards naturalism, if not materialism; to the exclusion of a vital element in education—the force of the idea.

Madame de Stael has a remarkable passage concerning this tendency in English philosophy which, though we may not be disposed to admit her conclusions *en bloc*, should certainly give us pause, and lead us to consider whether we should not wisely modify the tendencies of our national thought by laying ourselves open to foreign influences:—

Madame de Stael upon Locke.—'Hobbes prit a la lettre la philosophie qui fait deriver toutes nos idees des impressions des sens; ii n'en craignit point les consequences, et il a dit hardiment *que l'ame etait, soumise a la necessite comme la societe au despotisme.* Le culte des taus les sentiments eleves et purs est tellement consolide en Angleterre par les institutions politiques et religieuses, que les speculations de l'esprit tournent autour de ces imposantes colonnes sans

jamais les ebranler. Hobbes eut done peu de parti-
sans dans son pays; mais l'influence de Locke fut
plus universelle. Comme son caractere etait morale
et religieuse, il ne se permit aucun des raisonnements
corrupteurs qui derivaient necessairement de sa
metaphysique; et la plupart de ses compatriotes, en
l'adoptant, ont eu comme lui la noble inconsequence
de separer les resultats des principes, tandis que Hume
et les philosophes frarn;ais, apres avoir admisle systeme,
l'ont applique d'une maniere beaucoup plus logique.

'La metaphysique de Locke n'a eu d'autre effet
sur les esprits, en Angleterre, que de ternir un peu
leur originalite naturelle; quand meme elle desse
cherait la source des grandes pensees philosophiques,
elle ne saurait detruire le sentiment religieux, qui
sait si bien y suppleer; mais cette metaphysique recue
clans le reste de l'Europe, l'Allemagne exceptee, a ete
l'une des principales causes de l'immoralite dont on
s'est fait une theorie pour en mieux assurer la pratique.'

Our Educational Efforts lack Definite Aim.—
It is well that we should recognise the continuity of
English educational thought, and perceive that we
have in Spencer and Bain the lineal descendants of
the earlier philosophers. Probably the chief source
of weakness in our attempt to formulate a science of
education is that we do not perceive that education is
the outcome of philosophy. We deal with the issue
and ignore the source. Hence our efforts lack continuity and definite aim. We are content to pick
up a suggestion here, a practical hint there, without
even troubling ourselves to consider what is that
scheme of life of which such hints and suggestions
are the output.

We are on the Verge of Chaos.—Mr Green-street's translation of M. Fouillée's remarkable work[1] should not be without its effect upon the burning questions of the hour. As the translator well says in his preface: 'The spirit of reform is in the air; the question of the retention of Greek at the Universities is but a ripple of the great wave that seems ready to burst upon us and to obliterate the characteristic features of our national system of education. . . . A glance at the various forms of the educational systems obtaining in Europe and America is sufficient to betray to the observant eye how near to the verge of chaos we are standing.'

But also in the Throes of an Educational Revolution.—These are words of insight and wisdom, but let us not therefore despair as though the end of all things were at hand. The truth is, we are in the throes of an educational revolution; we are emerging from chaos rather than about to plunge into it; we are beginning to recognise that education is the applied science of life, and that we really have existing material in the philosophy of the ages and the science of the day to formulate an educational code whereby we may order the lives of our children and regulate our own. We need not aspire to a complete and exhaustive code of educational laws. This will come to us duly when humanity has, so to speak, fulfilled itself. Meantime, we have enough to go on with if we would believe it What we have to do is to gather together and order our resources; to put the first thing foremost and all things in sequence, and to see that education is neither more nor less than the practical application of our philosophy. Hence, if

[1] *Education from a National Standpoint.*

our educational thought is to be sound and effectual we must look to the philosophy which underlies it, and must be in a condition to trace every counsel of perfection for the bringing-up of children to one or other of the two schools of philosophy of which it must needs be the outcome.

Is our System of Education to be the Issue of Naturalism or Idealism?—Is our system of education to be the issue of naturalism or of idealism, or is there indeed a *media via*? This is practically the question which M. Fouillée sets himself to answer in the spirit of a philosophical educationalist. He examines his premises and draws his deductions with a candour, culture, and philosophic insight which carry the confidence of the reader. No doubt he is of a mind with that umpire in a cricket-match who lays down the dictum that one must be quite fair to both sides with a *little* leaning to one's own. M. Fouillée takes sides with classical as preferred to scientific culture. But he is not a mere partisan; he has philosophic reasons for the faith that is in him, and his examination of the question of national education is full of instruction and inspiration for the thoughtful parent as well as for the schoolmaster.

The Ethical View in Education.—M. Fouillée gives in his preamble a key to his treatment of the subject. He says,

"On this as on all great questions of practical philosophy Guyau has left his mark. . . . He has treated the question from the highest standpoint, and has treated it in a strictly scientific form. 'Given the hereditary merits and faults of a race, how far can we modify existing heredity by means of education for a new heredity?' For the problem is nothing less than this. It is not merely a matter of the instruction of individuals, but of the preservation and improvement of the race. Education must therefore be based upon the physiological and moral laws of the culture of races. . . . The ethnical is the true point of view. By means of education we must create such hereditary tendencies as will be useful to the race both physically and intellectually."

M. Fouillée begins at the beginning. He examines the principle of selection, and shows that it is a working principle, not only in animal, but in intellectual, aesthetic, and moral life. He demonstrates that there is what may be called psychological selection, according to whose laws those *ideas* which are the fittest rule the world; and it is in the light of this truth, of the natural selection of ideas and of their enormous force, that he would examine the vexed question of the subjects and methods of education.

No Attempt has been made to Unify Education.—M. Fouillée complains with justice that no attempt has been made to harmonise or unify education as a whole in any one civilised nation. Controversy rages round quite secondary questions—whether education shall be literary or scientific? And, again, whether the ancient or the modern languages shall be taught? But science and literature do not exhaust the field. Our author introduces a new candidate. He says,

"In this volume we shall inquire if the link between science and literature is not to be found in the knowledge of man, of society, of the great laws of the universe—*i.e.*, in morals and social science and aesthetics—in a word, in philosophy."

Claims of Philosophy as an Educational Agent.—Now this is the gist of the teaching which we have laboured to advance in the *Parents' Union* and its various agencies. 'The proper study of mankind is man,' is one of those 'thoughts beyond their thought' which poets light upon; and I am able to add my personal testimony to the fact that under no other study with which I am acquainted is it possible to trace such almost visible expansion of mind and soul in the young student as in this of philosophy.

A peculiarly interesting and original line of thought, worked out very fully in this volume, is, that just as the child with an individual bent should have that bent encouraged and 'educated,' so of a nation:—

'If social science rejects every mystical interpretation of the common spirit animating a nation, it by no means rejects the reflected consciousness or spontaneous divination, possessed by every nation, of the functions which have devolved upon it.'

A Nation should be Educated for its Proper Functions.—Here is a most fruitful suggestion. Think of the fitness of a scheme of physical, intellectual, and moral training, based upon our ideal of the English character and of the destiny of the English nation.

The chapter on '*Power of Education and of Idea-Forces—Suggestions—Heredity*' is very valuable, as utilising a floating nebulre of intuitions, which are coming upon us in connection with the hundred and one hypnotic marvels of the day. M. Fouillée maintains that—

'The power of instruction and education, denied

by some and exaggerated by others, being nothing but the power of ideas and sentiments, it is impossible to be too exact in determining at the outset the extent and limits of this force. This psychological problem is the foundation of pedagogy.'

M. Fouillée Neglects the Physiological Basis of Education.—In a word, M. Fouillée returns boldly to the Platonic philosophy; the *idea* is to him all in all, in philosophy and education. But he returns empty-handed. The wave of naturalism, now perhaps on the ebb, has left neither flotsam nor jetsam for him, save for stranded fragments of the Darwinian theory. Now, it is to this wave of thought, naturalistic, materialistic, what you will, that we owe the discovery of the physiological basis of education.

While we believed that thought was purely volatile, incapable of impact upon matter, or of being acted upon by matter, our theories of education were necessarily vague. We could not catch our Ariel; how, then, could we school him? But now, the physiologists have taught us that our wilful sprite rests with the tips of his toes, at any rate, upon solid ground; nay more, his foothold is none so slight but that it leaves footmarks behind, an impress on that domain of the physical in which we are somewhat at home. The impalpable thoughts that we think leave their mark upon the quite palpable substance of the brain; set up, so the physiologists tell us, connections between the nerve-cells of which that organ is composed; in fact, to make a long story short, the cerebrum 'grows to the uses it is earliest and most constantly put to.' This fact opens up a function of education upon which M. Fouillée hardly touches, that most important function of the formation of habits—physical, intellectual, moral. As has been well said, 'Sow an act, reap a habit; sow a habit, reap a character; sow a character, reap a destiny.' And a great function of the educator is to secure that acts shall be so regularly, purposefully, and methodically sown that the child shall reap the habits of the good life, in thinking and doing, with the minimum of conscious effort.

The Minor Moralities become Matters of Habit.—We are only now beginning to discover how beneficial are the laws which govern our being. Educate the child in right habits and the man's life will run in them, without the constant wear and tear of the moral effort of decision. Once, twice, three times in a day, he will still, no doubt, have to choose between the highest and the less high, the best and the less good course. But all the minor moralities of life may be made habitual to him. He has been brought up to be courteous, prompt, punctual, neat, considerate; and he practises these virtues without conscious effort. It is much easier to behave in the way he is used to, than to originate a new line of conduct. And this is so, because it is graciously and mercifully ordered that there shall be a physical record and adaptation as the result of our educational efforts, and that the enormous strain of moral endeavour shall come upon us only occasionally. 'Sow a habit, reap a character'; that is, the formation of habits is one of the chief means whereby we modify the original hereditary disposition of the child until it becomes the character of the man.

The Idea which Initiates a Habit.—But even in this physiological work, the spiritual force of the

idea has its part to play. For a habit is set up by
following out an initial idea with a long sequence
of corresponding acts. You tell a child that the
Great Duke slept in so narrow a bed that he could
not turn over, because, said he, 'When you want
to turn over it's time to get up.' The boy does not
wish to get up in the morning, but he does wish to be
like the hero of Waterloo. You stimulate him to act
upon this idea day after day for a month or so, until
the habit is formed, and it is just as easy as not to
get up in good time.

Can Spirit act upon Matter?—The functions
of education may be roughly defined as twofold:
(*a*) the formation of habits; (*b*) the presentation of
ideas. The first depends far more largely than we
recognise on physiological processes. The second
is purely spiritual in origin, method, and result. Is
it not possible that here we have the meeting-point
of the two philosophies which have divided mankind
since men began to think about their thoughts and
ways? Both are right; both are necessary; both
have their full activity in the development of a
human being at his best. The crux of modern
thought, as indeed of all profound thought, is, Is it
conceivable that the spiritual should have any
manner of impact upon the material? Every
problem, from the education of a little child to the
doctrine of the Incarnation, turns upon this point.
Conceive this possibility and all is plain, from the unlawful marvels resulting from hypnotic suggestion to
the miracles of our faith. It becomes possible, though
not easy, to believe what we are told, that, by an effort
of passionate concentration of thought and feeling
the devout have arrived at the figure of the stigmata

upon hands and feet. With this key nothing is impossible to our faith; all we ask for is precedent. And, after all, this inter-action of forces is the most common and every-day of our experiences. What is it but the impact of spirit upon matter which writes upon the face of flesh that record of character and conduct which we call countenance? And not only upon the face; he is a dull scholar in the lore of human nature who can not read a man fairly well from a back view. The sculptor knows the trick of it. There is a statue of the late Prince Consort in Edinburgh in which representative groups pay homage to the Prince. Stand so as to get the back view of any one of them and the shoulders of scholar, soldier, peasant, artisan, tell unmistakably the tale of their several lives. What is this but the impress of spirit upon matter?

There is no Middle Way Open.—Anyway we are on the horns of a dilemma. There is no middle course open to us. The physiologists have made it absolutely plain that the brain is concerned with thinking. Nay, more, that thought may go on without any volition on the part of the thinker. Further, that much of our best work in art and literature is the result of what is called unconscious cerebration. Now, we must admit one of two things. Either thought is a process of the material brain, one more 'mode of motion,' as the materialists contend, or the material brain is the agent of the spiritual thought, which acts upon it, let us say, as the fingers of a player upon the keys of his instrument. Grant this and the whole question is conceded. The impact of the spiritual upon the material is an accepted fact.

The Individuality of Children is Safeguarded.—
As we have had occasion to say before, in this great
work of education parents and teachers are permitted
to play only a subordinate part after all. You may
bring your horse to the water, but you can't make him
drink; and you may present ideas of the fittest to the
mind of the child; but you do not know in the least
which he will take, and which he will reject And
very well for us it is that this safeguard to his individuality is implanted in every child's breast. Our
part is to see that his educational *plat* is constantly
replenished with fit and inspiring ideas, and then we
must needs leave it to the child's own appetite to
take which he will have, and as much as he requires.
Of one thing we must beware. The least symptom
of satiety, especially when the ideas we present are
moral and religious, should be taken as a serious
warning. Persistence on our part just then may end
in the child's never willingly sitting down to that dish
any more.

Importance of Salient Ideas.—The very limitations we see to our own powers in this matter of
presenting ideas should make us the more anxiously
careful as to the nature of the ideas set before our
children. We shall not be content that they learn
geography, history, Latin, what not,—we shall ask
what salient ideas are presented in each such study,
and how will these ideas affect the intellectual
and moral development of the child. We shall be in
a mood, that is, to go calmly and earnestly into the
question of education as presented by M. Fouillée.
We shall probably differ from him in many matters of
detail, but we shall most likely be inclined to agree
with his conclusion that, not some subject of mere

utility, but moral and social science conveyed by means of history, literature, or otherwise, is the one subject which we are not at liberty to leave out from the curriculum of 'a being breathing thoughtful breath.'

The tables of studies given in the Appendix are of extreme value. Every subject is treated from what may be called the ideal point of view.

A Scientific Spirit.—"Two things are necessary. First, we must introduce into the study of each science the philosophic spirit and method, general views, the search for the most general principles and conclusions. We must then reduce the different sciences to unity by a sound training in philosophy, which will be as obligatory to students in science as to students in literature. . . . Scientific truths, said Descartes, are battles won; describe to the young the principal and most heroic of these battles; you will thus interest them in the results of science, and you will develop in them a scientific spirit by means of the enthusiasm for the conquest of truth; you will make them see the power of the reasoning which has led to discoveries in the past, and which will do so again in the future. How interesting arithmetic and geometry might be if we gave a short history of their principal theorems; if the child were mentally present at the labours of a Pythagoras, a Plato, a Euclid, or in modern times of a Viete, a Descartes, a Pascal, or a Leibnitz. Great theories, instead of being lifeless and anonymous abstractions, would become human, living truths, each with its own history, like a statue by Michael Angelo, or like a painting by Raphael."

CHAPTER XIII

FAITH AND DUTY

Man lives by Faith, Godward and Manward

Things 'Sacred' and Things 'Secular' an Irreligious Classification.—There is a little involuntary resistance in our minds to any teaching which shall draw the deep things of our faith within the sphere of the laws which govern our development as human beings. We prefer that the commerce between God and the soul, in which is our life, should be altogether 'supernatural'; apart from the common laws of life, arbitrary, inexplicable, opposed to reason. If we err in this, it is in reverence we err. Our thought may be poor and crude, but all our desire is to hallow the divine Name, and we know no other way in which to set it apart But though we err in reverence, we do err, and in the spiritual, as in the natural world, the motive does not atone for the act We lose through this misconception of our relations with God the sense of unity in our lives. We become aware of an altogether unnatural and irreligious classification into things sacred and things secular. We are not in all things *at one* with God. There are beautiful lives in which there is no trace of this separation, whose aims are confined to the things we call sacred. But many thoughtful, earnest persons feel sorely the need of a conception of the divine relation which shall embrace the whole of human life, which shall make art, science, politics, all those cares and thoughts of men which are not rebellious, sacred also, as being all engaged in the great evolution, the evolution of the Kingdom of God.

Every Man develops his own Philosophy.— Our religious thought, as our educational thought, is, far more than we imagine, the outcome of our philosophy. And do not let us imagine that philosophy is not for the general run of men, but only for the few. On the contrary, there is no living soul who does not develop his own philosophy of life—that which he appropriates of the current thought of his time, modified by his own experiences.

It would be interesting to trace the effect upon religious thought of the two great schools of philosophy—the Idealistic and the Naturalistic; but that is beyond the writer's power, and beyond our purpose here; we must confine ourselves to what is immediately practical. The present day crux is, that naturalistic philosophy being in the ascendant, and the things of our religion being altogether idealistic, many noble natures are in revolt, feeling that they cannot honestly accept as truth that which is opposed to human reason. Others, to whom their religious faith is the first thing, but who are yet in touch with the thought and discovery of the day, affect an only half-honest com promise with themselves, and say that there are certain questions which they will not examine; matters secular alone being open to searching scrutiny. Now, it is not, as we so often hear, that the times are out of joint, that Christianity is effete, that there is any inherent antagonism between the facts of natural and the facts of spiritual life. It is our own philosophy which needs to be adjusted. We have somehow managed to get life out of focus; we have begun with false initial ideas, and have taken the logical inferences from these for essential truth. We have not perceived that the concern of the reasoning powers is not with moral or spiritual truth, or even with what we call facts, but is, simply, with the *logical* inferences from any premisses whatever accepted by the mind.

All Intercourse of Thought belongs to the Realm of Ideas.—In our examination of M. Fouillée's *Education from a National Standpoint*, we made some attempt to show that the two schemes of philosophy, which have hitherto divided the world, have done so because both are right, and neither is exclusively right. Matter and spirit, force and idea, work together in the evolution of character. The brain, somehow, makes material record of those ideas which inspire the life. But the brain does not originate those ideas. They are spiritual in their nature, and are spiritually conveyed, whether by means of the printed page, the glance of an eye, the touch of a hand, or in that holy mystery of the inbreathing of the Divine Spirit, of which we cannot tell whence it comes nor whither it goes. Once we recognise that all thoughts that breathe and words that burn are of their nature spiritual, and appeal to the spiritual within us—that, in fact, all intercourse of thought and feeling belongs to the realm of ideas, spiritually conveyed, the great mysteries of our religion cease to be hedged off from our common experiences. If the friend who sits beside us deals with us, spirit with spirit, by means of quick interchange of ideas, is it hard to believe that just so is the intercourse between the Spirit of God and the spirit of man? The more perfect the sympathy between human souls, the less the need for spoken words. How easy to go on from this to the thought of that most intimate and blissful of all intercourse, the converse between the devout soul and its God.

It is Obvious and Natural that the Father of Spirits should keep Open Access to the Spirits of Men.—Nothing can be more obvious, real, natural, necessary, than that the Father of spirits should graciously keep open such intimate access to, and converse with, the spirits of men.

> 'I would that one would grant me,
>   O my Lord,
> To find Thee only.
>
> .   .   .   .
>
> That Thou alone wouldst speak to me, and I to Thee,
> As a lover talking to his loved one,
> A friend at table with his friend,'[1]

is ever the aspiration of the devout soul. This continuous aspiration towards closest communion is, spoken or unspoken, the prayer of faith. A vain and fond imagination, says the sceptic, begotten of the heart, as when Narcissus became enamoured of his reflected image! What have we to say in reply? Nothing. He who does not perceive that he loves in his brother, not the material form, but the spiritual being of which this form is one expression, how can he understand that the Spirit of God should draw with irresistible drawings the spirit of man, which is

[1] "The Imitation of Christ" (rhythmic translation).

indeed the whole man? For, after all, what is the body but the garment which the spirit shapes to its uses?

Easy Tolerance Commends itself to many Minds.—To accept the outward seeming, to ignore the spiritual reality, is the easier way. To say that prayer is flung, as a child flings his kite, into the air, only to come down again; to say that men are the creatures of circumstances, with no power to determine their own fate; that this belief and that are equal verities, and that the worship of Christ or of Buddha is a mere affair of climate and conditions; this easy tolerance commends itself to many minds in these days.

Thackeray on the Easy and Sceptical Attitude. —'And to what does this easy and sceptical life lead a man? . . . To what, we say, does this scepticism lead? It leads a man to shameful loneliness and selfishness, the more shameful because it is so good-humoured and conscienceless and serene. Conscience!' What is conscience? Why accept remorse? What is public or private faith? Mythuses alike enveloped in enormous tradition. If, seeing and acknowledging the lies of the world, Arthur, as see them you can with only too fatal a clearness, you submit to them without any protest further than a laugh; if, plunged yourself in easy sensuality, you allow the whole wretched world to go past groaning by you unmoved; if the fight for the truth is taking place, and all men of honour are on the ground armed on the one side or the other, and you alone are to lie on your balcony and smoke your pipe out of the noise and the danger, you had better have died, or never have been at all, than be such a sensual coward.'[1]

Man lives by Faith, Godward and Manward.—

[1] *Pendenis.* -Thackeray.

Canon Beeching's *Eleven Sermons on Faith* are in refreshing contrast with this sort of modern Sadduceeism. In his view, faith is not mystic, supernatural, an exceptional development; it is the common basis of our dealings with each other. Credit, trust, confidence—the framework of society rests upon these. 'I cannot trust you'—what worse thing can we say to one another? The law recognises every man's right to the confidence of his fellow-men, and will have a man accounted innocent until he is proved guilty. Our whole commercial and banking systems, what are they but enormous systems of *credit*, and only one in a hundred, or one in a thousand, fails to sustain this credit. Family and social life rest upon credit of another sort, let us call it moral credit; and only one in a hundred or one in a thousand forfeits the trust. If one here and there give occasion for jealousy, mistrust, suspicion, why, the exception proves the rule. In his dealings with men, man lives by credit; in his dealings with God, man lives by faith. Let us use the same word in both cases, and say that man is a spiritual being, and in all his relations, Godward or manward, he lives by faith. How simple and easy a thing faith becomes! How especially easy to the children who trust everybody and offer a confiding hand to any guide. Could we only rid ourselves of the materialistic notion that spiritual things are not to be understood by us, and that to believe in God is altogether a different thing from to trust a friend, how easy we should find the questions which we allow to stagger our faith.

Faith is the Simple Trust of Persons in a Person.—But the Kingdom of God is coming upon us with power. Let us only break down this foolish barrier of the flesh; let us perceive that our relations with each other are the relations of spirit with spirit, and that spoken and written words are no more than the outward and visible signs of ideas spiritually conveyed, and how inevitable, incessant, all-encompassing, becomes the presence of God about us. Faith is, then, the simple trust of person in Person. We realise with fearful joy that He is about our path, and about our bed, and spieth out all our ways—not with the austere eye of a judge, but with the caressing, if critical, glance of a parent. How easy, then, to understand the never-ceasing, ever-inspiring intercourse of the Divine Spirit with the spirit of man—how, morning by morning, He awakeneth *our* ear, also; how His inspiration and instruction come in the direction, and in the degree, in which the man is capable of receiving them. It is no longer a puzzle to us that the uninstructed savage shows sweet traits of pity and generosity,' for His God doth instruct him and doth teach him.' We are not confounded when we hear of a righteous man who lifts up his face to Heaven, and says, 'There is no God'; because we know He maketh His sun to shine upon the evil and upon the good, and that just that measure of moral light and leading which a man lays himself open to receive is freely given to him. He may shut his eyes and say 'There is no sun,' but none the less is he warmed and fed and comforted by the light he denies. This is the faith in which we would bring up our children, this strong, passionate sense of the dear nearness of our God; firm in this conviction, the controversies of the day will interest but not exercise us, for we are on the other side of all doubt once we know Him in whom we have believed.

Faith, a Lore of the Soul which demands Study.—Faith comes by hearing, and hearing by the Word of God. We advance in this lore of the soul only in proportion as we make it our study; and all of us who have the bringing-up of children must needs be thankful for every word of help and insight which shall open our eyes to the realities which are spiritually discerned. In this view parents will be glad to read and ponder the Sermons before us. Profound thought is conveyed in language of very great simplicity and purity. The sermons are written from the standpoint of present-day thought, are not at all emotional, nor even hortatory, but they are very strengthening and refreshing. You read and go on your way rejoicing in a strong sense of the reality of things unseen. Perhaps this result is due to Mr Beeching's presentation of the *naturalness* of faith.

The Naturalness of Faith.—"It is noticeable that while our Lord is always demanding Faith, He offers no definition of the Faith He requires; so that there is a presumption that He meant by Faith just what men ordinarily mean by it. And the presumption is increased when it is remembered that Faith in our Lord began with being faith in human qualities before those qualities were seen to be divine. The faith of the Apostles increased under our Lord's careful training, both in depth and breadth; but between the first attraction that drew (say) Peter from his nets, and the last declaration of his worship upon the shores of Gennesaret, there was no breach of continuity. Indeed, as if to assure us that the Apostle's human faith had not after the Resurrection 'changed to something else,' and become an indefinite theological virtue, we find the word used to express it which, of all the words which labour to express faith, is the one most deeply tinged with human feeling: "Simon, son of Jonas, *lovest* thou me more than these?" We must ask, therefore, what, as between man and man, is commonly meant by Faith, and then we can examine whether our explanation fits the several groups of passages in the Gospels."

Faith is no Self-originated Impulse.—The above extract from the very thoughtful and instructive preface illustrates what we mean by the naturalness of faith; not that which comes of itself and by itself, but that which is acceptable, fit, and proper to our nature whenever and whencesoever it arrive. 'For,' as Mr Beeching says, 'as faith is itself no self-originated impulse, but the springing up of a man's heart in response to the encircling pressure of the 'Everlasting Arms,' so its reward is to feel more deeply and ever more deeply their divine support.'

The eleven sermons are upon The Object of Faith, The Worship of Faith, The Righteousness of Faith, The Food of Faith, National Faith, The Eye of Faith, The Ear of Faith, The Activity of Faith, The Gentleness of Faith, The Discipline of Faith, Faith in Man.

The Compassion of Christ.—In his examination of 'The Object of Faith,' Mr Beeching asks: 'What, then, is He like; what kind of countenance is it that shines out upon us from the Gospel pages? Let us turn to them and see.' And we read the story of how Jesus, being moved with compassion, touched the eyes of the two blind men by the wayside going out from Jericho. How Christ had compassion on other things besides bodily sickness. 'Christ has compassion also on ignorance; on the aimless wandering of men after their own desires, without a Master to follow: on the weariness of spirit that such a life brings about.' Again, 'Christ has compassion not only on sickness and ignorance, but on sin—on the sinner who repents.' And we read the story of the woman whose sins, which were many, were forgiven, for she loved much. Again, we see the countenance of Christ as it is turned upon that young man of whom it is said, 'Then Jesus, looking upon him, loved him.' 'Compassion, then, for suffering and ignorance, and sin that repents, love for enthusiasm, this we have seen in the face of Christ.' One more divine regard we are invited to contemplate; how the Lord turned and looked upon Peter. 'Can you imagine with what a face our Lord looked upon Peter, who had thrice denied Him, after confidently affirming that he would go with Him to death? Would that that face would shine upon us with whatever reproach when we in word or deed deny Him, that so we too may remember and weep.' How the heart rises to such teaching as this—the simple presentation of Christ as He walked among men. Well did our Lord say: 'I, if I be lifted up, will draw all men unto Me.' The pity of it is that He, the altogether lovely, is so seldom lifted up to our adoring gaze. Perhaps, when our teachers invite us to behold the face of Christ, we shall learn the full interpretation of that profound word. He will draw all men, because it is not possible for any human soul to resist the divine loveliness once it is fairly and fully presented to his vision.

The Worship of Faith.—The sermon on the 'Worship of Faith' sets forth that 'To worship Christ is to bow down with love and wonder and thankfulness, before the most perfect goodness that the world has ever seen, and to believe that that goodness was the express image of God the Father.' All aims and all ideals that are not the aims and ideals of Christ, are distinctly opposed to such worship, and the man who entertains these alien ideals may not call himself a Christian. After examining that attitude of the spirit towards Christ which belongs to the worship of faith, the rest of the sermon is very practical. 'Work is Worship,' is the key-note: one longs that a writer who knows so well how to touch the secret springs had taken this opportunity to move us to that 'heart's adoration,' which is dearer to God; but, indeed, the whole volume has this tendency. It is well to be reminded that 'the thorough and willing performance of any duty, however humble or however exalted, is like the offering of incense to Christ, well-pleasing and acceptable.'

The sermon on the 'Righteousness of Faith' is extremely important and instructive. The writer dwells on the 'deplorable cant' with which we pronounce ourselves 'miserable sinners,' combining the 'sentiments of the Pharisees in the parable with the expressions of the publican.'

Righteousness is a certain Disposition of the Spirit of Man to the Spirit of God.—"Christ's language about man's sinfulness is altogether free from vagueness and hyperbole; when He blames He blames for definite faults which we can appreciate, and He is so far from declaring that men can do no good thing, that He assumes always that man in his proper state of dependence upon God has the power to do righteousness. 'Whosoever shall do the will of My Father, which is in heaven, the same is My brother, and sister, and mother.' . . . But the question remains, How, considering our actual shortcomings, can any of us be spoken of by Christ as righteous here and now? This is the question in answer to which St Paul wrote two of his greatest Epistles. His answer was, that according to Christ, a man is accounted righteous, not from a consideration of his works, but from a consideration of his faith in God. Human righteousness is not a verdict upon the summing up of a life, but it is reckoned to a man at any moment from a certain disposition of his spirit to the Spirit of God; a disposition of trust, love, reverence, the disposition of a dutiful son to a good father. . . . Righteousness, in the only sense in which it is possible for men, means believing and trusting God."

The Teaching of these Sermons should be Helpful to Parents.—I have not space to take up in detail all the teaching of this inspiring little volume; but I commend it to parents. Who, as they have need to nourish the spiritual life in themselves? Who, as they, have need to examine themselves as to with how firm a grasp they hold the mysteries of our faith? Who, as they, need to have their ideas as to the supreme relationship so clear that they can be translated into baby speech? Besides, we have seen that it is the duty of the educator to put the first thing foremost, and all things in sequence; only one thing is needful—that we 'have faith in God'; let us deliver our thoughts from vagueness and our ways from variableness, if we would help the children towards this higher life. To this end we gladly welcome teaching which is rather nourishing than stimulating, and which should afford real help towards 'sober walking in pure Gospel ways.'

CHAPTER XIV

PARENTS ARE CONCERNED TO GIVE THE HEROIC IMPULSE [1]

Heroic Poetry Inspires to Noble Living.—"To set forth, as only art can, the beauty and the joy of living, the beauty and the blessedness of death, the glory of battle and adventure, the nobility of devotion—to a cause, an ideal, a passion even—the dignity of resistance, the sacred quality of patriotism, that is my ambition here," says the editor of *Lyra Heroica* in his preface. We all feel that some such expression of the 'simpler sentiments, more elemental emotions' should be freely used in the education of children—that, in fact, heroic poetry contains such inspiration to noble living as is hardly to be found elsewhere; and also we are aware that it is only in the youth of peoples that these elemental emotions find free expression in song. We look at our own ballad literature and find plenty of the right material, but it is too occasional and too little connected; and so, though we would prefer that the children should imbibe patriotism and heroism at the one fountain-head, we think it cannot be done.

[1] *History of Early English Literature*. By Stopford A. Brooke. 2 vols. Macmillan & Co.

We have no truly English material, so we say, for education in this kind, and we fall back on the Homeric myths in one or other of the graceful and spirited renderings which have been made specially for children.

Beowulf, our English Ulysses.—But what if it should turn out that we have our own Homer, our own Ulysses? Mr Stopford Brooke has made a great discovery for us, who look at all things from the child standpoint. Possibly he would not be gratified to know that his *History of Early English Literature*, invaluable addition as it is to the library of the student and the man of letters, should be appropriated as food for babes. All the same, here is what we have long wanted. The elemental emotions and heroic adventures of the early English put into verse and tale, strange and eerie as the wildest fairy tale, yet breathing in every line the English temper and the English virtue that go to the making of heroes. Not that Beowulf, the hero of the great poem, was precisely English, but where the English came from, there dwelt he, and Beowulf was early adopted as the national hero, whose achievements were sung in every hall.

Beowulf is Prudent and Patient.—The poem, says Mr Stopford Brooke, consisting of three thousand one hundred and eighty-three lines, is divided into two parts by an interval of fifty years; the first, containing Beowulf's great deeds against the monster Grendel and his dam; the second, Beowulf's conquest of the Fire-drake and his death and burial. We are told that we may fairly claim the poem as English, that it is in our tongue and in our country alone that it is preserved. The hero Beowulf comes of brave and noble parents, and mildness and more than mortal daring meet in him. When he comes to Hrothgar to conquer Grendel, it is of his wise counsel as much as of his strength that we hear. The queen begs him to be friendly in council to her sons, saying to him, 'Thou holdest thy faith with patience and thy might with prudence of mind. Thou shalt be a comfort to thy people and a help to heroes.' None, it is said, could order matters more wisely than he. When he is dying he looks back on his life, and that which he thinks of the most is not his great war deeds, but his patience, his prudence, his power of holding his own well and of avoiding new enmities.

'Have Patience of thy Woes.'—'Each of us must await the close of life,' says he; 'let him who can, gain honour before he die. That is best for a warrior when he is dead. But do thou throughout this day have patience of thy woes; I look for that from thee.' Such the philosophy of this hero, legendary or otherwise, of some early century after Christ, before His religion had found its way among those northern tribes.

'I Swore no False Oaths.'—Gentle, like Nelson, he had Nelson's iron resolution. What he undertook to do he went through without a thought, save of getting to the end of it. Fear is wholly unknown to him, and he seems, like Nelson, to have inspired his captains with his own courage. 'I swore no false oaths,' he said when dying; so also he kept his honour in faithfulness to his lord. On foot, alone, in front, while life lasted, he was his king's defence. He kept it in equal faithfulness when his lord was dead, and that to his own loss, for when the kingdom was offered to him he refused, and trained Heardreg, the king's son, to war and learning, guarded him kindly with honour, and avenged him when he was slain. He kept it in generosity, for he gave away all the gifts that he received; in courtesy, for he gave even to those who had been rude to him; and he is always gentle and grave with women. Above all, he kept it in war, for these things are said of him: 'So shall a man do when he thinks to gain praise that shall never end, and cares not for his life in battle.' 'Let us have fame or death,' he cries, and when Wiglaf comes to help him against the dragon, and Beowulf is wrapped in the flame, Wiglaf recalls to him the aim of his whole life:—

'Bear thyself Well.'—'Beowulf, beloved, bear thyself well. Thou wert wont to say in youth that thou wouldst never let honour go. Now, strong in deeds, ward thy life, firm-souled prince, with all thy might, I will be thy helper.' 'These,' adds Mr Stopford Brooke, 'are the qualities of the man and the hero, and I have thought it worth while to dwell on them, because they represent the ancient English ideal, the manhood which pleased the English folk even before they came to Britain, and because in all our histories since Beowulf's time, for twelve hundred years or so, they have been repeated in the lives of the English warriors by land and sea whom we chiefly honour.'

The English Ideal.—'But it is not only the idea of a hero which we have in Beowulf, it is also the idea of a king, the just governor, the wise politician, the builder of peace, the defender of his own folk at the price of his life, "the good king, the folk king, the beloved king, the war ward of his land, the winner of treasure for the need of his people, the hero who thinks in death of those who sail the sea, the gentle and terrible warrior, who is buried amid the tears of his people."'

We owe Mr Stopford Brooke much gratitude for bringing this heroic ideal of the youth of our nation within reach of the unlearned. But what have we been about to let a thousand years and more go by without ever drawing on the inspiration of this noble ideal in giving impulse to our children's lives? We have many English heroes, it may be objected: we have no need of this resuscitated great one from a long-buried past. We have indeed heroes galore to be proud of, but somehow they have not often been put into song in such wise as to reach the hearts of the children and the unlearned.

Children should be in Touch with Beowulf.— We have to thank Tennyson for our Arthur, and Shakespeare for our Henry the Fifth, but we imagine that parents will find their children's souls more in touch with Beowulf than with either of these, no doubt because the legends of a nation's youth are the pages of history which most easily reach a child; and Beowulf belongs to a younger stage of civilisation than even Arthur. We hope the author of *Early English Literature* will sometime give us the whole of the poem translated with a special view to children, and interspersed with his own luminous teaching as we have it here. The quaintness of the metre employed gives a feeling of eld which carries the reader back, very successfully, to the long ago of the poem.

We have already quoted largely from this *History of Early English Literature*, but perhaps a fuller extract will give a better idea of the work and of its real helpfulness to parents. The cost of the two rather expensive volumes should be well repaid if a single child were to be fired with emulation of the heroic qualities therein sung:—

Action of the Poem.—'The action of the poem now begins with the voyage of Beowulf to the Danish coast. The hero has heard that Hrothgar, the chief of the Danes, is tormented by Grendel, a man-devouring monster. If Hrothgar's warriors sleep in Heorot—the great hall he has built—they are seized, torn to pieces, and devoured. "I will deliver the king," thought Beowulf, when he heard the tale from the roving seamen. "Over the swan road I will seek Hrothgar; he has need of men." His comrades urged him to the adventure, and fifteen of them were willing to fight it out with him. Among the rest was a sea-crafty man who knew the ocean-paths. Their ship lay drawn up on the beach, under the high cliff. Then—

'There the well-geared heroes
Stepped upon the stem, while the stream of ocean
Whirled the sea against the sand. To the ship, to its breast.
Bright and carved things of cost carried then the heroes
And the armour well-arrayed. So the men outpushed,
On desired adventure, their tight ocean wood.
Swiftly went above the waves, with a wind well-fitted,
Likest to a fowl, the Floater, foam around its neck,
Till about the same time, on the second day,
The up-curved prow had come on so far,
That at last the seamen saw the land ahead;
Shining sea-cliffs, soaring headlands,
Broad sea-nesses. So the Sailor of the Sea
Reached the sea-way's end.'

Beowulf, 1. 211.

'This was the voyage, ending in a fiord with two high sea-capes at its entrance. The same kind of scenery belongs to the land whence they had set out. When Beowulf returns over the sea the boat groans as it is pushed forth. It is heavily laden; the hollow,

under the single mast with the single sail, holds eight
horses, swords and treasure and rich armours. The
sail is hoisted, the wind drives the foam-throated bark
over the waves, until they see the Geats' Cliffs—the
well-known sea-nesses. The keel is pressed up by
the wind on the sand, and the "harbour-guard, who
had looked forth afar o'er the sea with longing for
their return"—one of the many human touches of the
poem—"fastens the wide-bosomed ship with anchoring
chains to the strand, lest the violence of the waves
should sweep away the winsome boat." . . . At the
end of the bay into which Beowulf sails is a low shore,
on which he drives his ship, stem on. Planks are
pushed out on either side of the prow; the Wederfolk
slipped down on the shore, tied up their sea-wood;
their battle sarks clanged on them as they moved.
Then they thanked the gods that the war-paths had
been easy to them. . . . On the ridge of the hill above
the landing-place the ward of the coast of the
Scyldings sat on his horse, and saw the strangers bear
their bright shields over the bulwarks of the ship to
the shore. He rode down, wondering, to the sea, and
shook mightily in his hands his heavy spear, and
called to the men—

> 'Who are ye of men, having arms in hand,
> Covered with your coats of mail. Who your keel afoaming
> O'er the ocean street thus have urged along.
> Hither on the high sea!'

> .   .   .   .
> 'Never saw I greater
> Earl upon this earth than is one of you;
> Hero in his harness. He is no home-stayer,
> 'Less his looks belie him, lovely with his weapons.
> Noble is his air!'
>
> *Beowulf,* 11. 237-247.

'Beowulf replies that he is Hrothgar's friend, and comes to free him from "Grendel, the secret foe on the dark nights." He pities Hrothgar, old and good. Yet, as he speaks, the Teutonic sense of the inevitable Wyrd passes by in his mind, and he knows not if Hrothgar can ever escape sorrow. "If ever," he says, "sorrow should cease from him, release ever come, and the welter of care become cooler." The coastguard shows them the path, and promises to watch over their ship. The ground rises from the shore, and they pass on to the hilly ridge, behind which lies Heorot.'

Our Gentle Forefathers.—Old English Riddles. —*The History of the Early English Literature* takes us into other pleasant places. Here are two or three specimens of the riddles of the old bards, and in riddle and saga we get most vivid pictures of their life and thoughts, the ways and words of the forefathers whom we are too ready to think of as 'rude' but who are here portrayed to us as gentle, mild and large of soul; men and women whom we, their posterity, may well delight to honour.

I. Here is Cynewulf's Riddle of the Sword.

'I'm a wondrous wight for warstrife shapen;
By my Lord beloved, lovelily adorned:
Many coloured is my corslet, and a clasping wire
Glitters round the gem of death which my wielder gave to me:
He who whiles doth urge me, wide-wanderer that I am,
With him to conquest.
     Then I carry treasure,
Cold above the garths, through the glittering day;
I of smiths the handiwork! Often do I quell
Breathing men with battle edges! Me bedecks a king
With his hoard and silver; honours me in hall,
Doth withhold no word of praise! Of my ways he boasts
'Fore the many heroes, where the mead they drink.

In restraint he lulls me, then he lets me loose again,
Far and wide to rush along; me the weary with wayfarings,
Cursed of all weapons.'

Riddle xxi.

II. The helmet speaks:

"Wretchedness I bear;
Wheresoe'er he carries me, he who clasps the spear!
On me, still upstanding, smite the streams (of rain);
Hail, the hard grain (helms me), and the hoar-frost covers me;
And the (flying) snow (in flakes) falls all over me."

Riddle lxxix., 6-10.

It is unnecessary to say a word about the literary value and importance of Mr Stopford Brooke's great work. 'There is nothing like leather,' and to parents all things present themselves as they may tell on education. Here is a very treasure-trove.

CHAPTER XV

IS IT POSSIBLE?

The Attitude of Parents towards Social Questions

A Moral Crisis.—The economic aspects of the great philanthropic scheme[1] which brought timely relief to the national conscience before the setting in of the hard winter of 1891, are, perhaps, outside our province; but it has educational aspects which we are, in some measure, bound to discuss. In the first place, the children in many homes hear 'I do not believe that' it is possible for the leopard to change his spots. General Booth's scheme brought this issue before us with startling directness; and what the children hear said to-day at the table and by the fireside about all such philanthropic effort, will probably influence for their lives their attitude towards all philanthropic and all missionary endeavour. Not only so, but we ourselves, who stand in some measure *in loco parentis* to the distressed in mind, body, or estate, are compelled to examine our own position. How far do we give, and work, for the ease of our own conscience, and how far do we believe in the possibility of the instant and utter restoration of the morally degraded, are

[1] Issue of *Darkest England.*

questions which, to-day, force themselves upon us. We must be ready with a yea or a nay; we must take sides, for or against such possibilities as should exalt philanthropic effort into a burning passion. The fact is, that great scheme forced a sort of moral crisis upon us whose effects are continually in evidence.

We, too, Love our Brother.—Whether or no the scheme commends itself to us for its fitness, seasonableness, and promise, one thing it assuredly did: it revealed us to ourselves, and that in an agreeable light. It discovered to us that we, too, love our brother; that we, too, yearn over 'the bruised' with something, however little, of the tenderness of Christ The brotherhood of man is no fancy bred in the brain; and we have loved our brother all the time—the sick, the poor, the captive, and the sinner, too; but the fearful, and unbelieving, and slothful amongst us—that is, the most of us—have turned away our eyes from beholding evils for which we saw no help. But when a promise of deliverance was offered, more adequate, conceivably, than any heretofore proposed, why, the solidarity of humanity asserts itself; our brother who is bruised is not merely near and dear; he is our very self, and whoso will ease and revive him is our deliverer too.

The 'Idol of Size.'—The first flush of enthusiasm subsided, we ask, Are we not, after all, led away by what Coleridge calls the 'Idol of Size'? Wherein does this scheme differ from ten thousand others, except in the colossal scale on which the experiment is to be tried? And perhaps we should concede at the outset that this hope of deliverance is 'the same, only more so,' as is being already worked out effectually in many an otherwise sunless corner of the great vineyard. Indeed, the great project has its great risks—risks which the quieter work escapes. All the same, there are aspects in which the remedy, because of its vastness and inclusiveness, is new.

Hitherto we have helped the wretched *in* impossible circumstances, not *out of* them. Our help has been as a drop in the bucket, reaching to hundreds or thousands only of the lost millions. Even so, we cannot keep it up; we give to-day, and withhold to-morrow; worse than all, our very giving is an injury, reducing the power and the inclination for self-help. Or, do we start some small amateur industry by way of making our people *independent*? This pet industry may sometimes be a transparent mask for almsgiving, and an encroachment upon regular industries and the rights of other workers.

Cui Bono?—Now and then is a gleam of hope, now and then a soul and body snatched into safety; but the hardest workers are glad of the noise of the wheels to keep the eternal *Cui bono?* Out of their ears. There is so much to be done, and so little means of doing it But this scheme—what with the amplitude of its provisions, what with the organisation and regimentation it promises, the strong and righteous government, the moral compulsion to well-doing—considering these, and the enormous staff of workers already prepared to carry it out, the dreariest pessimist amongst us concedes that General Booth's scheme *may* be worth trying. 'But,' he says, 'but—

DO WE BELIEVE IN CONVERSION?'

Can Character be Changed?—Everything turns on the condition the originator wisely puts first. There is the *crux*. Given money enough, land enough, men enough, fully equip and officer this teeming horde of incapables, and some sort of mechanical drill may be got through somehow. But, 'when a man's own character and defects constitute the reasons for his fall, that character must be changed and that conduct altered if any permanent beneficial results are to be obtained.' The drunkard must be made sober; the criminal, honest; the impure, clean. Can this be done? Is the crucial question.

The Question of the Age.—Is it possible that a man can emerge altogether out of his old self and become a new creature, with new aims, new thoughts, even new habits? That such renovation is possible is the old contention of Christianity. Here, and not on the ground of the inspiration of the sacred text, must the battle be fought out. The answer to the one urgent question of the age, What think ye of Christ? Depends upon the power of the idea of Christ to attract and compel attention, and of the indwelling of Christ to vivify and elevate a single debased and torpid human soul.

Many of us believe exultingly that the 'all power' which is given into the hands of our Master includes the power of upright standing, strength, and beauty, for every bruised human reed. That this is so, we have evidence in plenty, beginning with ourselves. But many others of us, and those not the less noble, consider, with Robert Elsmere, that 'miracles do not happen.'

The Essential Miracle.—The recorded miracles serve as pegs for the discussion; the essential miracle is the utter and immediate renovation of a human being. Upon this possibility the saving of the world must hang; and this many cannot receive, not because they are stiff-necked and perverse, but because it is dead against natural law as they know it. Proofs? Cases without end? The whole history of the Christian Church in evidence? Yes; but the history of the Church is a chequered one; and, for individual cases, we do not doubt the veracity of the details; only, nobody knows the whole truth; some preparation in the past, some motive in the present inadvertently kept out of sight, may alter the bearings of any such case.

The Honest Sceptic.—This is, roughly, the position of the honest sceptic, who would, if he could, believe heartily in General Booth's scheme, and, by consequence, in the convertibility of the entire human race. To improve the circumstances, even of millions, is only a question of the magnitude of the measures taken, the wisdom of the administration. But human nature itself, depraved human nature, is, to him, the impossible quantity. *Can* the leopard change his spots?

THE LAW AGAINST US—HEREDITY.

The Vicious by Inheritance.—Who are they whom General Booth cheerfully undertakes to re-fashion and make amenable to the conditions of godly and righteous and sober living? Let us hear the life history of many of them in his own words:—

'The rakings of the human cesspool.'

'Little ones, whose parents are habitually drunk. . . . Whose ideas of merriment are gained from the familiar spectacle of the nightly debauch.'

'The obscenity of the talk of many of the children of some of our public schools could hardly be outdone even in Sodom and Gomorrah.'

And the childhood—save the word!—of the children of to-day reproduces the childhood of their parents, their grandparents, who knows? Their great grand-parents. These are, no doubt, the worst; but the worst must be reckoned with first, for if these slip through the meshes of the remedial net, the masses more inert than vicious slide out through the breaks. In the first place, then, the scheme embraces the vicious by inheritance; proposes to mix up with the rest a class whose sole heritage is an inconceivable and incalculable accumulation of vicious inclinations and propensities. And this, in the face of that con-ception of heredity which is quietly taking possession of the public mind, and causing many thoughtful parents to abstain from very active efforts to mould the characters of their children.

Those of us whose attention has been fixed upon the working of the law of heredity until it appears to us to run its course, unmodified and unlimited by other laws, may well be pardoned for regarding with doubtful eye a scheme which has, for its very first condition, the regeneration of the vicious; of the vicious by inherited propensity.

THE LAW AGAINST US—HABIT.

The Vicious by Inveterate Habit.—Use is second nature, we say. Habit is ten natures; habit begins as a cobweb, and ends as a cable. 'Oh, you'll get used to it,' whatever it is. Dare we face the habits in which these people have their being? It is not only the obscene speech, the unholy acts; that which signifies is the manner of thoughts we think; speech, act, are the mere outcome; it is the habitual thought of a man which shapes that which we call his character. And these, can we reasonably doubt that every imagination of their heart is only evil continually? We say, use is second nature, but let us consider what we mean by the phrase; what is the philosophy of habit so far as it has been discovered to us. The seat of habit is the brain; the actual grey nervous matter of the cerebrum. And the history of a habit is shortly this: 'The cerebrum of man grows to those modes of thought in which it is habitually exercised.' That 'immaterial' thought should mould the 'material' brain need not surprise nor scandalise us, for do we not see with our eyes that immaterial thought moulds the face, forms what we call countenance, lovely or loathsome according to the manner of thought it registers? The how of this brain growth is not yet in evidence, nor is this the time and place to discuss it; but, bearing in mind this structural adaptation to confirmed habit, what chance, again, we say, has a scheme which has for its first condition the regeneration of the vicious, vicious not only by inherited propensity, but by unbroken inveterate habit?

THE LAW AGAINST US—UNCONSCIOUS CEREBRATION.

Thoughts Think Themselves.—Those who are accustomed to write know what it is to sit down and 'reel off' sheet after sheet of matter without plan or premeditation, clear, coherent, ready for press, hardly needing revision. We are told of a lawyer who wrote in his sleep a lucid opinion throwing light on a most difficult case; of a mathematician who worked out in his sleep a computation which baffled him when awake. We know that Coleridge dreamed 'Kubla Khan' in an after-dinner nap, line by line, and wrote it down when he awoke. What do these cases and a thousand like them point to? To no less than this: that, though the all-important *ego* must, no doubt, 'assist' at the thinking of the initial thought on a given subject, yet, after that first thought or two, 'brain' and 'mind' manage the matter between them, and the thoughts, so to speak, think themselves; not after the fashion of a pendulum which moves to and fro, to and fro, in the same interval of space, but in that of a carriage rolling along the same road, but into ever new developments of the landscape. An amazing thought—but have we not abundant internal evidence of the fact? We all know that there are times when we cannot get rid of the thoughts that *will think themselves* within us, though they drive away sleep and peace and joy. In the face of this law, benign as it eases us of the labour of original thought and decision about the everyday affairs of life, terrible when it gets beyond our power of control and diversion, what hope for those in whose debauched brain vile thoughts, involuntary, automatic, are for ever running with frightful rapidity in the one well worn track? Truly, the *in*-look is appalling. What hope for these?

Vicious Imaginations.—And what of a scheme whose first condition is the regeneration of the vicious—vicious, not only by inherited propensity, and by unbroken inveterate habit, but reduced to that state of, shall we say, inevitable viciousness—when 'unconscious cerebration,' with untiring activity, goes to the emanation of vicious imaginations? All these things are against us.

THE LAW FOR US—LIMITATIONS TO THE DOCTRINE OF HEREDITY.

But the last word of Science, and she has more and better words in store, is full of hope. The fathers have eaten sour grapes, but it is not inevitable that the children's teeth be set on edge. The soul that sinneth it shall die, said the prophet of old, and Science is hurrying up with her 'Even so.'

Acquired Modification not Transmitted.—The necessary corollary to the latest presentation of the theory of evolution is—*acquired modifications of structure are not transmitted*. All hail to the good news; to realise it, is like waking up from a hideous nightmare. This, definitely, is our gain; the man who by the continuous thinking of criminal thoughts has modified the structure of his brain so as to adapt it to the current of such thoughts, does not necessarily pass on this modification to his child. There is no necessary adaptation in the cerebrum of the new-born child to make place for evil thoughts. In a word, the child of the vicious may be born as fit and able for good living as the child of the righteous. Inherent modifications are, it is true, transmitted, and the line between inherent and acquired modifications may not be easy to define. But, anyway, there is hope to go on with. The child of the wicked may have as good a start in life, so far as his birthright goes, as the child of the just.

Education Stronger than Nature.—The child's future depends not upon his lineage so much as upon his bringing-up, for education is stronger than nature, and no human being need be given over to despair. We need not abate our hope of the regeneration of the vicious for the bugbear of an inheritance of irresistible propensity to evil.

THE LAW FOR US—'ONE CUSTOM OVERCOMETH ANOTHER.'

But habit! It is bad enough to know that use is second nature, and that man is a bundle of habits; but how much more hopeless to look into the *rationale* of habit, and perceive that the enormous strength of the habit that binds us connotes a structural modification, a shaping of the brain tissues to the thought of which the habit is the outward and visible sign and expression. Once such growth has taken place, is not the thing done, so that it can't be undone—has not the man taken shape for life when his ways of thinking are registered in the substance of his brain?

Not so; because one habit has been formed and registered in the brain is no reason at all why another and contrary habit should not be formed and registered in its turn. To-day is the day of salvation, physically speaking, because a habit is a thing of *now*; it may be begun in a moment, formed in a month, confirmed in three months, become the character, the very man, in a year.

Natural Preparation for Salvation.—There is growth to the new thoughts in a new tract of the brain, and, 'One custom overcometh another'; here is the *natural* preparation for salvation. The words are very old, the words of Thomas a Kempis, but the perception that they have a literal physical meaning has been reserved for us to-day. Only one train of ideas can be active at one time; the old cell connections are broken, and benign Nature is busy building up the waste places, even be they the waste places of many generations. NO ROAD is set up in the track where unholy thoughts carried on their busy traffic. New tissue is formed; the wound is healed, and, save, perhaps, for a scar, some little tenderness, that place is whole and sound as the rest.

This is how one custom overcometh another: there is no conflict, no contention, no persuasion. Secure for the new idea a weighty introduction, and it will accomplish all the rest for itself. It will feed and grow; it will increase and multiply; it will run its course of its own accord; will issue in that current of automatic unconscious involuntary thought of the man which shapes his character. Behold, a new man! Ye must be born again, we are told; and we say, with a sense of superior knowledge of the laws of Nature, How can a man be born again? Can he enter the second time into his mother's womb and be born? This would be a miracle, and we have satisfied ourselves that 'miracles do not happen.'

Conversion no Miracle.—And now, at last, the miracle of conversion is made plain to our dull understanding. We perceive that conversion, however sudden, is no miracle at all—using the word *miracle* to describe that which takes place in opposition to natural law. On the contrary, we find that every man carries in his physical substance the gospel of perpetual, or of always possible, renovation; and we find how, from the beginning, Nature was prepared with her response to the demand of Grace. Is conversion possible? We ask; and the answer is, that it is, so to speak, a function for which there is latent provision in our physical constitution, to be called forth by the touch of a potent idea. Truly His commandment is exceeding broad, and grows broader day by day with each new revelation of Science.

Many Conversions in a Lifetime.—A man may, most men do, undergo this process of renovation many times in their lives; whenever an idea strong enough to divert his thoughts (as we most correctly say) from all that went before is introduced, the man becomes a new creature; when he is 'in love,' for example; when the fascinations of art or of nature take hold of him; an access of responsibility may bring about a sudden and complete conversion:—

> The breath no sooner left his father's body
> But that his wildness, mortified in him,
> Seem'd to die too; yea, at that very moment,
> Consideration, like an angel came
> And whipped the offending Adam out of him;
> Leaving his body as a paradise
> To envelop and contain celestial spirits.

Here is a picture—psychologically true, anyway; Shakespeare makes no mistakes in psychology—of an immediate absolute conversion. The conversion may be to the worse, alas, and not to the better, and the value of the conversion must depend upon the intrinsic worthiness of the idea by whose instrumentality it is brought about. The point worth securing is, that man carries in his physical structure the conditions of renovation; conditions, so far as we

can conceive, always in working order, always ready
to be put in force.

**'Conversion' is not Contrary to Natural
Law.**—Wherefore 'conversion' in the Biblical sense,
in the sense in which the promoters of this scheme
depend upon its efficacy, though a miracle of divine
grace in so far as it is a sign and a marvel, is no
miracle in the popular sense of that which is outside
of and opposed to the workings of 'natural law.'
Conversion is entirely within the divine scheme of
things, even if we choose to limit our vision of that
scheme to the 'few, faint, and feeble' flashes, which
Science is as yet able to throw upon the mysteries
of being. But is this all? Ah, no; this is no more
than the dim vestibule of Nature to the temple of grace;
we are not concerned, however, to say one word here
of how 'great is the mystery of godliness'; of the
cherishing of the Father, the saving and the indwelling
of the Son, the sanctifying of the Spirit; neither need
we speak of 'spiritual wickedness in high places.' The
aim of this slight essay is to examine the assertion
that what we call conversion is contrary to natural
law; and we do this with a view, not to General
Booth's scheme only, but to all efforts of help.

Hope shows an ever stronger case for the regeneration of the vicious. Not only need we be no more
oppressed by the fear of an inheritance of invincible
propensities to evil, but the strength of life-long habit
may be vanquished by the power of an idea, new
habits of thought may be set up on the instant, and
these may be fostered and encouraged until that
habit which is ten natures is the habit of the new life,
and the thoughts which, so to speak, think themselves
all day long are thoughts of purity and goodness.

THE LAW FOR US—POTENCY OF AN IDEA.

'Hath not a Jew eyes? hath not a Jew hands, organs, dimensions,
senses, affections, passions?'

Conditions of the Potency of an Idea.—In effecting the renovation of a man the external agent is ever
an idea, of such potency as to be seized upon with
avidity by the mind, and, therefore, to make an impression upon the nervous substance of the cerebrum. The
potency of an idea depends upon the fact of its being
complementary to some desire or affection within the
man. Man wants knowledge, for example, and power,
and esteem, and love, and company; also he has
within him capacities for love, esteem, gratitude, reverence, kindness. He has an unrecognised craving for
an object on which to spend the good that is in him.

Fitness of the Ideas included in Christianity.—
The idea which makes a strong appeal to any one of
his primal desires and affections must needs meet with
a response. Such idea and such capacity are made
for one another; apart, they are meaningless as ball
and socket; together, they are a *joint*, effective in a
thousand ways. But the man who is utterly depraved
has no capacity for gratitude, for example? Yes, he
has; depravity is a disease, a morbid condition; beneath is the man, capable of recovery. This is hardly
the place to consider them, but think for a moment of
the fitness of the ideas which are summed up in the
thought of Christ to be presented to the poor degraded
soul: divine aid and compassion for his neglected
body; divine love for his loneliness; divine forgiveness
in lieu of the shame of his sin; divine esteem for his
self-contempt; divine goodness and beauty to call forth
the passion of love and loyalty that is in him; the

Story of the Cross, the lifting up, which perhaps no human soul is able to resist if it be fitly done. The divine idea once received, the divine life is imparted also, grows, is fostered and cherished by the Holy Ghost. The man is a new creature, with other aims, and other thoughts, and a life out of himself. The old things have passed away, and all things have become new—the physical being embodying, so to speak, the new life of the spirit.

We may well believe, indeed, that 'conversion' is so proper to the physical and spiritual constitution of man that it is inevitable to all of us if only the ideas summed up in Christ be fitly introduced to the soul.

The question then turns, not upon the possibility of converting the most depraved, nor upon the potency of the ideas to be presented, but altogether upon the power of putting these ideas so that a man shall recognise and seize upon the fulness of Christ as the necessary complement to the emptiness of which he is aware.

THE HABITS OF THE GOOD LIFE.

Curative Treatment Necessary.—The man converted, the work is not done. These sinners exceedingly are not only sinful, but diseased; morbid conditions of brain have been set up, and every one of them needs individual treatment, like any other sick man, for disease slow of cure. For a month, three months, six months, it will not do to let one of them alone. Curative *treatment* is an absolute condition of success, and here is where human co-operation is invited in what is primarily and ultimately the work of God. There are places in the brain where ill thoughts have of old run their course;

and these sore places must have time, blessed time, wherein to heal. That is to say, all traffic in the old thoughts must be absolutely stopped at whatever cost.

Think of the Army of Vigilance which must be ever on the alert to turn away the eyes of the patients from beholding evil; for, a single suggestion, of drink, of uncleanness, and, *presto*, the old thoughts run riot, and the work of healing must begin anew. There is no way to keep out the old, but by administering the thoughts of the new life watchfully, one by one, as they are needed, and can be taken; offering them with engaging freshness, with comforting fitness, until at last the period of anxious nursing is over, the habits of the good life are set up, and the patient is able to stand on his own feet and labour for his own meat. This is no work to be undertaken whole-sale. The spiritual care of a multitude diseased, even physically diseased, of sin, is no light thing. And if it be not undertaken systematically, and carried out efficiently, the whole scheme must of necessity fall through. Who is sufficient for these things? No one perhaps; but a following of a great corps of nurses trained to minister to minds diseased, and with the experience and the method belonging to a professional calling, is surely a fitting qualification for the Herculean task.

THE EASE OF DISCIPLINE.

How readily we can understand how, in the days when monarchs were more despotic than they are now, one and another would take refuge in a convent for the ease of doing the will of another rather than his own! Is not this the attraction of conventual life to-day, and is not this why the idea of the Salvation Army is powerfully attractive to some of us who know, all the same, that we (individually) should be wrong to lay down our proper function of ordering and acting out our own lives?

The Relief of Inclusion in a Strong Organisation.—But for these, strong of impulse and weak of will, who have no power at all to do the good they vaguely and feebly desire, oh, the ease of being taken up into a strong and beneficent organisation, of having their comings and goings, their doings and havings, ordered for them! Organisation, regimentation, we are reminded, make a hero of Tommy Atkins. And these all have it in them to be heroes, because restlessness, rebellion, once subdued, they will rejoice more than any others in the ease of simply doing as they are bidden. Here is a great secret of power, to treat these, lapsed and restored, like children; for what is the object of family discipline, of that obedience which has been described as 'the whole duty of a child'? Is it not to ease the way of the child, while will is weak and conscience immature, by setting it on the habits of the good life where it is as easy to go right as for a locomotive to run on its lines? Just such present relief from responsibility, such an interval for development, do these poor children of larger growth demand for their needs; and any existing possibility of ordering and disciplining this mixed multitude must needs appear to us a surpassing adaptation of 'supply' to 'demand.'

Work and Fresh Air are Powerful Agents.— The saving grace of work, and the healing power of the fresh air, again, should do their part in the restoration of the 'submerged.' But it is not our part to examine the methods proposed by General Booth, or to adumbrate his chances of success. Our concern is solely with the children. The attitude of thought towards all good work which children will henceforth take may depend very much upon how far the underlying principles are made clear to them in one typical instance. Whatever the agency, let children be assured that the work is the work of God, to be accomplished in the strength of God, according to the laws of God: that it is our part to make ourselves acquainted with the laws we would work out, and that, having done all, we wait for the inspiration of the divine life, even as the diligent farmer waits upon sunshine and shower.

CHAPTER XVI

DISCIPLINE

A Serious Study for Parents

Discipline is not Punishment.—'What part does Discipline play in your system of education?' We should hail the query as manifesting a cheering degree of interest if we were not quite sure that our interlocutor uses discipline as a euphuism for punishment. That conviction puts one's mind into the attitude of protest. In the first place, we have no system of education. We hold that great things, such as nature, life, education, are 'cabined, cribbed, confined,' in proportion as they are systematised. We have a *method* of education, it is true, but method is no more than a way to an end, and is free, yielding, adaptive as Nature herself. Method has a few comprehensive laws according to which details shape themselves, as one naturally shapes one's behaviour to the acknowledged law that fire burns. System, on the contrary, has an infinity of rules and instructions as to what you are to do and how you are to do it. Method in education follows Nature humbly; stands aside and gives her fair play.

A Method is not a System.—System leads Nature: assists, supplements, rushes in to undertake those very tasks which Nature has made her own since the world was. Does Nature endow every young thing, child or kitten, with a wonderful capacity for inventive play? Nay, but, says System, I can help here; I will invent games for the child and help his plays, and make more use of this power of his than unaided Nature knows how. So Dame System teaches the child to play, and he enjoys it; but, alas, there is no play in him, no initiative, when he is left to himself; and so on, all along the lines. System is fussy and zealous and produces enormous results—in the teacher!

A Wise Passiveness.—Method pursues a 'wise passiveness.' You watch the teacher and are hardly aware that he is doing anything. The children take the initiative, but, somehow, the result here is in these and not in the teacher. They develop, become daily more and more of persons, with

> 'The reason firm, the temperate will,
> Endurance, foresight, strength, and skill.'

Such as these are the golden fruits which ripen under the eyes of the parent, who is wise to discriminate between the *role* of Nature and that of the educator, who follows sympathetically and dutifully the lead of the great mother.

'Oh, then you have no discipline. I thought not. I daresay it would answer very well to leave children to themselves and make them happy. Children are always good when they are happy, are they not?' Not so fast, dear reader. He who would follow a great leader must needs endeavour himself, *Ohne hast ohne Rast;* and the divine lead which we call Nature is infinitely blessed in the following, but the way is steep to tread and hard to find, and this uphill work is by no means to be confounded with leisurely strolling in ways of our own devising.

The parent who would educate his children, in any large sense of the word, must lay himself out for high thinking and lowly living; the highest thinking indeed possible to the human mind and the simplest, directest living.

This thought of discipline, for example, is one of the large comprehensive ideas which must inform and direct the life, rather than be gathered up into a rule, easy to remember and easy to apply, now and then. If Tommy is naughty, whip him and send him to bed—is a ready-reckoner kind of rule, handy to have about one, and is the sort of thing which many people mean by discipline. Now we would not say that punishment is never to be used, very much otherwise. Neither would we say that physic is never to be taken. But punishment, like physic, is a casualty only of occasional occurrence at the worst, and punishment and physic alike are reduced to a minimum in proportion as we secure healthy conditions of body and mind. We are not anxious to lay down canons for punishment. Mr Herbert Spencer has not perhaps said the last word, but he has given us a quite convenient rule to go on with.

Punishment by Consequences.—A child should be punished by the natural consequences of his offence. To carry this suggestion out *au pied de la lettre* would often enough mean lasting, even fatal, injury to the child, bodily and mental. You cannot let the indolent child be punished by ignorance, or the wilful and adventurous child break a limb;

but, so far as punishments have been allowed to become necessary, the nature of the offence gives one a clue to a suitable punishment. The child who does not eat his porridge goes without his plum. This is, anyway, a punishment in kind, perhaps the nearest approach to natural consequences which it is advisable to try.

Children rather Enjoy Punishments.—But parents should face the fact that children rather enjoy punishments. In these they find the opportunities, so frequent in story-books, so rare in real life, for showing a fine pluck. The child who is in punishment is very commonly enjoying himself immensely, because he is respecting himself intensely.

Heroism in Bearing Penalties.—There is a bit of heroism in the bearing of a penalty which is very apt to do away with any sense of contrition for the offence; and the plucky little fellow, who takes his punishment with an air, is by no means a bad and hardened young offender; but is an economist of opportunities, making the best of what comes to hand for his own real education. His mother's distress, his father's disapproval, these are quite different matters, and carry no compensating sense of hardihood. Reflections like these lead one to spare the rod, not at all out of over-sensibility to the child's physical suffering, for we must have him endure hardness if we mean to make a man of him, but purely because it is not easy to find a punishment that does not defeat its own ends.

Wrongdoing followed by its own Penalties.—The light smart slap with which the mother visits the little child when he is naughty, is often both effective and educative. It changes the current of baby's thoughts, and he no longer wishes to pull his sister's hair. But should not the slap be a last resort when no other way is left of changing his thoughts? With the older child a theory of punishment rests less upon the necessity to change the culprit's thoughts than upon the hope of forming a new association of ideas, that is, of certain pains and penalties inevitably attached to certain forms of wrongdoing. This, we know too well, is a teaching of life, and is not to be overlooked in education. The experience of each of us goes to prove that every breach of law, in thought, or deed, is attended by its own penalties, immediate or remote, and the child who is not brought up to know that 'due follows deed, in course,' is sent out to his first campaign undrilled and untrained, a raw recruit.

Our contention is twofold: (*a*), that the need for punishment is mostly preventable; and (*b*), that the fear of punishment is hardly ever so strong a motive as the delight of the particular wrongdoing in view.

Punishment is not Reformative.—If punishment were necessarily reformative, and able to cure us all of those 'sins we have a mind to,' why, the world would be a very good world; for no manner of sin escapes its present punishment. The fact is, not that punishment is unnecessary or that it is useless, but that it is inadequate and barely touches our aim; which is, not visitation for the offence, but the correction of that fault of character of which the offence is the outcome. Jemmy tells lies and we punish him; and by so doing we mark our sense of the offence; but, probably, no punishment could be invented drastic enough to cure Jemmy of telling lies in the future; and this is the thing to be aimed at. No, we must look deeper; we must find out what weak place in character, what false habit of thinking, leads Jemmy to tell lies, and we must deal with this false habit in the only possible way, by forming the contrary habit of true thinking, which will make Jemmy grow up a true man. 'I think I have never told a lie since,' said a lady, describing the single conversation in which her father cured her, when she was a child, of lying by setting up an altogether new train of thought.

Good Habits the best Schoolmasters.—Not mere spurts of occasional punishment, but the incessant watchfulness and endeavour which go to the forming and preserving of the habits of the good life, is what we mean by discipline; and, from this point of view, never were there such disciplinarians as the parents who labour on the lines we would indicate. Every habit of courtesy, consideration, order, neatness, punctuality, truthfulness, is itself a schoolmaster, and orders life with the most unfailing diligence.

A habit is so easily formed, so strong to compel. There are few parents who would not labour diligently if for every month's labour they were able to endow one of their children with a large sum of money. But, in a month, a parent may begin to form a habit in his child of such value that money is a bagatelle by comparison. We have often urged that the great discovery which modern science has brought to the aid of the educator is, that every habit of the life sets up, as it were, a material record in the brain tissues. We all know that we think as we are used to think and act as we are used to act. Ever since man began to notice the ways of his own mind, this law of habit has been matter of common knowledge, and has been more or less acted upon by parents and other trainers of children. The well-brought-up child has always been a child carefully trained in good habits. But it is only within our own day that it has been possible to lay down definite laws for the formation of habits. Until now, the mother who wished to train her children in such and such a good habit has found herself hindered by a certain sense of casualty.

'Always Telling.'—'I'm sure I am always telling her'—to keep her drawers neat, or to hold up her head and speak nicely, or to be quick and careful about an errand, says the poor mother, with tears in her eyes; and indeed this, of 'always telling' him or her is a weary process for the mother; dull, because hopeless. She goes on 'telling' to deliver her own soul, for she has long since ceased to expect any result: and we know how dreary is work without hope. But, perhaps, even his mother does not know how unutterably dreary is this 'always telling,' which produces nothing, to the child. At first he is fretful and impatient under the patter of idle words; then he puts up with the inevitable; and comes at last hardly to be aware that the thing is being said. As for any impression on his character, any habit really formed, all this labour is without result; the child does the thing when he cannot help it, and evades as often as he can. And the poor disappointed mother says, 'I'm sure I've tried as much as any mother to train my children in good habits, but I have failed.' She is not altogether dispirited, however. The children have not the habits she wished to train them in; but they grow up warm-hearted, good-natured, bright young people, by no means children to be ashamed of. All the same, the mother's sense of failure is a monition to be trusted.

Our failures in life are, perhaps, due, for the most part, to the defects of our qualities; and, therefore, it is not enough to send children into the world with just the inheritance of character they get from their parents.

Some Practical Counsels.—Let me offer a few definite practical counsels to a parent who wishes to deal seriously with a bad habit. *First.*—Let us remember that this bad habit has made its record in the brain. *Second.*—There is only one way of obliterating such record; the absolute cessation of the habit for a considerable space of time, say some six or eight weeks. *Third.*—During this interval new growth, new cell connections, are somehow or other taking place, and the physical seat of the evil is undergoing a natural healing. *Fourth.*—But the only way to secure this pause is to introduce some new habit as attractive to the child as is the wrong habit you set yourself to cure. *Fifth.*—As the bad habit usually arises from the defect of some quality in the child it should not be difficult for the parent who knows his child's character to introduce the contrary good habit. *Sixth.*—Take a moment of happy confidence between parent and child; introduce, by tale or example, the stimulating idea; get the child's will with you. *Seventh.*—Do not tell him to do the new thing, but quietly and cheerfully see that he does it on all possible occasions, for weeks if need be, all the time stimulating the new idea, until it takes great hold of the child's imagination. *Eighth.*—Watch most carefully against any recurrence of the bad habit. *Ninth.*—Should the old fault recur, do not condone it. Let the punishment, chiefly the sense of your estrangement, be acutely felt. Let the child feel the shame not only of having done wrong, but of having done wrong when it was perfectly easy to avoid the wrong and do the right. Above all, 'watch unto prayer' and teach your child dependence upon divine aid in this warfare of the spirit; but, also, the absolute necessity for his own efforts.

An Inquisitive Child.—Susie is an inquisitive little girl. Her mother is surprised and not always delighted to find that the little maid is constantly on voyages of discovery, of which the servants speak to each other as prying and poking. Is her mother engaged in talk with a visitor or the nurse—behold, Susie is at her side, sprung from nobody knows where. Is a confidential letter being read aloud—Susie is within earshot. Does the mother think she has put away a certain book where the children cannot find it—Susie volunteers to produce it. Does she tell her husband that cook has asked for two days' leave of absence—up jumps Susie, with all the ins and outs of the case. 'I really don't know what to do with the child. It is difficult to put down one's foot and say you ought not to know this or that or the other. Each thing in itself is harmless enough; but it is a little distressing to have a child who is always peering about for gossipy information.' Yes it is tiresome, but is not a case for despair, nor for thinking hard things of Susie, certainly not for accepting the inevitable.

The Defect of her Quality.—Regarding this tiresome curiosity as the defect of its quality, the mother casts about for the quality, and, behold, Susie is reinstated. What ails the child is an inordinate desire for knowledge, run to seed, and allowed to spend itself on unworthy objects. When the right moment comes, introduce Susie to some delightful study, of Nature, for example, which will employ all her prying proclivities. Once the new idea has taken possession of the little girl, a little talk should follow about the unworthiness of filling one's thoughts with trifling matters so that nothing really interesting can get in. For weeks together see that Susie's mind is too full of large matters to entertain the small ones; and, once the inquisitive habit has been checked, encourage the child's active mind to definite progressive work on things worth while. Susie's unworthy curiosity will soon cease to be a trial to her parents.

CHAPTER XVII

SENSATIONS AND FEELINGS

Sensations Educable by Parents

Common-sense.—Children whose parents have little theoretic knowledge of the values of the various food-stuffs are often thoroughly nourished; their parents rely on what they call common-sense; and the result is, on the whole, better than if scientific consideration were given to the family dietary. But this common-sense has usually scientific opinion for its basis, though the fact may be forgotten, and when scientific opinion has become the groundwork of habit it is of more value, and works in a more simple way, than while it is still in the stage of experiment. In the same way it is a good thing to have such an acquaintance with the functions of human nature that we act on our knowledge unconsciously, and do not even know that we possess it. But if we have no such floating capital of cognisance we must study the subject, even if we have to make experiments. Most people suppose that the sensations, feelings, and emotions of a child are matters that take care of themselves. Indeed, we are apt to use the three terms indiscriminately, without attaching very clear ideas to them. But they cover, collectively, a very important educational field; and though common-sense, that is to say, judgments formed upon inherited knowledge, often helps us to act wisely without knowing why, we shall probably act more wisely if we act reasonably.

Origin of Sensations.—Let us consider, first, the subject of sensations. We speak of sensations of cold, and sensations of heat, and sensations of pain, and we are quite right. We also speak of sensations of fear and sensations of pleasure, and we are commonly wrong. The sensations have their origin in impressions received by the several organs of sense—eye, tongue, nostrils, ear, and the surface of the external skin—and are conveyed by the sensory nerves, some to the spinal cord and some to the lower region of the brain. Many sensations we know nothing about; when we become aware of our sensations, it is because communications are sent by nerve fibres, acting as telegraph wires, from the sensorium to the thinking brain; and this happens when we give our *attention* to any one of the multitudinous messages carried by the sensory nerves. The physiology of the senses is too complicated a subject to touch upon here, but it is deeply interesting, and perhaps no better introduction exists than Professor Clifford's little book, *Seeing and Thinking* (Macmillan). Now, the senses are the Five Gateways of Knowledge, to quote the title of a little book which many of us have used in early days; and an intelligent person should be aware of, and capable of forming judgments upon, the sensations he receives.

Sensations should be treated as of Objective Interest.—We all recognise that the training of the senses is an important part of education. One caution is necessary: from the very first a child's sensations should be treated as matters of objective and not of subjective interest. Marmalade, for example, is interesting, not because it is 'nice'—a fact not to be dwelt upon at all—but because one can discern in it different flavours and the modifying effect of the oil secreted in the rind of the orange. We shall have occasion to speak more of this subject later; but a useful piece of education is this of causing a child's interest to centre in the objects which produce his sensations and not in himself as the receiver of those sensations.

Object-Lessons in Disfavour.—The purpose of so-called object-lessons is to assist a child, by careful examination of a given object, to find out all he can about it through the use of his several senses. General information about the object is thrown in, and lodges only because the child's senses have been exercised and his interest aroused. Object-lessons are a little in disfavour just now, for two reasons. In the first place, miserable fragments are presented to the children which have little of the character of the object *in situ*, and are apt to convey inadequate, if not wrong, ideas. In the next place, object-lessons are commonly used as a means to introduce children to hard words, such as opaque and translucent, which never become part of their living thought until they pick them up for themselves incidentally as they have need of them. But the abuse of this kind of teaching should not cause us to overlook its use. No child can grow up without daily object teaching, whether casual or of set purpose; and the more thorough this is, the more intelligent and observant will he become. It is singular how few people are capable of developing an intelligent curiosity about the most attractive objects, except as their interest is stimulated from without

A Baby's Object-Lesson.—The baby is a wonderful teacher in this matter of object-lessons. To be sure, his single pupil is his own small self; but his progress is amazing. At first he does not see any difference between a picture of a cow and the living animal; big and little, far and near, hard and soft, hot and cold, are all alike to him; he wishes to hold the moon in his pinafore, to sit on the pond, to poke his finger into the candle, not because he is a foolish little person, but because he is profoundly ignorant of the nature of the contents of this unintelligible world. But how he works! He bangs his spoon to try if it produces sound; he sucks it to try its flavour; he fumbles it all over and no doubt finds out whether it is hard or soft, hot or cold, rough or smooth; he gazes at it with the long gaze of infancy, so that he may learn the look of it; it is an old friend and an object of desire when he sees it again, for he has found out that there is much joy in a spoon. This goes on with great diligence for a couple of years, at the end of which time baby has acquired enough knowledge of the world to conduct himself in a very dignified and rational way.

Nature's Teaching.—This is what happens under Nature's teaching; and for the first five or six years of his life, everything, especially everything in action, is an object of intelligent curiosity to the child—the street or the field is a panorama of delight, the shepherd's dog, the baker's cart, the man with the barrow, are full of vivid interest. He has a thousand questions to ask, he wants to know about everything; he has, in fact, an inordinate appetite for knowledge. We soon cure all that: we occupy him with books instead of things; we evoke other desires in place of the desire to know; and we succeed in bringing up the unobservant man (and more unobservant woman), who discerns no difference between an elm, a poplar and a lime tree, and misses very much of the joy of living. By the way, why is it that the baby does not exercise with purpose his organ of smell? He screws up a funny little nose when he is taught to sniff at a flower, but this is a mere trick; he does not naturally make experiments as to whether things are odorous, while each of his other senses affords him keen joy. No doubt the little nose is, involuntarily, very active; but can his inertness in this matter be a hereditary failing? It may be that we all allow ourselves to go about with obtuse nostrils. If so, this is a matter for the attention of mothers, who should bring up their children not only to receive, which is involuntary and vague, but to perceive odours from the first.

Education of the Senses.—Two points call for our attention in the education of the senses; we must assist the child to educate himself on Nature's lines, and we must take care not to supplant and crowd out Nature and her methods with that which we call education. Object-lessons should be incidental; and this is where the family enjoys so great an advantage over the school. It is almost impossible that the school should give any but set lessons; but this sort of teaching in the family falls in with the occurrence of the object The child who finds that wonderful and beautiful object, a 'paper' wasp's nest, attached to a larch-twig, has his object-lesson on the spot from father or mother. The grey colour, the round symmetrical shape, the sort of cup-and-ball arrangement, the papery texture, the comparative size, the comparative smoothness, the odour or lack of odour, the extreme lightness, the fact that it is not cold to the touch—these and fifty other particulars the child finds out unaided, or with no more than a word, here and there, to direct his observation. One does not find a wasp's nest every day, but much can be got out of every common object, and the commoner the better, which falls naturally under the child's observation, a piece of bread, a lump of coal, a sponge.

Advantages of Home Teaching.—In the first place, it is unnecessary in the family to give an exhaustive examination to every object; one quality might be discussed in this, another quality in that. We eat our bread and milk, and notice that bread is absorbent; and we overhaul our experience to discover other things which we know to be absorbent also; and we do what we can to compare these things as to whether they are less absorbent or more absorbent than bread. This is exceedingly important: the unobservant person states that an object is light, and considers that he has stated an ultimate fact: the observant person makes the same statement, but has in his mind a relative scale, and his judgment is of the more value because he compares, silently, with a series of substances to which this is relatively light.

Positive and Comparative Terms.—It is important that children should learn to recognise that high, low, sweet, bitter, long, short, agreeable, etc., etc., are comparative terms; while square, round, black, white, are positive terms, the application of which is not affected by comparison with other objects.

Indiscriminate Use of Epithets.—Care in this matter makes for higher moral, as well as intellectual development: half the dissensions in the world arise from an indiscriminate use of epithets. 'Would you say your bread (at dinner) was light or heavy?' The child would probably answer, 'Rather light.' 'Yes, we can only say that a thing is light by comparing it with others; what is bread light compared with?' 'A stone, a piece of coal, of cheese, of butter of the same size.' 'But it is heavy compared with?' 'A piece of sponge cake, a piece of sponge, of cork, of pumice,' and so on. 'What do you think it weighs?' 'An ounce,' 'an ounce and a half.' 'We'll try after dinner; you had better have another piece and save it,' and the weighing after dinner is a delightful operation. The power of judging of weight is worth cultivating. We heard the other day of a gentleman who was required at a bazaar to guess the weight of a monster cake; he poised it and said it weighed eighteen pounds fourteen ounces, and it did exactly. *Caeteris paribus,* one has a greater respect for the man who made this accurate judgment than for the vague person, who suggested that the cake might weigh ten pounds.

Judgment as to Weight.—Letters, book parcels, an apple, an orange, a vegetable marrow, fifty things in the course of the day, give opportunities for this kind of object teaching; *i.e.* the practice of forming judgments as to the relative and absolute weight of objects by the irresistance, that is their opposition to our muscular force, perceived by our sense of touch. By degrees the children are trained to observe that the relative weights of objects depend upon their relative density, and are introduced to the fact that we have a standard of weight.

Judgment as to Size.—In the same way children should be taught to measure objects by the eye. How high is that candlestick? How long and broad that picture-frame? And so on—verifying their statements. What is the circumference of that bowl? of the clock-face? of that flower-bed? How tall is So-and-so, and So-and-so? How many hands high are the horses of their acquaintance? Divide a slip of wood, a sheet of paper into halves, thirds, quarters by the eye; lay a walking-stick at right angles with another; detect when a picture, curtain, etc., hangs out of the perpendicular. This sort of practice will secure for children what is called a correct, or true, eye.

Discrimination of Sounds.—A quick and true ear is another possession that does not come by Nature, or anyway, if it does, it is too often lost. How many sounds can you distinguish in a sudden silence out of doors? Let these be named in order from the less to the more acute. Let the notes of the birds be distinguished, both call-notes and song-notes; the four or five distinct sounds to be heard in the flow of a brook. Cultivate accuracy in distinguishing footfalls and voices; in discerning, with their eyes shut, the direction from which a sound proceeds, in which footsteps are moving. Distinguish passing vehicles by their sounds; as lorry, brougham, dog-cart. Music is, no doubt, the means *par excellence* for this kind of ear culture. Mrs Curwen's 'Child Pianist' puts carefully graduated work of this kind into the hands of parents; and, if a child never become a performer, to have acquired a cultivated and correct ear is no small part of a musical education.

Discrimination of Odours.—We do not attach enough importance to the discrimination of odours, whether as a safeguard to health or as a source of pleasure. Half the people one knows have nostrils which register no difference between the atmosphere of a large, and so-called 'airy,' room, whose windows are never opened, and that of a room in which a through current of air is arranged for at frequent intervals: and yet health depends largely on delicate perception as regards the purity of the atmosphere. The odours which result in diphtheria or typhoid are perceptible, however slight, and a nose trained to detect the faintest malodorous particles in food, clothing, or dwelling, is to the possessor a safeguard from disease.

Then, odours enter more readily than other sense perceptions into those—

'Sensations sweet,
Felt in the blood, and felt along the heart,'

which add so much to the sum of our happiness, because they unite themselves readily with our purely incorporeal joys by links of association. 'I never smell woodruff without being reminded—' is the sort of thing we hear and say continually, but we do not trouble ourselves to realise that we owe a double joy to the odour of the woodruff (or it may be, alas! a reflected sorrow)—the joy of the pleasant influences about us when we pluck the flower, and the possibly more personal joy of that other time with which we associate it. Every new odour perceived is a source, if not of warning, of recurrent satisfaction or interest. We are acquainted with too few of the odours which the spring-time offers. Only this spring the present writer learned two peculiarly delightful odours quite new to her, that of young larch twigs, which have much the same kind and degree of fragrance as the flower of the syringa, and the pleasant musky aroma of a box-hedge. Children should be trained to shut their eyes, for example, when they come into the drawing-room, and discover by their nostrils what odorous flowers are present; should discriminate the garden odours let loose by a shower of rain:—

'Houses and rooms are full of perfumes, the shelves are crowded with perfumes,
I breathe the fragrance myself and know it and like it.

'The atmosphere is not a perfume, it has no taste of the distillation, it is odourless,
It is for my mouth for ever, I am in love with it.

'The sniff of green leaves, and dry leaves, and of the shore, and dark-coloured sea-rocks, and of hay in the barn.'

—The American poet has, perhaps, done more than any other to express the pleasure to be found in odours. This is one direction in which much remains to be done; we have not yet arrived even at a scale of odours, as of sound and of colour.

Discrimination of Flavour.—Flavour, again, offers a wide range for delicate discrimination. At first sight it would appear difficult to cultivate the sense of flavour without making a child more or less of a gourmand; but the fact is, that the strong flavours which titillate the palate destroy the power of perception. The young child who lives upon milk-foods has, probably, more pleasure in flavour than the diner-out who is familiar with the confections of a *cordon bleu*. At the same time, one would prefer to make flavour a source of interest rather than of sensuous pleasure to children: it is better that they should try to discern a flavour with their eyes shut, than that they should be allowed to think or say that things are 'nice' or 'nasty.' This sort of fastidiousness should be cried down. It is not well to make a child eat what he does not like, as that would only make him dislike that particular dish always; but to let him feel that he shows a want of self-control and manliness, when he expresses distaste for wholesome food, is likely to have a lasting effect.

Sensory Gymnastics.—We have barely touched on the sorts of object-lessons, appealing now to one sense and now to another, which should come incidentally every day in the family. We are apt to regard an American Indian as a quite uneducated person; he is, on the contrary, highly educated in so far as that he is able to discriminate sensory impressions, and to take action upon these, in a way which is bewildering to the book-learned European. It would be well for parents to educate a child, for the first half-dozen years of his life, at any rate, on 'Red Indian' lines. Besides the few points we have mentioned, he should be able to discriminate colours and shades of colour; relative degrees of heat in woollen, wood, iron, marble, ice; should learn the use of the thermometer; should discriminate objects according to their degrees of hardness; should have a cultivated eye and touch for texture; should, in fact, be able to get as much information about an object from a few minutes' study as to its form, colour, texture, size, weight, qualities, parts, characteristics, as he could learn out of many pages of a printed book. We approach the subject by the avenue of the child's senses rather than by that of the objects to be studied, because just now we have in view the occasional test exercises, the purpose of which is to give thorough culture to the several senses. An acquaintance with Nature and natural objects is another thing, and is to be approached in a slightly different way. A boy who is observing a beetle does not consciously apply his several senses to the beetle, but lets the beetle take the initiative, which the boy reverently follows: but the boy who is in the habit of doing sensory daily gymnastics will learn a great deal more about the beetle than he who is not so trained.

Sensory Games.—Definite object-lessons differ from these incidental exercises in that an object is in a manner exhausted by each of the senses in turn, and every atom of information it will yield got out of it. A good plan is to make this sort of a lesson a game. Pass your object round—a piece of bread, for example—and let each child tell some fact that he discovers by touch; another round, by smell; again, by taste; and again, by sight. Children are most ingenious in this kind of game, and it affords opportunities to give them new words, as friable, elastic, when they really ask to be helped to express in a word some discovery they have made. Children learn in this way to think with exactitude, to distinguish between friable and brittle; and any common information that is offered to them in the course of these exercises becomes a possession for ever. A good game in the nature of an object-lesson, suitable for a birthday party, is to have a hundred objects arranged on a table, unknown to the children; then lead the little party into the room, allow them three minutes to walk round the table; afterwards, when they have left the room, let them write or tell in a corner, the names of all the objects they recollect. Some children will easily get fifty or sixty.

No doubt the best and happiest exercise of the senses springs out of a loving familiarity with the world of nature, but the sorts of gymnastics we have indicated render the perceptions more acute, and are greatly enjoyed by children. That the sensations should not be permitted to minister unduly to the subjective consciousness of the child is the great point to be borne in mind.

CHAPTER XVIII

SENSATIONS AND FEELINGS

Feelings Educable by Parents

'These beauteous forms
Through a long absence, have not been to me
As is a landscape to a blind man's eye;
But oft, in lonely rooms, and 'mid the din
Of towns and cities, I have owed to them,
In hours of weariness, sensations sweet
Felt in the blood, and felt along the heart;
And passing even into my purer mind,
With tranquil restoration:—feelings, too,
Of unremembered pleasure: such, perhaps,
As have no slight or trivial influence
On that best portion of a good man's life,
His little, nameless, unremembered acts
Of kindness and of love.'

W. WORDSWORTH, *Tintern Abbey.*

Reflected Sensations. — Insight — the, so to speak, scientific grip of a great poet—is amongst those 'more things' in heaven and earth than our philosophy has dreamed of. Wordsworth tells us that, after the lapse of years, those beauteous forms (of Tintern Abbey) gave him sensations. Now we are apt to think that sensations can only be immediate, perceived on the instant that the object is present to the senses; but the poet is, as usual, absolutely right: we may have, so to speak, reflected sensations, as well as those that are immediate; because a conscious sensation depends upon the recognition of an impression in the sensory centres, and this recognition may be evoked, not only by an immediate sensation, but by an association which recalls the image once permanently impressed by the original sensation. Wordsworth is exquisitely right when he speaks of the repeated enjoyment of sensations sweet. 'In lonely rooms and 'mid the din of towns and cities,' some sudden touch of the chords of association has brought to him the soothing joy of a picture—'Forms' with every grace of symmetry, harmony, venerable antiquity, in the ever fresh and gracious setting of a beautiful landscape. The eye of his mind is infinitely gladdened; the ear of his mind, no longer conscious of the din of cities, hears the chord struck by the Wye in its flow, and the notes of the birds and the lowing of the cattle and the acuter notes of the insect world. Again he perceives the odour of the meadowsweet, he touches the coolness of the grass; and all these are as absolutely sensations as when they were for the first time conveyed to his consciousness by the sensory organs.

Open-air Memories should be Stored.—We have in these few lines a volume of reasons why we should fill for children the storehouse of memory with many open-air images, capable of giving them reflected sensations of extreme delight. Our constant care must be to secure that they do look, and listen, touch, and smell; and the way to this is by sympathetic action on our part: what we look at they will look at; the odours we perceive, they, too, will get. We heard, the other day, of a little girl who travelled in Italy with her parents in the days of dignified family travelling-carriages. The child's parents were conscientious, and time was precious, not by any means to be wasted on the mere idleness of travelling; so the governess and the little girl had the coupe to themselves, and in it were packed all the paraphernalia of the schoolroom; and the little girl did her sums, learned her geography, probably the counties of England, and all the rest of it, with the least possible waste of time in idle curiosity as to what the 'faire londes' through which she was passing might be like. A story like this shows that we are making advances, but we are still far from fully recognising that our part in the education of children should be thoughtfully subordinated to that played by Nature herself.

Memories of Delight a Source of Physical Well-being and of Mental Restoration.—To continue our study of this amazingly accurate, as well as exquisitely beautiful, psychological record: —the poet goes on to tell us that these sensations sweet are 'felt in the blood and felt along the heart,' a statement curiously true to fact; for a pleasurable sensation causes the relaxation of the infinitesimal nerve fibres netted around the capillaries; the blood flows freely, the heart beats quicker, the sense of well-being is increased; gaiety, gladness, supervene; and the gloom of the dull day, and the din of the busy city, exist for us no more; that is to say, memories of delight are, as it were, an elixir of life, capable, when they present themselves, of restoring us at any moment to a condition of physical well-being.

But even this is not the whole. Wordsworth

speaks of these memories as 'passing into my purer mind with tranquil restoration'—purer, because less corporeal, less affected by physical conditions, but all the same so intimately related to the physical brain, that the condition of the one must rule the other. Mind and brain, perhaps, have been alike fagged by the insistent recurrence of some one line of thought; when, suddenly, there flashes into the 'purer mind' the cognition of images of delight, presented in consequence of a touch to some spring of association: the current of thought is diverted into new and delightful channels; and weariness and brain fag give place to 'tranquil restoration.'

If mere sensations are capable of doing so much for our happiness, our mental refreshment, and our physical well-being, both at the time of their reception and for an indefinite number of times afterwards, it follows that it is no small part of our work as educators to preserve the acuteness of the children's perceptions, and to store their memories with images of delight.

Sensations and Feelings Distinguished.—The poet pursues the investigation and makes a pointed distinction; he not only recovers 'sensations sweet,' but 'feelings, too, of unremembered pleasure.' Very few persons are capable of discriminating between the sensations and the feelings produced by an image recovered by some train of association. Wordsworth's psychology is not only delicately nice, but very just, and the distinction he draws is important to the educator. The truth is, 'the feelings' are out of fashion at present: *The Man of Feeling* is a person of no account; if he still exists he keeps in the shade, being aware, through a certain quickness of perception which belongs to him, that any little efflorescence proper to his character would be promptly reduced to pulp by some wielder of a sledge-hammer. *The Man of Feeling* has himself to thank for this; he allowed his feelings to become fantastic; his sweet sensibilities ran away with him; he meant pathos and talked bathos; he became an exaggerated type, and, in self-preservation, Society always cuts off the offending limb, so *The Man of Feeling* is no more.

The Feelings should be Objective, not Subjective.—Nor is this the only charge that 'the feelings' have to sustain. So long as the feelings remain objective, they are, like the bloom to the peach, the last perfection of a beautiful character; but when they become subjective, when every feeling concerns itself with the ego, we have, as in the case of sensations, morbid conditions set up; the person begins by being 'over sensitive,' hysteria supervenes, perhaps melancholia, an utterly spoilt life. George Eliot has a fine figure which aptly illustrates this subjective condition of the feelings. She tells us that a philosophic friend had pointed out to her that whereas the surface of a mirror or of a steel plate may be covered with minute scratches going in every direction, if you hold a lighted candle to the surface all these random scratches appear to arrange themselves and radiate from the central flame; just so with the person whose feelings have been permitted to minister to his egoistic consciousness: all things in heaven and earth are 'felt' as they affect his own personality.

What the Feelings are and are not.—What are the feelings? Perhaps they are best expressed in

Coleridge's phrase of 'a vague appetency of the mind'; and we may do something to clear our thoughts by a negative examination. The feelings are *not* sensations, because they have no necessary connection with the senses; they are to be distinguished from the two great affections (of love and justice) because they are not actively exercised upon any objects; they are distinct from the desires because they demand no gratification; and they are distinguishable from the intellectual operations which we call thought, because while thought proceeds from an idea, is active, and arrives at a result, the feelings arrive from perceptions, are passive, and not definitely progressive.

Every Feeling has its Positive and its Negative.—Every feeling has its positive and its negative, and these in almost infinitely varying degrees: pleasure, displeasure; appreciation, depreciation; anticipation, foreboding; admiration, contempt; assurance, hesitancy; diffidence, complacency; and so on, through many more delicate *nuances* of feeling that are nameable, and yet more, so delicate that language is too rough an instrument for their expression.

The Feelings not Moral or Immoral.—It will be observed that all these feelings have certain conditions in common; none are distinctly moral or immoral; they have not arrived at the stage of definite thought; they exist vaguely in what would appear to be a semi-conscious intellectual region. Why, then, need we concern ourselves about this little known tract of that *terra incognita* which we call human nature? This 'why' is the question of the prose-philosopher—our poet sees deeper. In one of the most exquisitely discriminating passages in the whole field of poetry, he speaks of feelings of unremembered pleasure as having no slight or trivial influence on a good man's life, as the sources of 'little nameless unremembered acts of kindness and of love.'

Connection between Unremembered Feelings and Acts.—Even the feeling of '*unremembered pleasure*'—for it is possible to have the spring of association touched so lightly that one recovers the feeling of former pleasure without recovering the sensation, or the image which produced the sensation, but only just the vague feeling of the pleasure, as when one hears the word 'Lohengrin' and does not wait, as it were, to recover the sensation of musical delight, but just catches a waft of the pleasure which the sensation brought—the feeling of unremembered pleasure, intangible, indefinite, as it is, produces that glow of the heart which warms a good man to 'acts of kindness and of love,' as little, as nameless, and as unremembered as the feelings out of which they spring.

These Trifling Acts the Best Portion of a Good Man's Life.—Nameless as they are, the poet does not hesitate to rank these trifling acts as the 'best portion of a good man's life.' But it is only out of the good man's heart that these good issues come, because, as we have said, the feelings are not in themselves moral; they act upon that which is there, and the point brought before us is, that the influence of the feelings is, at the same time, powerful and indirect. Why should the recollection of Tintern Abbey cause a good man to do some little kind thing? We can only give the ultimate answer that 'God has made us so,' that a feeling of even unremembered pleasure prompts the good man to give forth out of the good treasure of his heart in kindness and in love. We have but to think of the outcome of feelings at the negative pole to convince us of the nice exactitude of the poet's psychology. Suppose, that we are not exactly displeased, but unpleased, dull, not quickened by any feeling of pleasure: let us ask ourselves if, in this condition of our feelings, we are prompted to any outpouring of love and kindness upon our neighbours.

The Perception of Character one of our Finest Feelings.—Here is another aspect of the feelings, of very great importance to us who have the education of children.

> 'I do not like you, Doctor Fell,
> The reason why I cannot tell,'

is a feeling we all know well enough, and is, in fact, that intuitive perception of character—one of our finest feelings and best guides in life—which is too apt to be hammered out of us by the constant effort to beat down our sensibilities to the explicit and definite. One wonders why people complain of faithless friends, untrustworthy servants, and disappointed affections. If the feelings were retained in truth and simplicity, there is little doubt that they would afford for each of us such a touchstone of character in the persons we come in contact with, that we should be saved from making exigeant demands on the one hand, and from suffering disappointment on the other.

The Orator Plays upon Feelings.—The orator plays, by preference, upon the gamut of the feelings. He throws in arguments by the way; brightens his discourse with graphic word-picture, metaphor, simile;

but for his final effect he relies upon the impression he has been able to make upon the feelings of his audience, and the event proves him to be right.

Enthusiasm.—Not only our little nameless acts, but the great purposes of our lives, arise out of our feelings. Enthusiasm itself is not thought, though it arises when we are

'Stung with the rapture of a sudden thought';

it is a glowing, malleable condition of the forces of our nature, during which all things are possible to us, and we only wait for a lead. Enthusiasm in its earliest stage is inconsequent, incoherent, devoid of purpose, and yet is the state out of which all the great purposes of life shape themselves. We feel, we think, we say, we do; this is the genesis of most of our activities.

In Educating the Feelings we Modify the Character.—But our feelings, as our thoughts, depend upon what we are; we feel in all things as ''tis our nature to,' and the point to be noticed is that our feelings are educable, and that in educating the feelings we modify the character. A pressing danger of our day is that the delicate task of educating shall be exchanged for the much simpler one of blunting the feelings. This is the almost inevitable result of a system where training is given *en masse*; but not the necessary result, because the tone of feeling of a headmaster or mistress is almost with certainty conveyed, more or less, to a whole school. Still, perhaps, the perfect bloom of the feelings can only be preserved under quite judicious individual culture, and, therefore, necessarily devolves upon parents.

The Sixth Sense of Tact.—The instrument to be employed in this culture is always the same—the blessed sixth sense of Tact. It is possible to call up the feeling one desires by a look, a gesture; to dissipate it entirely by the rudeness of a spoken word. Our silence, our sympathy, our perception, give place and play to fit feelings, and, equally, discourage and cause to slink away ashamed the feeling which should not have place.

Beware of Words.—But let us beware of words; let us use our eyes and our imagination in dealing with the young; let us see what they are feeling and help them by the flow of our responsive feeling. But words, even words of praise and tenderness, touch this delicate bloom of nature as with a hot finger, and behold! It is gone. Let us consider carefully what feelings we wish to stimulate, and what feelings we wish to repress in our children, and then, having made up our minds, let us say nothing. We all know the shrinking, as of a sore place, with which children receive some well-meant word from a tactless friend.

A Feeling is Communicated by Sympathy.—The sense of spiritual touch is our only guide in this region of the feelings, but with this alone we may tune the spirits of the children to great issues, believing that they are capable of all things great. We wish them to revere. Now, reverence is a feeling before it becomes a thought or an act, and it is a communicable feeling, but communicable, like the light of a torch, only by contact. The sentiment of reverence fills our own souls when we see a bird on its nest, an old man at his cottage door, a church in which have centred the aspirations of a village for many an age; we feel, and the children feel our feeling, and they feel too; a feeling is communicated by sympathy, but perhaps in no other way. The ignoble habit of depreciation is in the first place a feeling. It is quite easy to put the children into that other attitude of feeling called forth by the fitness and goodness of the thing regarded, and we all know that it is easy to appreciate or depreciate the same thing. These two feelings alone illustrate the importance of the delicate culture we have in view, for among the minor notes of character none tend more to differentiate persons than this of perceiving cause of satisfaction in an object or a person, or of perceiving cause of dissatisfaction in the same object or person.

Persons are Differentiated by their Powers of Appreciation or Depreciation.—An appreciative habit of feeling is a cause of tranquil joy to its possessor, and of ease and contentment to the people connected with him. A depreciative habit, on the contrary, though it affords a little pleasurable excitement because it ministers to the vanity of the *ego* (I dislike this person or this thing, therefore I know better or am better than others), disturbs tranquillity and puts the person out of harmony with himself and with his surroundings; no stable joy comes of depreciation. But even in dealing with feelings of this class we must remember that tact, sympathy and communicable feeling are our only implements; the feelings are not thoughts to be reasoned down; they are neither moral nor immoral to challenge our praise or our blame; we cannot be too reticent in our dealings with them in children, nor too watchfully aware that the least inadvertence may bruise some tender blossom of feeling.

Some Danger in Persiflage.—This is the risk
which attends the habit of persiflage and banter in
family talk; a little is thoroughly good and wholesome, but this kind of play should be used with very
great tact, especially by the elders. Children understand each other so well that there is far less risk of
hurt feelings from the tormenting schoolboy than
from the more considerate elder.

**To Deal with the Feelings of the Young a
Delicate Task.**—There is only one case in which the
feelings may not have free play, and that is when they
reflect the consciousness of the *ego*. What are commonly called sensitive feelings—that is, susceptibility
for oneself and about oneself, readiness to perceive
neglect or slight, condemnation or approbation—
through belonging to a fine and delicate character,
are in themselves of less worthy order, and require
very careful direction lest morbid conditions should
be set up. To ignore wisely is an art, and the girl who
craves to know what you thought of her when she
said this or did the other, need not be told brutally
that you did not think of her at all; it is quite enough
for her to perceive that your regard is fixed upon
something impersonal both to her and you; she takes
the hint and looks away from herself, and nothing is
said to cause her pain. It appears to be an immutable
law that our feelings, as our sensations, must find their
occupation in things without; the moment they are
turned in upon themselves harm is done. The task
of dealing with the susceptibilities of young people is
one of the most delicate that falls to us elders, whether
we be parents or friends. Undiscriminating sympathy
is very perilous, and bluntness of perception is very
damaging; we are between Scylla and Charybdis, and

must needs walk humbly and warily in this delicate work of dealing with the feelings of children and young people. Our only safeguard is to cherish in ourselves 'the soft, meek, tender soul,' sensitive to the touch of God, and able to deal in soft, meek, tender ways with children, beings of fine and delicate mould as they are.

CHAPTER XIX

'WHAT IS TRUTH?'

Moral Discrimination required by Parents

We are as a Nation Losing and Gaining in Truthfulness.—It is said that we English are no longer to be characterised as a truth-speaking people. This is a distressing charge, and yet we cannot put it away from us with a high hand. Possibly we are in a stage of civilisation which does not tend to produce the fine courage of absolute truthfulness. He who is without fear is commonly without falsehood; and a nation brought up amid the chivalries of war dares to be true. But we live in times of peace; we are no longer called on to defend the truth of our word by the strength of our hand. We speak with very little sense of responsibility, because no one calls us to account; and, so far as we are truth-tellers, we are so out of pure truth of heart and uprightness of life. That is, we may be, as a nation, losing the habit of truth to which the nation's childhood was trained, in ways however rough and ready; but we are growing up, and the truth that is among us is perhaps of a higher quality than the more general truthfulness of earlier days. Now, truth is indeed the white flower of a blameless life, and not the mere result of a fearless habit. The work before us is to bring up our children to this higher manner of truth. We no longer treat this or that particular lie or bit of deceit as a local ailment, for which we have only to apply the proper lotion or plaster; we treat it as symptomatic, as denoting a radical defect of character which we set ourselves to correct.

Opinion without knowledge, says Darwin, has no value, and to treat the tendency to untruthfulness that children often show, one should have a great deal of knowledge of a special kind. To treat a child *de novo*, place him under a moral microscope, record our observations, and formulate opinions based upon that child, and as many more as we can get into focus, is, it may be, useful and important public work. But it is work for the trained expert, rather than for the busy parent or teacher.

The Child a Human Being, perhaps at his Best. —It is not sufficient to bring unaided common-sense and good intentions to this most delicate art of child-study. We cannot afford to discard the wisdom of the past and begin anew with the effort to collect and systematise, hoping to accomplish as much and more in our short span than the centuries have brought us. For, indeed, the child is a human being, immature, but yet, perhaps, a human being at his best. Who amongst us has such gifts of seeing, knowing, comprehending, imagining, such capacities for loving, giving, believing, as the little child in the midst! We have no higher praise for our wisest and best than that they are fresh and keen as little children in their interests and loves.

In the Matter of Lying: Two Theories.— In this matter of lying, for example, unaided common-sense is likely to start on one of two theses: either the child is born true and you must keep him so; or the child is born false, and you must cure him of it. Popular opinion leans strongly to the first theory in these days; and as we perceive only that which we believe, the tendency is, perhaps, to take the absolute truthfulness and honour of children a little too much for granted. If you would have children true, you must, of course, treat them as if they were true and believe them to be true. But, all the same, wisdom may not play the ostrich. In the last generation, people accepted their children as born false, and what more likely to make them so than this foregone conclusion? Possibly some falling off in truthfulness in our day is traceable to the dogmatic teaching upon which our forebears were brought up.

A Child is Born without Virtue or Vice.— The wisdom of the ages—*i.e.* philosophy, and the science of the present, especially physiology, and more particularly what we may call psycho-physiology—show us that both these positions are wrong, and that all theories founded upon either position, or upon any midway point between the two, must needs be wrong too. A child is born neither true nor false. He is absolutely without either virtue or vice when he comes into the world. He has tendencies, indeed, but these are no more either virtuous or vicious than is the colour of his eyes. Even the child of a liar is not necessarily born a liar, because we are assured acquired tendencies are not transmitted. But there is this to be said. The child born of a family which has from generation to generation been in a subject position may have less predisposition to truthfulness than the child of a family which has belonged for generations to the ruling class. As in the natural world all substances must be reduced to their elements before they can be chemically dealt with, so in the moral world, if we wish to treat an offence, it is best to trace it to that elemental property of human nature of which it is the probable outcome.

Lying is not Elemental, but Secondary and Symptomatic.—Now, lying, even in its worst forms, is by no means elemental. Ambition is elemental, avarice, vanity, gratitude, love and hate. But lying arises from secondary causes. The treatment is all the more difficult. It is no longer a case of—the child has lied, punish him; but, where is the weak place in his character, or what is the defect in his education, which has induced this lying habit, if it be a habit? How shall we, not punish the lie, but treat the failing of which it is symptomatic? From this point of view let us consider the extremely interesting classification of lies presented to us by an American educationalist.[1]

1. Pseudophobia.—Treatment.—Janet *thinks* she *may* have glanced at Mary's slate and seen the answer to her sum. A comparison of the two slates shows that she has not done so, and that Janet, in the effort to save herself from a lie, has actually told one. This sort of morbid conscientiousness is Argus-eyed for other forms of sin. I knew a sick girl of fourteen who was terribly unhappy because she was not able to kneel up in bed when she said her prayers. Was this the 'unpardonable sin'? She asked in unaffected

[1] Professor G. Stanley Hall, in an article which appeared in the American Journal of Psychology. Jan. 1891. The headings are from Professor Stanley Hall's classification,

terror. I agree with the writer in question, as to the frequent occurrence of this form of distress, and also in tracing it, not to moral but to physical causes. I should say, too, it is more common in girls than in boys, and in the home-taught than in the school-taught child. Healthy interests, out-of-door life, engrossing and delightful handiworks, general occupation with things rather than with thoughts, and avoidance of any word or hint that may lead to self-consciousness or the habit of introspection, will probably do much to carry the young sufferer through a difficult stage of life.

2. The Lie Heroic.—The lie heroic is, *par excellence,* the schoolboy's lie, and has its rise, not in any love for lying, but in a want of moral balance; that is to say, the boy has been left to form his own code of ethics. 'Who spilled the ink?' little Tom Brown is asked. 'I did,' he says, because Jack Spender, the real culprit, is his particular hero at the moment. Faithfulness to a friend is a far higher virtue in Tom's eyes than mere barren truthfulness. And how is Tom to know, if he has not been taught, that it is unlawful to cherish one virtue at the expense of another? Considering how little clear, definite, authoritative teaching children receive on ethical questions, the wonder is that most persons do elaborate some kind of moral code, or code of honour, for themselves.

3. Truth for Friends, Lies for Enemies.—A lie under this head differs from the lie heroic chiefly in that it need not bring any risk to the speaker. This class of lies, again, points to the moral ignorance which we are slow to recognise in children because we confound innocence with virtue. It is quite natural for a child to believe that truth is relative, and not absolute, and that whether a lie is a lie or not depends on whom you are speaking to. The children are in the position of 'jesting Pilate.' What is truth? They unconsciously ask.

4. Lies inspired by Selfishness.—This is a form of lying for which superficial treatment is quite idle. The lie and the vice of which it is the instrument are so allied that those two cannot be put asunder. Professor Stanley Hallwell points out that school is a fertile field for this kind of lying. But it is the selfishness and not the lying that must be dealt with. Cure the first, and the second disappears, having no further occasion. How? This is a hard question. Nothing but a strong impulse to the heroism of unselfishness, initiated and sustained by the grace of God, will deliver boy or girl from the vice of selfishness of which lying is the ready handmaid. But let us not despair; *every* boy and girl is open to such impulse, is capable of heroic effort. Prayer and patience, and watchfulness for opportunities to convey the stimulating idea—these will not be in vain. *Every* boy and girl is a hero *in posse*. There is no worse infidelity than that which gives up the hope of mending any flaw of character, however bad, in a young creature. All the same, happy those parents who have not allowed selfishness and virtue (whether in the form of truthfulness, or under some other name) to come to hand to hand conflict. It is easy to give direction to the tendencies of a child; it is agonisingly difficult to alter the set of character in a man.

5. Deceptions of Imagination and Play—Due to an Unfed Imagination—Lessons in Truth

Telling.—I passed little Muriel in the park one day; the child was not looking; her companion was unknown to me. I was engaged with my companion, and believed that Muriel had not noticed me. The little girl went home and told her mother that I had kissed her and asked various questions about the family health. What could be the child's motive? She had none. Her active imagination rehearsed the little dialogue which most naturally would have taken place; and this was so real to her that it obscured the fact. The reality, the truth, to Muriel, was what she imagined had taken place. She had probably no recollection whatever of the actual facts. This sort of failure in verbal truthfulness is excessively common in imaginative children, and calls for prompt attention and treatment; but not on the lines a hasty and righteous parent might be inclined to adopt. Here is no call for moral indignation. The parents and not the child are in fault. The probability is that the child's ravenous imagination is not duly and daily supplied with its proper meat, of fairy tale in early days, of romance, later. Let us believe of the children that trailing clouds of glory do they come from the place where all things are possible, where any delightful thing may happen. Let us believe that our miserable limitations of time and space and the laws of matter irk them inconceivably, imprison the free soul as a wild bird in a cage. If we refuse to give the child outlets into the realms of fancy, where everything is possible, the delicate Ariel of his imagination will still work within our narrow limits upon our poor tasks, and every bit of our narrow living is played over with a thousand variations, apt to be more vivid and interesting than the poor facts, and, therefore, more likely to remain with the child as the facts which he will produce when required to speak the truth. What is the cure? Give the child free entrance into, abundant joyous living in, the kingdom of make-believe. Let him people every glen with fairies, every island with Crusoes. Let him gift every bird and beast with human interests, which he will share when the dear fairy godmother arrives with an introduction. Let us be glad and rejoice that all things are possible to the children, recognising, in this condition of theirs, their fitness to receive and believe and understand, as, alas! we cannot do, the things of the kingdom of God. The age of faith is a great sowing time, doubtless designed, in the Divine scheme of things, especially that parents may make their children at home in the things of the Spirit before contact with the world shall have materialised them.

At the same time the more imaginative the child, the more essential is it that the boundaries of the kingdom of make-believe should be clearly defined: and exact truthfulness insisted upon in all that concerns the narrower world where the grown-ups live. It is simply a matter of careful education; daily lessons in exact statement, without any horror or righteous indignation about misstatements, but warm, loving encouragement to the child who gives a long message quite accurately, who tells you just what Miss Brown said and no more, just what happened at Harry's party without any garnish. Every day affords scope for a dozen little lessons at least, and, gradually, the more severe beauty of truth will dawn upon the child whose soul is already possessed by the grace of fiction.

6. Pseudomania.—We have little to say on this score, except to counsel parents to keep watch at the place of the letting out of waters. No doubt the condition is pathological, and calls for curative treatment rather than punishment. But we believe it is a condition which need never be set up. The girl who has been able to win esteem for what she really is and really does, is not tempted to 'pose,' and the boy who has found full outlet for his energies, physical and mental, has no part of himself left to spend upon 'humbugging.' This is one of the cases which show how important it is for parents to acquaint themselves with that delicate borderland of human nature which touches the material and the spiritual. How spiritual thought and material brain interact; how brain and nerves are inter-dependent; how fresh air and wholesome food affect the condition of the blood which nourishes the nerves; how the nerves again may bear tyrannous sway over all that we include under 'bodily health'; these are matters that the parent should know who would avoid the possibility of the degradation described as Pseudomania from being set up in any one of his children.

Signs of Pseudomania.—It is as well that those who have to do with young people should be familiar with one or two marked signs of this mentally diseased condition; as, the furtive glance from under half-closed lids, shot up to see how you are taking it all; the flowing recital, accompanied by a slightly absent pre-occupied look, which denotes that the speaker is in the act of inventing the facts he relates.

It is not necessary to enlarge upon *palliatives, lies of terror,* or one or two more classes of lies which seem to be of frequent occurrence, as *lies of display* (boast ing), *lies of carelessness* (inaccuracy), and, worst of all, lies of *malice* (false witness).

Children must be Trained to Truthfulness.—It is well, however, to commend the subject to the attention of parents; for, though one child may have more aptitude than another, neither truthfulness nor the multiplication table come by nature. The child who appears to be perfectly truthful is so because he has been carefully trained to truthfulness, however indirectly and unconsciously. It is more important to cultivate the habit of truth than to deal with the accident of lying.

Moral teaching must be as simple, direct and definite as the teaching which appeals to the intellect; presented with religious sanctions, quickened by religious impulses, but not limited to the prohibitions of the law nor to the penalties which overtake the transgressor.

CHAPTER XX

SHOW CAUSE WHY

Parents responsible for Competitive Examinations

We have been asking, Why?—We have been asking, Why? Like Mr Ward Fowler's Wagtail, for a long time. We asked, Why? about linen underclothing, and behold it is discarded. We asked, Why? About numberless petticoats, and they are going. We are asking—Why? About carpets and easy chairs, and all manner of luxurious living; and probably the year 1910 will see of these things only the survivals. It is well we should go about with this practical Why? Rather than with the 'Why does a wagtail wag its tail?' manner of problem. The latter issues in vain guesses, and the pseudo-knowledge which puffeth up. But if, Why? Leads us to—'Because we should not; then let us do the thing we should.' This manner of Why? Is like a poker to a dying fire.

Tom goes to School to get a good place in Class.—Why is Tom Jones sent to school? That he may be educated, of course, say his parents. And Tom is dismissed with a fervent hope that he may take a good place. But never a word about the delights of learning, or of the glorious worlds of Nature and of thought to which his school studies will presumably prove an open sesame. 'Mind you be a good boy and get a good place in your class,' is Tom's valediction; and his little soul quickens with purpose. He won't disappoint father, and mother shall be proud of him. He'll be the top boy in his class. Why, he'll be the top boy in the whole school, and get prizes and things, and won't that be jolly! Tommy says nothing of this, but his mother sees it in his eyes and blesses the manly little fellow. So Tommy goes to school, happy boy, freighted with his father's hopes and his mother's blessings.

Tom passes his 'Exams.'—By-and-by comes a report the main delight of which is, that Tommy has gained six places; more places are gained, prizes, removes—by-and-by scholarships. Before he is twelve Tommy is able to earn the whole of his future schooling by his skill in that industry of the young popularly known as *Exams*. Now he aims at larger game; 'exams' still, but 'exams' big with possibilities, 'exams' which will carry him through his University career. His success is pretty certain, because you get into the trick of 'exams' as of other crafts. His parents are congratulated, Tom is more or less of a hero in his own eyes and in those of his compeers. Examinations for ever! Hip, hip! Never was a more facile way for a youth to distinguish himself, that is, if his parents have sent him into the world blessed with any inheritance of brains. For the boy not so blessed—why, he may go to the Colonies and that will make a man of him.

So do the Girls.—The girls come in a close second. The 'Junior,' the 'Senior,' the 'Higher,' the 'Intermediate,' the 'B.A.,' and what else you will, mark the epochs in most girls' lives. Better, say you, than having no epochs at all. Unquestionably, yes. But the fact that a successful examination of one sort or another is the goal towards which most of our young people are labouring with feverish haste and with undue anxiety, is one which possibly calls for the scrutiny of the investigating Why?

In the first place, people rarely accomplish beyond their own aims. Their aim is a pass, not knowledge; 'they cram to pass and not to know; they do pass and they don't know,' says Mr Ruskin; and most of us who know the 'candidate' will admit that there is some truth in the epigram. There are, doubtless, people who pass and who also know, but, even so, it is open to question, whether passing is the most direct, simple, natural and efficacious way of securing knowledge, or whether the persons who pass *and* know are not those keen and original minds which would get blood out of a stone,—anyway, sap out of sawdust.

The Tendency of Grind.—Again—except for the fine power of resistance possessed by the human mind, which secures that most persons who go through examination grind come out as they went in, absolutely unbiassed towards any intellectual pursuits whatever—except for this, the tendency of the grind is to imperil that individuality which is the one incomparably precious birthright of each of us. The very fact of a public examination compels that all who go in for it must study on the same lines.

No Choice as to the Matter or Manner of Studies.—It will be urged that there is no necessary limitation to studies outside the examination syllabus, nor any restrictions whatever as to the direction of study even upon the syllabus; but this is a mistake.

Whatever public examinations a given school takes, the whole momentum of pupils and staff urges towards the great issue. As to the manner of study, this is ruled by the style of questions set in a given subject; and Dry-as-dust wins the day because it is easier and fairer to give marks upon definite facts than upon mere ebullitions of fancy or genius. So it comes to pass that there is absolutely no choice as to the matter or manner of their studies for most boys and girls who go to school, nor for many of those who work at home. For so great is the convenience of a set syllabus that parents and teachers are equally glad to avail themselves of it.

Tyranny of Competitive Examination Supported by Parents.—It appears, then, that the boy is in bondage to the schoolmaster, and the schoolmaster to the examiner, and the parents do no more than acquiesce. Would parents be astounded if they found themselves in this matter a little like the man who had talked prose all his life without knowing it? The tyranny of the competitive examination is supported for the most part by parents. We do not say altogether. Teachers do their part manfully; but, in the first place, teachers unsupported by parents have no power at all in the matter; not a single candidate could they present beyond their own sons and daughters; in the next place, we do not hesitate to say that the whole system is forced upon teachers (though, perhaps, by no means against their will) by certain ugly qualities of human nature as manifested in parents. Ignorance, idleness, vanity, avarice, do not carry a pleasant sound; and if we, who believe in parents, have the temerity to suggest such shadows to the father basking in the sunshine of his boy's success, we would add that the rest of us who are not parents are still more to blame; that it is terribly hard to run counter to the current of the hour; and that 'harm is wrought through want of thought.'

The Evil Lies in the Competition.—Ignorance is excusable, but wilful ignorance is culpable, and the time has come for the thoughtful parent to examine himself and see whether or no it be his duty to make a stand against the competitive examination system. Observe, the evil lies in the competition, not in the examination. If the old axiom be true, that the mind can know nothing but what it can produce in the form of an answer to a question put by the mind itself, it is relatively true that knowledge conveyed from without must needs be tested from without Probably, work on a given syllabus tested by a final examination is *the* condition of definite knowledge and steady progress. All we contend for is that the examination shall not be competitive.

Examination Necessary—but should Include the whole School.—It will be urged that it is unfair to rank such public examinations as the Universities' Local—which have done infinitely much to raise the standard of middle-class education, especially amongst girls, and upon which neither prize nor place depends—as competitive examinations. They are rarely competitive, it is true, in the sense of any extraneous reward to the fortunate candidate; but, happily, we are not so far gone from original righteousness but that Distinction is its own reward. The pupil is willing to labour, and rightly so, for the honour of a pass which distinguishes him among the *elite* of his school. The schools themselves compete (*con+petere*=to seek with) as to which shall send in the greatest number of candidates and come out with the greatest number of Honours, Scholarships, and what not. These distinctions are well advertised, and the parent who is on the look-out for a school for his boy is all too ready to send him where the chances of distinction are greatest. Examinations which include the whole school, and where every boy has his place on the list, higher or lower, are another thing; though these also appeal to the emulous principle, they do not do so in excess, the point to be noted.

The Primary Desires.—But why should so useful an incentive to work as a competitive examination be called in question? There are certain facts which may be predicated of every human being who is not, as the country folk say, 'wanting.' Everyone wants to get on; whatever place we occupy we aim at the next above it. Everyone wants to get rich, or, anyway, richer; whether the wealth he chooses to acquire be money or autographs. Everyone wants the society of his fellows; if he does not, we call him a misanthrope and say, to use another popular and telling phrase, 'He's not quite right.' We all want to excel, to do better than the rest, whether in a tennis-match or an examination. We all want to know, though some of us are content to know our neighbours' affairs, while others would fain know about the stars in their courses. We all, from the sergeant in his stripes to the much-decorated commanding officer, want people to think well of us. Now the several desires, of power, of wealth, of society, of excelling, of knowledge, of esteem, are primary springs of action in every human being. Touch any one of them, in savage or in *savant*, and you cannot fail of a response. The Russian moujik besieges a passing traveller with questions about the lands he has seen, because he *wants to know*. The small boy gambles with his marbles because he *wants to get*. The dairymaid dons a new bow because she *wants to be admired*, the only form of esteem to which she is awake. Tom drives when the children play horses because he *wants to rule*. Maud works herself into a fever for her examination because she *wants to excel*, and 'to pass' is the hall-mark of excellence, that is, of those who excel.

Neither Virtuous nor Vicious.—Now these desires are neither virtuous nor vicious. They are common to us all and necessary to us all, and appear to play the same part towards our spiritual being that the appetites do to our material existence; that is, they stimulate us to the constant effort which is the condition of progress, and at the same time the condition of health. We know how that soul stagnates which thinks nothing worth an effort

They Stimulate to Effort.—He is a poor thing who is content to be beaten on all hands. We do not quarrel with the principle of emulation any more than we do with that of respiration. The one is as natural and as necessary as the other, and as little to be brought before a moral tribunal. But it is the part of the educator to recognise that a child does not come into the world a harp with one string; and that the perpetual play upon this one chord through all the years of adolescence is an evil, not because emulation is a vicious principle, but because the balance of character is destroyed by the constant stimulation of this one desire at the expense of the rest.

Curiosity as Active as Emulation.—Equally strong, equally natural, equally sure of awakening a responsive stir in the young soul, is the divinely implanted principle of curiosity. The child *wants* to *know*; wants to know incessantly, desperately; asks all manner of questions about everything he comes across, plagues his elders and betters, and is told not to bother, and to be a good boy and not ask questions. But this only sometimes. For the most part we lay ourselves out to answer Tommy's questions so far as we are able, and are sadly ashamed that we are so soon floored by his insatiable curiosity about natural objects and phenomena. Tommy has his reward.

Extent of a Child's Knowledge.—The most surprising educational feat accomplished amongst us is the amount of knowledge, about everything within his range, which Tommy has acquired by the end of his sixth year. 'Why, he knows as much as I do, about'—this, and that, and the other, says his astonished and admiring father. "Take him to the seaside, and in a week he will tell you all about trawling and mackerel fishing, the ways of the fisher-folk, and all that his inquisitive mind can find out unaided. He would tell all about sand, and shells, and tides, and waves, only, poor little boy, he must have help towards this manner of knowledge, and there is no one to give it to him. However, he finds out all that he can about all that he sees and hears, and does amass a surprising amount of exact knowledge about things and their properties.

Why the Schoolboy is no longer Curious.—When Tommy goes to school, his parents find themselves relieved of the inconvenience of his incessant Why? They are probably so well pleased to be let off that it does not occur to them to ask themselves, Why Tommy no longer wonders Why? Up to this period Nature has been active. She has been allowed to stimulate that one of his desires most proper to minister to his mental growth: just as, if let alone, she would give him that hearty appetite which should promote his physical growth. She has it all her own way. The desire of knowledge is that spring of action most operative in Tommy's childhood. But he goes to school. Knowledge is a pure delight to Tommy. Let his lessons approach him on the lines of his nature—not on the lines proper for certain subjects of instruction—and the little boy has no choice. He cannot help learning and loving to learn, "cos 'tis his nature to.'

This, of presenting knowledge to Tommy on the lines of his nature, is, however, a difficult and delicate task. Not every schoolmaster, any more than every parent, is keen to give Tommy what he wants in this matter of needful knowledge. So, once upon a time, let us suppose, there arose a pedagogue to whom was discovered a new and easier way. The morning had seen the poor man badly baffled by the queries of boys who *wanted to know.* How was a man, who had pretty well done with fresh studies for his own part, to keep up with these eager intelligences? In a vision of the night it is disclosed to Cognitus that there is another and an easier way. The desire of knowledge is not the only desire active in the young bosom.

Every Boy Wants to Excel.—Just as much as he wants to know, he wants to excel, to do better than the rest. 'Every soul of them wants to be first in one way or another—first in games, if not in class.'

Now, Cognitus was a philosopher; he knew that, as a rule, but one desire is supremely active at one time in the breast of boy or man. Kindle their emulation, and all must needs do the same thing in the same way to see who can do it best. The boys will no longer *want to know*; they will get their due share of learning in regular ways, and really get on better than if they were moved by the restless spirit of inquiry. *Eureka!* A discovery; honour and renown for master and boys—no need for cane or imposition, for emulation is the best of all disciplinarians—and steady-going, quiet work, without any of the fatiguing excursions into new fields to which the craving for knowledge leads. 'How pleased the parents will be, too,' says Cognitus, for he knows that paternal love, now and then, looks for a little sustenance from paternal vanity, that the child who does well is dear.

Emulation an Easier Spring to Work than Curiosity.—Nay, who knows but the far-seeing Cognitus beheld, as in a vision, the scholarships and money awards which should help to fill the pocket of Paternus, or should, any way, lessen the drain thereupon. Here, indeed, is a better way, upon which Paternus and Cognitus may well consent to walk together. Every one is happy, everyone content, nobody worried, a great deal of learning got in. What would you have more? Just one thing, honoured Cognitus—that keen desire for knowledge, that same incessant Why? with which Tommy went to school, and which should have kept him inquisitive about all things good and great and wise throughout the years given to him wherein to lay the groundwork of character, the years of his youth.

But the Boy no longer Wants to Know.—We cannot put our finger upon Cognitus, and are pretty sure that he arrived by a consensus of opinion, and through considerable urgency on the part of parents. No one is to blame for a condition of things which is an enormous advance upon much of what went before. Only, knowledge is advancing, and it is full time that we reconsider our educational principles and recast our methods. We absolutely must get rid of the competitive examination system if we would not be reduced to the appalling mediocrity which we see, in China, for example, to have befallen an examination-ridden empire.

An Examination-ridden Empire.—Probably the world has never seen a finer body of educationalists than those who at the present moment man our schools, both Boys' and Girls'. But the originality, the fine initiative, of these most able men and women is practically lost. The schools are examination-ridden, and the heads can strike out no important new lines. Let us begin our efforts by believing in one another, parents in teachers and teachers in parents. Both parents and teachers have the one desire, the advance of the child along the lines of character. Both groan equally under the limitations of the present system. Let us have courage, and united and concerted action will overthrow this Juggernaut that we have made.

CHAPTER XXI

A SCHEME OF EDUCATIONAL THEORY PROPOSED
TO PARENTS

Each Class in Society should have its Ideal.—
One of Mr Matthew Arnold's discriminating utterances may help us in the effort to define anew the
scope and the methods of education. In *A French
Eton* (page 61) he says:—'The education of each
class in society has, or ought to have, its ideal,
determined by the wants of that class, and by its
destination. Society may be imagined so uniform
that one education shall be suitable for all its
members; we have not a society of that kind, nor
has any European country. . . . Looking at English
society at this moment one may say that the ideal
for the education of each of its classes to follow, the
aim which the education of each should particularly
endeavour to reach, is different'

This remark, to which we can give only a doubtful
assent, helps us, nevertheless, to define our position.
In this matter of class differentiation we believe we
have scientific grounds for a line of our own. The
Fathers (why should we not have Fathers in education as well as in theology?) worked out, for the most

part, their educational thought with an immediate view to the children of the poor.

Poor Children need a Vocabulary.—Because the children that he had to deal with had a limited vocabulary, and untrained observing powers, Pestalozzi taught them to see and then to say: 'I see a hole in the carpet. I see a small hole in the carpet. I see a small round hole in the carpet. I see a small round hole with a black edge in the carpet,' and so on; and such training may be good for such children. But what is the case with the children we have to deal with? We believe to-day on scientific grounds in the doctrine of heredity, and certainly in this matter experience supports our faith.

Children of Educated Parents do not.—*Punch* has hit off the state of the case. 'Come and see the puff-puff, dear.' 'Do you mean the *locomotive*, grandmamma?' As a matter of fact, the child of four and five has a wider, more exact vocabulary in everyday use than that employed by his elders and betters, and is constantly adding to this vocabulary with surprising quickness; *ergo*, to give a child of this class a vocabulary is no part of direct education. Again, we know that nothing escapes the keen scrutiny of the little people. It is not their perceptive powers we have to train, but the habit of methodical observation and accurate record.

Generations of physical toil do not tend to foster imagination. It may be good, then, for the children of the working classes to have games initiated for them, to be carried through little dramatic plays until, perhaps, in the end they will be able to invent such little dramas for themselves!

This, true of Imagination.—But the children of

the cultured classes—why, surely their danger is rather to live too much in realms of fancy. A single sentence in lesson or talk, the slightest sketch of a historical character, and they will play at it for a week, inventing endless incidents. Like Tennyson, when he was a child, they will carry on a story of the siege and defence of a castle (represented by a mound, with sticks for its garrison) for weeks together; and a child engrossed with these larger interests feels a sensible loss of dignity when he flaps his wings as a pigeon or skips about as a lamb, though, no doubt, he will do these things with pleasure for the teacher he loves. Imagination is ravenous for food, not pining for culture, in the children of educated parents, and education need not concern herself directly, for them, with the development of the conceptive powers. Then with regard to the child's reasoning powers, most parents have had experiences of this kind. Tommy is five. His mother had occasion to talk to him about the Atlantic Cable, and said she did not know how it was insulated; Tommy remarked next morning that he had been thinking about it, and perhaps the water itself was an insulator. So far from needing to develop their children's reasoning powers, most parents say—'Oh, wad the gods the giftie gie us' —to answer the everlasting 'why' of the intelligent child.

The Development of Faculties Important for Ignorant and Deficient Children.—In a word, to develop the child's so-called faculties is the main work of education when *ignorant* or otherwise *deficient* children are concerned; but the children of educated parents are never *ignorant* in this sense. They awake to the world all agog for knowledge, and with keen-edged faculties; therefore the principle of heredity causes us to re-cast our idea of the office of education, and to recognise that the child of intelligent parents is born with an inheritance of self-developing faculties.

But not for Children of Educated Parents.— Thus education naturally divides itself into education for the children of *lettered*, and education for the children of *unlettered* parents. In fact, this class question, which we are all anxious to evade in common life, comes practically into force in education. It is necessary to individualise and say, this part of education is the most important for *this* child, or *this* class, but may be relegated into a lower place for another child or another class.

The Educator should form Habits.—If science limits our range of work as regards the development of so-called faculties, it extends it in equal measure with regard to habit. Here we have no new doctrine to proclaim. 'One custom overcometh another,' said Thomas a Kempis, and that is all we have to say; only, physiologists have made clear to us the *rationale* of this law of habit. We know that to form in his child right habits of thinking and behaving is a parent's chief duty, and that this can be done for every child definitely and within given limits of time. But this question has been already dealt with, and we need do no more than remind parents of what they already know.

Should Nourish with Ideas.—To nourish a child daily with loving, right, and noble ideas we believe to be the parent's next duty. The child having once received the Idea will assimilate it in his own way, and work it into the fabric of his life; and a single sentence from his mother's lips may give him a bent that will make him, or may tend to make him, painter or poet, statesman or philanthropist. The object of lessons should be in the main twofold: to train a child in certain mental habits, as attention, accuracy, promptness, etc., and to nourish him with ideas which may bear fruit in his life.

Our Main Objects.—There are other educational principles which we bear in mind and work out, but for the moment it is worth while for us to concentrate our thought upon the fact that one of our objects is to accentuate the importance of education under the two heads of the *formation of habits* and the *presentation of ideas*; and, as a corollary, to recognise that the *development of faculties* is not a supreme object with the cultivated classes, because this is work which has been done for their children in a former generation.

We recognise Material and Spiritual Principles of Human Nature.—But how does all this work? Is it practical? Is it the question of to-day? It must needs be practical because it gives the fullest recognition to the two principles of human nature, the *material* and the *spiritual*. We are ready to concede all that the most advanced biologist would ask of us. Does he say, 'Thought is only a mode of motion?' If so, we are not dismayed. We know that ninety-nine out of a hundred thoughts that pass through our minds are involuntary, the inevitable result of those modifications of the brain tissue which habit has set up. The mean man thinks mean thoughts, the magnanimous man great thoughts, because we all think as we are accustomed to think, and Physiology shows us why. On the other hand, we recognise that greater is the spirit within us than the matter which it governs. Every habit has its beginning. The beginning is the *idea* which comes with a stir and takes possession of us.

We recognise the Supreme Educator.—The *idea* is the motive power of life, and it is because we recognise the spiritual potency of the idea that we are able to bow reverently before the fact that God the Holy Spirit is Himself the Supreme Educator, dealing with each of us severally in the things we call sacred and those we call secular. We lay ourselves open to the spiritual impact of ideas, whether these be conveyed by the printed page, the human voice, or whether they reach us without visible sign.

Studies are Valued as they present Fruitful Ideas.—But ideas may be evil or may be good; and to choose between the ideas that present themselves is, as we have been taught, the one responsible work of a human being. It is the power of choice that we would give our children. We ask ourselves, 'Is there any fruitful idea underlying this or that study that the children are engaged in?' We divest ourselves of the notion that to develop the faculties is the chief thing; and a 'subject' which does not rise out of some great thought of life we usually reject as not nourishing, not fruitful; while we usually, but not invariably, retain those studies which give exercise in habits of clear and orderly thinking. We have some gymnastics of the mind whose object is to exercise what we call faculties as well as to train in the habit of clear and ordered thinking. Mathematics, grammar, logic, etc., are not purely disciplinary; they do develop, if a bull may be allowed intellectual muscle. We by no means reject the familiar staples of education, in the school sense, but we prize them even more for the record of intellectual habits they leave in the brain tissue than for their distinct value in developing certain 'faculties.'

Nature-Knowledge.—Thus our first thought with regard to Nature-knowledge is that the child should have a living personal acquaintance with the things he sees. It concerns us more that he should know bistort from persicaria, hawkweed from dandelion, and where to find this and that, and how it looks, living and growing, than that he should talk about *epigynous* and *hypogynous*. All this is well in its place, but should come quite late, after the child has seen and studied the living growing thing *in situ*, and has copied colour and gesture as best he can.

Object-Lessons.—So of object-lessons; we are not anxious to develop his observing powers on little bits of everything, which he shall describe as opaque, brittle, malleable, and so on. We would prefer not to take the edge off his curiosity in this way; we should rather leave him receptive and respectful for one of those opportunities for asking questions and engaging in talk with his parents about the lock in the river, the mowing machine, the ploughed field, which offer real seed to the mind of a child, and do not make him a priggish little person able to tell all about it.

We trust much to Good Books.—Once more, we know that there is a storehouse of thought wherein we may find all the great ideas that have moved the world. We are above all things anxious to give the child the key to this storehouse. The education of the day, it is said, does not produce *reading* people. We are determined that the children shall love books, therefore we do not interpose ourselves between the book and the child. We read him his *Tanglewood Tales*, and when he is a little older his *Plutarch*, not trying to break up or water down, but leaving the child's mind to deal with the matter as it can.

We do not recognise 'Child-Nature.'—We endeavour that all our teaching and treatment of children shall be on the lines of nature, *their* nature and ours, for we do not recognise what is called 'Child-nature.' We believe that children are human beings at their best and sweetest, but also at their weakest and least wise. We are careful not to dilute life for them, but to present such portions to them in such quantities as they can readily receive.

We are Tenacious of Individuality: we consider Proportion.—In a word, we are very tenacious of the dignity and individuality of our children. We recognise steady, regular growth with no *transition* stage. This teaching is up to date, but it is as old as common sense. Our claim is that our common sense rests on a basis of Physiology, that we show a reason for all that we do, and that we recognise 'the science of the proportion of things,' put the first thing foremost, do not take too much upon ourselves, but leave time and scope for the workings of Nature and of a higher Power than Nature herself.

We think that Children have a Right to Knowledge.—Much guidance and stimulation are afforded by another principle. We are not anxious to contend with Kant that the mind possesses certain a *priori* knowledge; nor with Hume that it holds innate ideas. The more satisfying proposition seems to be that the mind has, as it were, prehensile adaptations to each department of universal knowledge. We find that children lay hold of all knowledge which is fitly presented to them with avidity, and therefore we maintain that a wide and generous curriculum is due to them.

CHAPTER XXII

A CATECHISM OF EDUCATIONAL THEORY

Character an Achievement.—As the philosophy which underlies any educational or social scheme is really the vital part of that scheme, it may be well to set forth, however meagrely, some fragments of the thought on which we found our teaching.

We believe—

That disposition, intellect, genius, come pretty much by nature.

That *character* is an achievement, the one practical achievement possible to us for ourselves and for our children.

That all real advance, in family or individual or nation, is along the lines of character.

That, therefore, to direct and assist the evolution of character is the chief office of education.

But perhaps we shall clear the ground better by throwing a little of the teaching of the Union[1] into categorical form:—

Character and Disposition.

Origin of Conduct.—What is character?
The resultant or residuum of conduct.

[1] 'The Parents' National Educational Union.'

That is to say, a man is what he has made himself by the thoughts which he has allowed himself, the words he has spoken, the deeds he has done.

How does conduct itself originate?

Commonly, in our habitual modes of thought. We think as we are accustomed to think, and, therefore, act as we are accustomed to act.

What, again, is the origin of these habits of thought and act?

Commonly, inherited disposition. The man who is generous, obstinate, hot-tempered, devout, is so, on the whole, because that strain of character runs in his family.

Means of Modifying Disposition.—Are there any means of modifying inherited dispositions?

Yes; marriage, for the race; education, for the individual.

Life-History of a Habit.

How may a bad habit which has its rise in an inherited disposition be corrected?

By the contrary good habit: as Thomas a Kempis has said, 'One custom overcometh another.'

Genesis of a Habit.—Trace the genesis of a habit.

Every act proceeds from a thought. Every thought modifies somewhat the material structure of the brain. That is, the nerve substance of the brain forms itself to the manner of thoughts we think. The habit of act rises from the habit of thought. The person who thinks, 'Oh, it will do'; 'Oh, it doesn't matter,' forms a habit of negligent and imperfect work.

Correction of Bad habit.—How may such habit be corrected?

By introducing the contrary line of thought, which will lead to contrary action. 'This *must* be done well, because—'

Is it enough to think such thought once?

No, the stimulus of the new idea must be applied until it is, so to speak, at home in the brain, and arises involuntarily.

Involuntary Thought.

What do you mean by involuntary thought?

The brain is at work unceasingly, is always thinking, or rather is always being acted upon by thought, as the keys of an instrument by the fingers of a player.

Is the person aware of all the thoughts that the brain elaborates?

No; only of those which are new and 'striking.' The old familiar 'way of thinking' beats in the brain without the consciousness of the thinker.

Conduct depends on Unconscious Cerebration.—What name is given to this unconscious thought?

Unconscious (or involuntary) cerebration.

Why is it important to the educator?

Because most of our actions spring from thoughts of which we are not conscious, or, anyway, which are involuntary.

Is there any means of altering the trend of unconscious cerebration?

Yes, by diverting it into a new channel.

The 'unconscious cerebration' of the greedy child

runs upon cakes and sweetmeats: how may this be corrected?

By introducing a new idea—the pleasure of giving pleasure with these good things, for example.

Springs of Action.

Is the greedy child capable of receiving such new idea?

Most certainly; because benevolence, the desire of benefiting others, is one of those springs of action in every human being that need only to be touched to make them act.

Give an example of this fact.

Benevolence.—Mungo Park, dying of thirst, hunger, and weariness in an African desert, found himself in the vicinity of a cannibal tribe. He gave himself up for lost, but a woman of the tribe found him, took compassion on him, brought him milk, hid him, and nourished him until he was restored and could take care of himself.

Are there any other springs of action which may be touched with effect in every human being?

Yes, such as the desire of knowledge, of society, of distinction, of wealth; friendship, gratitude, and many more. Indeed, it is not possible to incite a human being to any sort of good and noble conduct but you touch a responsive spring.

How, then, can human beings do amiss?

Malevolence.—Because the good feelings have their opposite bad feelings, springs which also await a touch. Malevolence is opposed to benevolence. It is easy to imagine that the unstable savage woman might have been amongst the first to devour the man she cherished, had one of her tribe given an impulse to the springs of hatred within her.

In view of these internal impulses, what is the duty of the educator?

To make himself acquainted with the springs of action in a human being, and to touch them with such wisdom, tenderness and moderation that the child is insensibly led into the habits of the good life.

Habits of the Good Life.

Habits of 'Well-brought-up' Persons.—Name some of these habits.

Diligence, reverence, gentleness, truthfulness, promptness, neatness, courtesy; in fact, the virtues and graces which belong to persons who have been 'well brought up.'

Is it enough to stimulate a spring of action—say, curiosity, or the desire of knowledge, once, in order to secure a habit?

No; the stimulus must be repeated, and action upon it secured over and over many times before a habit is formed.

What common error do people make about the formation of habits?

They allow lapses; they train a child to 'shut the door after him' twenty times, and allow him to leave it open the twenty-first.

With what result?

That the work has to be done over again, because the growth of brain tissue to the new habit (the forming of cell-connections) has been disturbed. The result would appear to be much the same as when the flesh-forming process which knits up a wound is disturbed.

Time should be given to the Forming of a Habit.—Then the educator should 'time' himself in forming habits? How long may it take to cure a bad habit, and form the contrary good one?

Perhaps a month or six weeks of careful incessant treatment may be enough.

But such treatment requires an impossible amount of care and watchfulness on the part of the educator?

Yes; but not more than is given to the cure of some bodily diseases—measles, or scarlet fever, for example.

Then the thoughts and actions of a human being may be regulated mechanically, so to speak, by setting up the right nerve currents in the brain?

This is true only so far as it is true to say that the keys of a piano produce music.

Thoughts Follow in Sequence.— But the thoughts, which may be represented by the fingers of the player, do they not also run their course without the consciousness of the thinker?

They do; not merely vague, inconsequent musings, but thoughts which follow each other with more or less logical sequence, according to the previous training of the thinker.

Would you illustrate this?

Mathematicians have been known to think out abstruse problems in their sleep; the bard improvises, authors 'reel off' without premeditation, without any deliberate intention to write such and such things. The thoughts follow each other according to the habit of thinking previously set up in the brain of the thinker.

Into new Developments.—Is it that the thoughts go round and round a subject like a horse in a mill?

No; the horse is rather drawing a carriage along the same high road, but into ever new developments of the landscape.

The Initial Thought.—In this light, the important thing is how you *begin* to think on any subject?

Precisely so; the initial thought or suggestion touches as it were the spring which sets in motion a possibly endless succession, or train, of ideas; thoughts which are, so to speak, elaborated in the brain almost without the consciousness of the thinker.

Are these thoughts, or successive ideas, random, or do they make for any conclusion?

They make for the logical conclusion which should follow the initial idea.

Then the reasoning power may be set to work involuntarily?

Yes; the sole concern of this power is, apparently, to work out the rational conclusion from any idea presented to it.

Makes for Logical Conclusions.—But surely this power of arriving at logical rational conclusions almost unconsciously is the result of education, most likely of generations of culture?

It exists in greater or less degree according as it is disciplined and exercised; but it is by no means the result of education as the word is commonly understood: witness the following anecdote:[1]

'When Captain Head was travelling across the Pampas of South America, his guide one day suddenly stopped him, and, pointing high into the air, cried out, "A lion!" Surprised at such an exclamation, accompanied with such an act, he turned up his eyes,

[1] From Thompson's *Laws of Thought*.

and with difficulty perceived, at an immeasurable height, a flight of condors soaring in circles in a particular spot. Beneath this spot, far out of sight of himself or guide, lay the carcass of a horse, and over this carcass stood, as the guide well knew, a lion, whom the condors were eyeing with envy from their airy height. The sight of the birds was to him what the sight of the lion alone would have been to the traveller, a full assurance of its existence. Here was an act of thought which cost the thinker no trouble, which was as easy to him as to cast his eyes upward, yet which from us, unaccustomed to the subject, would require many steps and some labour.'

'Reason' Acts without Volition.—Then is what is called 'the reason' innate in human beings?

Yes, it is innate, and is exercised without volition by all, but gains in power and precision in proportion as it is cultivated.

Not an Infallible Guide to Conduct.—If the reason, especially the trained reason, arrives at the right conclusion without any effort of volition on the part of the thinker, it is practically an infallible guide to conduct?

On the contrary, the reason is pledged to pursue a suggestion to its logical conclusion only. Much of the history of religious persecutions and of family and international feuds turns on the confusion which exists in most minds between that which is logically inevitable and that which is morally right.

But according to this doctrine any theory whatever may be shown to be logically inevitable?

Exactly so; the initial idea once received, the difficulty is, not to prove that it is tenable, but to restrain the mind from proving that it is so.

Can you illustrate this point?

The child who lets himself be jealous of his brother is almost startled by the flood of convincing proofs, that he does well to be angry, which rush in upon him. Beginning with a mere flash of suspicion in the morning, the little Cain finds himself in the evening possessed of irrefragable proofs that his brother is unjustly preferred to him: and,

> 'All seems infected that the infected spy,
> As all looks yellow to the jaundiced eye.'

But supposing it is true that the child has cause for jealousy?

Given the starting idea, and his reason is equally capable of proving a logical certainty, whether it is true or whether it is not true.

Is there any historical proof of this startling theory?

Confusion as to Logical and Moral Right.— Perhaps every failure in conduct, in individuals, and in nations, is due to the confusion which exists as to that which is logically right, as established by the reason, and that which is morally right, as established by external law.

Is any such distinction recognised in the Bible?

Distinctly so; the *transgressors* of the Bible are those who do that which is *right* in their own eyes —that is, that of which their reason approves. Modern thought considers, on the contrary, that all men are justified in doing that which is right in their own eyes, acting 'up to their lights,' 'obeying the dictates of their reason.'

For example?

A mother whose cruel usage had caused the death of her child was morally exonerated some time ago in a court of justice because she acted 'from a mistaken sense of duty.'

Error from Mistaken Sense of Duty.—But is it not possible to err from a mistaken sense of duty? Not only possible, but inevitable, if a man accept his 'own reason' as his lawgiver and judge. Take a test case, the case of the superlative crime that has been done upon the earth. There can be no doubt that the persons who caused the death of our Lord and Saviour Jesus Christ acted under a mistaken sense of duty. 'It is expedient that one man die for the people, and that the whole nation perish not,' said, most *reasonably*, those patriotic leaders of the Jews; and they relentlessly hunted to death this Man whose ascendency over the common people and whose whispered claims to kingship were full of elements of danger to the subject race. 'They know not what they do,' He said, who is the Truth.

Children should be taught Self-knowledge.

All this may be of importance to philosophers; but what has it to do with the bringing-up of children?

A Child should know what he is as a Human Being.—It is time we reverted to the teaching of Socrates. 'Know thyself,' exhorted the wise man, in season and out of season; and it will be well with us when we understand that to acquaint a child with himself—what he is as a human being—is a great part of education.

It is difficult to see why; surely much harm comes of morbid introspection?

Introspection is morbid or diseased when the person imagines that all which he finds within him is peculiar to him as an individual. To know what is common to all men is a sound cure for unhealthy self-contemplation.

How does it work?

This Knowledge a Safeguard.—To recognise the limitations of the reason is a safeguard in all the duties and relations of life. The man who knows that loyalty is his first duty in every relation, and that if he admit doubting, grudging, unlovely thoughts, he cannot possibly be loyal, because such thoughts once admitted will prove themselves to be right and fill the whole field of thought, why, he is on his guard and writes up 'no admittance' to every manner of mistrustful fancy.

That rule of life should affect the Supreme relationship?

Truly, yes; if a man will admit no beginning of mistrustful surmise concerning his father and mother, his child and his wife, shall he do so of Him who is more than they, and more than all, the 'Lord of his heart'? 'Loyalty forbids' is the answer to every questioning of His truth that would intrude.

Against 'Honest Doubt.'—But when others whom you must needs revere, question and tell you of their 'honest doubt'?

You know the history of their doubt, and can take it for what it is worth—its origin in the suggestion, which, once admitted, must needs reach a logical conclusion even to the bitter end. 'Take heed that ye *enter* not into temptation,' He said, who needed not that any should tell Him, for He knew what was in men.

Man as Free Agent.

If man is the creature of those habits he forms with care or allows in negligence, if his very thoughts are involuntary and his conclusions inevitable, he ceases to be a free agent. One might as well concede at once that 'thought is a mode of motion,' and cease to regard man as a spiritual being capable of self-regulation. Is not this the case?

It is hardly possible to concede too wide a field to biological research, if we keep well to the front the fact that man is a spiritual being whose material organs act in obedience to non-material ideas; that, for example, as the hand writes, so the brain thinks, in obedience to stimulating ideas.

Life Sustained upon Ideas.—Is the idea self originated?

Probably not; it would appear that, as the material life is sustained upon its appropriate food from without, so the immaterial life is sustained upon *its* food,—ideas spiritually conveyed.

May the words 'idea' and 'suggestion' be used as synonymous terms?

Only in so far as that ideas convey suggestions to be effected in acts.

What part does the man himself play in the reception of this immaterial food?

It is as though one stood on the threshold to admit or reject the viands which should sustain the family.

Volition in the Reception of Ideas.—Is this free-will in the reception or rejection of ideas the limit of man's responsibility in the conduct of his life?

Probably it is; for an idea once received must run its course, unless it be superseded by another idea, in the reception of which volition is again exercised.

Origin of Ideas.

How do ideas originate?

They appear to be spiritual emanations from spiritual beings; thus, one man conveys to another the idea which is a very part of himself.

How Ideas are Conveyed.—Is the intervention of a bodily presence necessary for the transmission of an idea?

By no means; ideas may be conveyed through picture or printed page; natural objects convey ideas, but, perhaps, the initial idea in this case may always be traced to another mind.

The Supreme Educator.—Then the spiritual sustenance of ideas is derived directly or indirectly from other human beings?

No; and here is the great recognition which the educator is called upon to make. God, the Holy Spirit, is Himself the supreme Educator of mankind.

How?

He openeth man's ear morning by morning, to hear so much of the best as the man is able to hear.

In things Natural and Spiritual.—Are the ideas suggested by the Holy Spirit confined to the sphere of the religious life?

No; Coleridge, speaking of Columbus and the discovery of America, ascribes the origin of great inventions and discoveries to the fact that 'certain ideas of the natural world are presented to minds already prepared to receive them by a higher Power than Nature herself.'

Is there any teaching in the Bible to support this view?

Yes; very much. Isaiah, for example, says that the ploughman knows how to carry on the successive operations of husbandry, 'for his God doth instruct him and doth teach him.'

Are all ideas which have a purely spiritual origin ideas of good?

Unhappily, no; it is the sad experience of mankind that ideas of evil also are spiritually conveyed.

What is the part of the man?

To choose the good and refuse the evil.

This View throws Light on Christian Doctrine. —Does this doctrine of ideas as the spiritual food needful to sustain the immaterial life throw any light on the doctrines of the Christian religion?

Yes; the Bread of Life, the Water of Life, the Word by which man lives, the 'meat to eat which ye know not of,' and much more, cease to be figurative expressions, except that we must use the same words to name the corporeal and the incorporeal sustenance of man. We understand, moreover, how ideas emanating from our Lord and Saviour, which are of His essence, are the spiritual meat and drink of His believing people. We find it no longer a 'hard saying,' nor a dark saying, that we must sustain our spiritual selves upon Him, even as our bodies upon bread.

Divine Co-operation in Education.—What practical bearing upon the educator has this doctrine of ideas?

He knows that it is his part to place before the child daily nourishment of ideas; that he may give the child the right initial idea in every study, and respecting each relation and duty of life; above all, he recognises the divine co-operation in the direction, teaching, and training of the child.

The Functions of Education.

How would you summarise the functions of education?

Education is a discipline—that is, the discipline of the good habits in which the child is trained. Education is a life, nourished upon ideas; and education is an atmosphere—that is, the child breathes the atmosphere emanating from his parents; that of the ideas which rule their own lives.

Part of Lessons in Education.—What part do lessons and the general work of the schoolroom play in education thus regarded?

They should afford opportunity for the discipline of many good habits, and should convey to the child such initial ideas of interest in his various studies as to make the pursuit of knowledge on those lines an object in life and a delight to him.

A Curriculum.—Has a child any natural fitness for knowledge?

Yes; it would appear that he has a natural affinity for all knowledge, and has a right to a generous curriculum of studies.

What duty lies upon parents and others who regard education thus seriously, as a lever by means of which character may be elevated, almost indefinitely?

Perhaps it is incumbent upon them to make conscientious endeavours to further all means used to spread the views they hold; believing that there is such 'progress in character and virtue' possible to the redeemed human race as has not yet been realised or even imagined. 'Education is an atmosphere, a discipline, a life.'

CHAPTER XXIII

WHENCE AND WHITHER

A Question for Parents.—1. Whence?

Progress of the Parents' National Educational Union.—'The Union goes on,' an observer writes, 'without puff or fuss, by its own inherent force'; and it is making singularly rapid progress. At the present moment thousands of children of thinking, educated parents, are being brought up, more or less consciously and definitely, upon the lines of the Union. Parents who read the *Parents' Review* or other literature of the Society, parents who belong to our various branches, or our other agencies, parents who are influenced by these parents are becoming multitudinous; and all have one note in common—the ardour of persons working out inspiring ideas.

Its Importance.—It is hardly possible to overestimate the force of this league of educated parents. When we think of the part that the children being brought up under these influences will one day play in the leading and ruling of the land, we are solemnised with the sense of a great responsibility, and it behoves us to put to ourselves, once again, the two searching queries by which every movement should from time to time be adjudged—Whence? And Whither?

Whence? The man who is satisfied with his dwelling-place has no wish to move, and the mere fact of a 'movement' is a declaration that we are not satisfied, and that we are definitely on our way to some other ends than those commonly accepted. In one respect only we venture boldly to hark back.

The Legacy of the Past.—Exceedingly fine men and women were brought up by our grandfathers and grandmothers, even by our mother's and fathers; and the wise and old amongst us, though they look on with great sympathy, yet have an unexpressed feeling that men and women were made on the old lines of a stamp which we shall find it hard to improve upon. This was no mere chance result, nor did it come out of the spelling-book or the Pinnock's Catechisms which we have long ago consigned to the limbo they deserve.

Children Responsible Persons.—The teaching of the old days was as bad as it could be, the training was hapazard work, reckless alike of physiology and psychology; but our grandfathers and grandmothers had one saving principle, which, for the last two or three decades, we have been, of set purpose, labouring to lose. They, of the older generation, recognised children as reasonable beings, persons of mind and conscience like themselves, but needing their guidance and control, as having neither knowledge nor experience. Witness the queer old children's books which have come down to us; before all things, these addressed children as reasonable, intelligent and responsible (terribly responsible!) persons. This fairly represents the note of home-life in the last generation. So soon as the baby realised his surroundings, he found himself a morally and intellectually responsible person. Now one of the secrets of power in dealing with our fellow-beings is, to understand that human nature does that which it is expected to do and is that which it is expected to be. We do not mean *believed* to do and to be, with the fond and foolish faith which Mrs. Hardcastle bestowed on her dear Tony Lumpkin. Expectation strikes another chord, the chord of '*I am, I can, I ought,*' which must vibrate in every human breast, for "tis our nature to.' The capable, dependable men and women whom we all know were reared upon this principle.

Now, we are not sure.—But now? Now, many children in many homes are still brought up on the old lines, but not with quite the unfaltering certitude of the old times. Other thoughts are in the air. A baby is a huge oyster (says one eminent psychologist) whose business is to feed, and to sleep, and to grow. Even Professor Sully, in his most delightful book,[1] is torn in two. The children have conquered him, have convinced him beyond doubt that they are as ourselves, only more so. But then he is an evolutionist, and feels himself pledged to accommodate the child to the principles of evolution. Therefore the little person is supposed to go through a thousand stages of moral and intellectual development, leading him from the condition of the savage or ape to that of the intelligent and cultivated human being. If children will not accommodate themselves pleasantly to this theory, why, that is their fault, and Professor

[1] *Studies of Children,* by Professor Sully (Longmans, 10s. 6d.).

Sully is too true a child-lover not to give us the children as they are, with little interludes of the theory upon which they ought to evolve. Now I have absolutely no theory to advance, and am, on scientific grounds, disposed to accept the theories of the evolutionary psychologists. But facts are too strong for me.

Intellectual Labour of the Child's First Year.— When we consider the enormous intellectual labour the infant goes through during his first year in accommodating himself to the conditions of a new world, in learning to discern between far and near, solid and flat, large and small, and a thousand other qualifications and limitations of this perplexing world, why, we are not surprised that John Stuart Mill should be well on in his Greek at five; that Arnold at three should know all the Kings and Queens of England by their portraits; or that a musical baby should have an extensive repertoire of the musical classics.

Intelligence of Children.—I was once emphasising the fact that every child could learn to speak two languages at once with equal facility, when a gentleman present stated that he had a son who was a missionary in Bagdad, married to a German lady, and their little son of three expressed all he had to say with equal fluency in three languages— German, English, and Arabic, using each in speaking to those persons whose language it was. 'Nana, which does God love best, little girls or little boys?', said a meditative little girl of four. 'Oh, little girls, to be sure,' said Nana, with a good-natured wish to please. 'Then if God loves little girls best, why was not God Himself a little girl?' Which of us who

have reached the later stages of evolution would
have hit upon a more conclusive argument? If the
same little girl asked on another occasion, watch-
ing the blackbirds at the cherries: 'Nana, if the
bees make honey, do the birds make jam?' it was
by no means an inane question, and only proves
that we older persons are dull and inappreciative
of such mysteries of Nature as that bees should
make honey.

Children highly Endowed but Ignorant.—This
is how we find children—with intelligence more
acute, logic more keen, observing powers more alert,
moral sensibilities more quick, love and faith and
hope more abounding; in fact, in all points like as
we are, only much more so; but absolutely ignorant
of the world and its belongings, of us and our ways,
and, above all, of how to control and direct and
manifest the infinite possibilities with which they are
born.

Happy and Good, or Good and Happy.—Our
conception of a child rules our relations towards him.
Pour s'amuser is the rule of child-life proper for the
'oyster' theory, and most of our children's books and
many of our theories of child-education are based
upon this rule. 'Oh! he's so happy,' we say, and
are content, believing that if he is happy he will be
good; and it is so to a great extent; but in the
older days the theory was, if you are good you will
be happy; and this is a principle which strikes the
keynote of endeavour, and holds good, not only
through the childish 'stage of evolution,' but for the
whole of life, here and hereafter. The child who has
learned to 'endeavour himself' (as the Prayer Book
has it) has learned to live.

Our Conception of the Child is Old, of Education New.—If our conception of *Whence?* As regards the child, as of—

> 'A Being, breathing thoughtful breath,
> A traveller betwixt life and death,'—

is old, that of our grandfathers, our conception of the aims and methods of education is new, only made possible within the late decades of the last century; because it rests one foot upon the latest advances in the science of Biology and the other upon the potent secret of these latter days, that matter is the all-serviceable agent of spirit, and that spirit forms, moulds, is absolute lord, over matter, as capable of affecting the material convolutions of the brain as of influencing what used to be called the heart.

Knowing that the brain is the physical seat of habit, and that conduct and character alike are the outcome of the habits we allow: knowing, too, that an inspiring idea initiates a new habit of thought, and, hence a new habit of life, we perceive that the great work of education is to inspire children with vitalising ideas as to the relations of life, departments of knowledge, subjects of thought: and to give deliberate care to the formation of those habits of the good life which are the outcome of vitalising ideas.

Divine Co-operation.—In this great work we seek and assuredly find the co-operation of the Divine Spirit, whom we recognise, in a sense rather new to *modern* thought, as the Supreme Educator of mankind in things that have been called secular, fully as much as in those that have been called sacred.

Two Educational Labours.—We are free to give

our whole force to these two great educational labours, of the inspiration of ideas and the formation of habits, because, except in the case of children somewhat mentally deficient, we do not consider that the 'development of faculties' is any part of our work; seeing that the children's so-called faculties are already greatly more acute than our own.

Test for Systems.—We have, too, in our possession, a test for systems that are brought under our notice, and can pronounce upon their educational value. For example, some time ago the London Board Schools held an exhibition of work; and great interest was excited by an exhibit which came from New York representing a week's work (on 'Herbartian' lines) in a school. The children worked for a week upon 'an apple.' They modelled it in clay, they painted it in brushwork, they stitched the outline on cardboard, they pricked it, they laid it in sticks (the pentagonal form of the seed vessel). Older boys and girls modelled an apple-tree and made a little ladder on which to run up the apple-tree and gather the apples, and a wheel-barrow to carry the apples away, and a great deal more of the same kind. Everybody said, 'How pretty, how ingenious, what a good idea!' and went away with the notion that here, at last, was education. But *we* ask, 'What was the informing idea?' The external shape, the internal contents of an apple,—matters with which the children were already exceedingly well acquainted. What mental habitudes were gained by this week's work? They certainly learned to look at the apple, but think how many things they might have got familiar acquaintance with in the time. Probably the children were not consciously bored, because the

impulse of the teachers' enthusiasm carried them on.
But, think of it—

> 'Rabbits hot and rabbits cold,
> Rabbits young and rabbits old
> Rabbits tender and rabbits tough,'

no doubt those children had enough—of apples anyway. This 'apple' course is most instructive to us
as emphasising the tendency in the human mind to
accept and rejoice in any neat system which will
produce immediate results, rather than to bring every
such little course to the test of whether it does or
does not further either or both of our great educational principles.

Advance with the Tide.—*Whither?* Our 'whence'
opens to us a 'whither' of infinitely delightful
possibilities. Seeing that each of us is labouring
for the advance of the human race through the
individual child we are educating, we consider carefully in what directions this advance is due, and
indicated, and we proceed of set purpose and
endeavour to educate our children so that they shall
advance with the tide. 'Can ye not discern the signs
of the times?' A new Renaissance is coming upon
us, of unspeakably higher import than the last; and
we are bringing up our children to lead and guide,
and by every means help in the progress—progress
by leaps and bounds—which the world is about to
make. But 'whither' is too large a question for the
close of a chapter.

CHAPTER XXIV

WHENCE AND WHITHER

2. Whither?

Physical and Psychical Evolutions.—The biologists leave thinking persons without hesitation in following the great *bouleversement* of thought, summed up in the term *evolution*. They are no longer able to believe otherwise than that man is the issue of processes, ages long in their development; and what is more, and even more curious, that each individual child, from the moment of his conception to that of his birth, appears in his own person to mark an incredible number of the stages of this evolutionary process. The realisation of this truth has made a great impression on the minds of men. We feel ourselves to be part of a process, and to be called upon, at the same time, to assist in the process, not for ourselves exactly, but for any part of the world upon which our influence bears; especially for the children who are so peculiarly given over to us. But there comes, as we have seen, a point where we must arise and make our protest. The physical evolution of man admits of no doubt; the psychical evolution, on the other hand, is not only *not proven*, but the whole weight of existing evidence appears to go into the opposite scale.

The Greatness of Children.—The age of materialism has run its course; we recognise matter as force, but as altogether subject force, and that it is the spirit of a man which shapes and uses his material substance in its own ways to its own ends. Who can tell the way of the spirit? Perhaps this is one of the ultimate questions upon which man has not yet been able to speculate to any purpose; but when we consider the almost unlimited powers of loving and trusting, of discriminating and of apprehending, of perceiving and of knowing, which a child possesses, and compare these with the blunted sensibilities and slower apprehension of the grown man or woman of the same calibre, we are certainly not inclined to think that growth from less to more, and from small to great, is the condition of the spiritual life: that is, of that part of us which loves and worships, reasons and thinks, learns and applies knowledge. Rather would it seem to be true of every child in his degree, as of the divine and typical Child, that He giveth not the Spirit by measure to him.

Wisdom, the Recognition of Relations.—It is curious how the philosophy of the Bible is always well in advance of our latest thought. 'He grew in wisdom and in stature,' we are told. Now what is wisdom, philosophy? Is it not the recognition of *relations*? First, we have to understand relations of time and space and matter, the natural philosophy which made up so much of the wisdom of Solomon; then, by slow degrees, and more and more, we learn that moral philosophy which determines our relations of love and justice and duty to each other: later, perhaps, we investigate the profound and puzzling subject of the inter-relations of our own most composite being, mental philosophy. And in all these and beyond all these we apprehend, slowly and feebly, the highest relation of all, the relation to God, which we call religion. In this science of the relations of things consists what we call wisdom, and wisdom is not born in any man,—apparently not even in the Son of man Himself.

Wisdom increases; Intelligence does not.—He grew in wisdom, in the sweet gradual apprehension of all the relations of life: but the power of apprehending, the strong, subtle, discerning spirit, whose function it is to grasp and understand, appropriate and use, all the relations which bind all things to all other things—this was not given to Him by measure; nor, we may reverently believe, is it so given to us.

Differences in Men.—That there are differences in the measures of men, in their intellectual and moral stature, is evident enough; but it is well that we should realise the nature of these differences, that they are differences in kind and not in degree; and depend upon what we glibly call the laws of heredity, which bring it to pass that man in his various aspects shall make up that conceivably perfect whole possible to mankind. This is a quite different thing from the notion of a small and feeble measure of heart and intellect in the child, to grow by degrees into the robust and noble spiritual development which, according to the psychical evolutionist, should distinguish the adult human being.

Ignorance is not Impotence.—These are quite practical and simple considerations for every one entrusted with the bringing up of a child, and are not to be set aside as abstract principles, the discussion of which should serve little purpose beyond that of sharpening the wits of the schoolmen. As a matter of fact, we do not *realise* children, we under-estimate them; in the divine words, we 'despise' them, with the best intentions in the world, because we confound the immaturity of their frames, and their absolute ignorance as to the relations of things, with spiritual impotence: whereas the fact probably is, that never is intellectual power so keen, the moral sense so strong, spiritual perception so piercing, as in those days of childhood which we regard with a supercilious, if kindly, smile.

All Possibilities Present in a Child.—A child is a person in whom all possibilities are present—present now at this very moment—not to be educed after years and efforts manifold on the part of the educator; but indeed it is a greater thing to direct and use this wealth of spiritual power than to develop the so-called faculties of the child. It cannot be too strongly urged that our education of children will depend, *nolens volens*, upon the conception we form of them. If we regard them as instruments fit and capable for the carrying out of the Divine purpose in the progress of the world, we shall endeavour to discern the signs of the times, perceive in what directions we are being led, and prepare the children to carry forward the work of the world, by giving them vitalising ideas concerning, at any rate, some departments of that work.

We Live for the Advancement of the Race.— Having settled it with ourselves that we and the children alike live for the advancement of the race, that our work is immediately with them, and, through them, mediately for all, and that they are perfectly fitted to receive those ideas which are for the inspiration of life, we must next consider in what directions we shall try to set up spiritual activities in the children.

Our Whence in the Potency of the Child, our Whither in the Thought of the Day.—We have sought to establish our *whence* in the potency of the child, we will look for our *whither* in the living thought of the day, which probably indicates the directions in which the race is making progress. We find that all men everywhere are keenly interested in science, that the world waits and watches for great discoveries; we, too, wait and watch, believing that, as Coleridge said long ago, great ideas of Nature are imparted to minds already prepared to receive them by a higher Power than Nature herself.

All Men are Interested in Science.—At a former meeting of the British Association, the President lamented that the progress of science was greatly hindered by the fact that we no longer have field naturalists—close observers of Nature as she is. A literary journal made a lamentable remark thereupon. It is all written in books, said this journal, so we have no longer any need to go to Nature herself. Now the knowledge of Nature which we get out of books is not real knowledge; the use of books is, to help the young student to verify facts he has already seen for himself. Let us, before all things, be Nature-lovers; intimate acquaintance with every natural object within his reach is the first, and, possibly, the best part of a child's education. For himself, all his life long, he will be soothed by—

> 'The breathing balm,
> The silence and the calm,
> Of mute, insensate things.'

Children Trained to Observe.—And for science, he is in a position to do just the work which is most needed; he will be a close, loving observer of Nature at first hand, storing facts, and free from all impatient greed for inferences.

A new Conception of Art; great Ideas demand great Art.—Looking out on the realm of Art again, we think we discern the signs of the times. Some of us begin to learn the lesson which a prophet has been raised up to deliver to this, or the last, generation. We begin to understand that mere technique, however perfect—whether in the rendering of flesh tints, or marbles, or of a musical composition of extreme difficulty—is not necessarily high Art. It is beginning to dawn upon us that Art is great only in proportion to the greatness of the idea that it expresses; while what we ask of the execution, the technique, is that it shall be adequate to the inspiring idea. But surely these high themes have nothing to do with the bringing up of children? Yes, they have; everything. In the first place, we shall permit no *pseudo* Art to be in the same house with our children; next, we shall bring our own facile tastes and opinions to some such searching test as we have indicated, knowing that the children imbibe the thoughts that are in us, whether we will or no; and lastly, we shall inspire our children with those great ideas which shall create a demand, anyway, for great Art.

Children should Learn to Care for Books.—In literature, we have definite ends in view, both for our own children and for the world through them. We wish the children to grow up to find joy and refreshment in the taste, the flavour of a *book*. We do not mean by a book any printed matter in a binding, but a work possessing certain literary qualities able to bring that sensible delight to the reader which belongs to a literary word fitly spoken. It is a sad fact that we are losing our joy in literary form. We are in such haste to be instructed by facts or titillated by theories, that we have no leisure to linger over the mere putting of a thought. But this is our error, for words are mighty both to delight and to inspire. If we were not as blind as bats, we should long ago have discovered a truth very fully indicated in the Bible—that that which is once said with perfect fitness can never be said again, and becomes ever thereafter a living power in the world. But in literature, as in art, we require more than mere form. Great ideas are brooding over the chaos of our thought; and it is he who shall say the thing we are all dumbly thinking, who shall be to us as a teacher sent from God.

Children must be Nurtured on the Best.—For the children? They must grow up upon the best. There must never be a period in their lives when they are allowed to read or listen to twaddle or reading-made-easy. There is never a time when they are unequal to worthy thoughts, well put; inspiring tales, well told. Let Blake's 'Songs of Innocence' represent their standard in poetry; De Foe and Stevenson, in prose; and we shall train a race of readers who will demand *literature*—that is, the fit and beautiful expression of inspiring ideas and pictures of life. Perhaps a printed form to the effect that gifts of books to the children will not be welcome in such and such a family, would greatly assist in this endeavour!

The Solidarity of the Race.—To instance one more point—there is a reaching out in all directions after the conception expressed in the words 'solidarity of the race.' We have probably never before felt as now in absolute relation with all men everywhere; everything human is precious to us, the past belongs to us as the present, and we linger tenderly over evidences of the personality of men and women who lived ages ago. An American poet expresses this feeling with Western intensity, but he does not exaggerate when he tells us that *he* is the soldier wounded in battle, *he* is the galley slave, and *he* is the hero come to the rescue, that every human pulse is *his* pulse, every fall *his* fall, and every moral victory *his* triumph. The present writer recollects the moment when the conviction of the common sisterhood of women was brought home to her in a way never to be forgotten. She was driving from station to station in London, and saw a drunken woman carried on a door. She knew by the shock of pain and the tears the sight brought that the woman was not outside of her, but was in some mysterious way part of her—her very self. This was a new perception to a girl, and one never again to be lost sight of. Such shocks of recognition probably come to most of us, and when they come to the Greathearts of the world we get our Elizabeth Frys, our Wilberforces, our Florence Nightingales. Deeds of pity have been done through all the Christian ages, and, indeed, wherever the human heart has had free play; but to feel pity for another and to be aware, however dimly, that that other is, part and lot, indissolubly bound up with ourselves—these are two things. We venture to believe that this is the stage which the education of mankind, as divinely conducted, has reached in our day. In other days, men did good for the love of God, or to save their own souls; they acted uprightly, because it behoved themselves to be just in all their dealings; but the motives which stir us in our relation to each other now are more intimate, tender, indefinable, soul-compelling. What the issues will be when we have learned to con understandingly this new page in the Book of Life we cannot foretell, but we may hope that the Kingdom of God is coming upon us.

Children should be Brought up to Live for All Men.—Studying reverently *these* signs of the times, what indications do we find for our guidance in the bringing up of children? The tender sympathy of the child must be allowed to flow in ways of help and kindness towards all life that anyway touches his. I knew a little girl of five, who came in from her walk under an obvious cloud of distress. 'What is the matter, H——?' she was asked. A quick little 'Nothing,' with the reticence of her family, was all that could be got out of her for some minutes; but a caress broke her down, and, in a passion of pity, she sobbed out, 'A poor man, no home, no food, no bed to lie upon!' Young as she was, the revelation of the common life in humanity had come upon her; she was one with the beggar and suffered with him. Children must, of course, be shielded from intense suffering, but woe to mother or nurse who would shield, by systematically hardening, the child's heart. This little girl had the relief of helping, and then the pain of sympathy ceased to be too much for her.

Children should not hear of 'Impostors.'—
Whatever our own opinion of the world and of human
nature, let us be careful how we breathe the word
'impostor' into the ear of a child, until he is old
enough to understand that if the man is an impostor,
that does but make him the object of a deeper pity
and a wiser help—a help whose object is not to relieve
but to reform.

To Serve is Promotion.—Again, children are
open to vanity as to all other evil dispositions
possible to human nature. They must be educated
to give and to help without any notion that to do so
is goodness on their part It is very easy to keep
them in the attitude of mind natural to a child, that
to serve is promotion to the person who serves, for
indeed he has no absolute claim to be in a position
to pour benefits upon another. The child's range
of sympathy must be widened, his love must go out
to far and near, rich and poor; distress abroad and
distress at home should appeal to him equally;
and always he should give some manner of help
at real cost to himself. When he is old enough, the
object-lessons of the newspapers should be brought
before him.

No Considerations of Expediency.—He should
know that atrocities in Armenia, for instance, are
the cause of real heart-trouble in English homes;
that there are cases of abstract right and wrong for
nations as for individuals, which admit of no considerations of expediency; that to succour our
neighbour in mortal distress is such an occasion,
and that he who has fallen among thieves is therefore our neighbour, whether as a nation or as an
individual. Do not let us bring up our children in

glass houses, for fear of the ravages of pity upon their tender hearts. Let them know of any distress which would naturally come before them, and let them ease their own pain by alleviating in some way the sufferings they sorrow for. Children were not given to us with infinite possibilities of love and pity that we might choke the springs of pity and train them into hardness of heart. It is our part, on the contrary, to prepare these little ministers of grace for the larger and fuller revelation of the kingdom of heaven that is coming upon us.

CHAPTER XXV

THE GREAT RECOGNITION REQUIRED OF PARENTS

Ruskin on the 'Vaulted Book.'—Mr. Ruskin
has done a great service to modern thought in inter-
preting for us the harmonious and ennobling scheme
of education and philosophy recorded upon one
quarter of what he calls the 'Vaulted Book,' that
is, the Spanish Chapel attached to the Church of
Sta. Maria Novella, in Florence.

Many of my readers have probably studied under
Mr. Ruskin's guidance the illuminating teaching of
the frescoes which cover roof and walls; but all will
like to be reminded of the lessons they have pondered
with reverence and wonder. "The descent of the
Holy Ghost is on the left hand (of the roof) as you
enter. The Madonna and Disciples are gathered in
an upper chamber: underneath are the Parthians,
Medes, Elamites, etc., who hear them speak in their
own tongues. Three dogs are in the foreground—
their mythic purpose, to mark the share of the lower
animals in the gentleness given by the outpouring of
the Spirit of Christ. . . . On this and the opposite
side of the Chapel are represented by Simon Memmi's
hand, the teaching power of the Spirit of God and
the saving power of the Christ of God in the world,

according to the understanding of Florence in his time.

"We will take the side of intellect first. Beneath the pouring forth of the Holy Spirit in the point of the arch beneath are the three Evangelical Virtues. Without these, says Florence, you can have no science. Without Love, Faith, and Hope—no intelligence. Under these are the four Cardinal Virtues . . . . . Temperance, Prudence, Justice, Fortitude. Under these are the great Prophets and Apostles. . . . . Under the line of Prophets, as powers summoned by their voices, are the mythic figures of the seven theological or spiritual and the seven geological or natural sciences; and under the feet of each of them the figure of its Captain-teacher to the world."

The Seven Natural Sciences.—I hope the reader will continue to study Mr. Ruskin's exposition of the 'Vaulted Book' in *Mornings in Florence*: it is wonderfully full of teaching and suggestion. Our immediate concern is with the seven mythic figures representing the natural sciences, and with the figure of the Captain-teacher of each. First, we have Grammar, a gracious figure teaching three Florentine children; and, beneath, Priscian. Next, Rhetoric, strong, calm, and cool; and below, the figure of Cicero with a quite beautiful face. Next, Logic, with perfect pose of figure and lovely contenance; and beneath her, Aristotle—intense keenness of search in his half-closed eyes. Next, Music, with head inclined in intent listening to the sweet and solemn strains she is producing from her antique instrument; and underneath, Tubal Cain, not Jubal, as the inventor of harmony—perhaps the most marvellous record that Art has produced of the impact of a great idea upon the soul of a man but semi-civilised. Astronomy succeeds, with majestic brow and upraised hand, and below her, Zoroaster, exceedingly beautiful—'the delicate Persian head made softer still by the elaborately wreathed silken hair.' Next, Geometry, looking down, considering some practical problem, with her carpenter's square in her hand, and below her, Euclid. And lastly, Arithmetic, holding two fingers up in the act of calculating, and under her, Pythagoras wrapped in the science of number.

> 'The thoughts of God are broader than the measures of
> man's mind,'

but here we have the breadth of minds so wide in the sweep of their intelligence, so profound in their insight, that we are almost startled by the perception that, pictured on these walls, we have indeed a true measure of the thoughts of God. Let us glance for a moment at the conception of education in our own century.

Education not Religious and Secular.—In the first place, we divide education into religious and secular. The more devout among us insist upon religious education as well as secular. Many of us are content to do without religious education altogether; and are satisfied with what we not only call secular but make secular, in the sense in which we understand the word, i.e. entirely limited to the uses of this visible world.

The Great Recognition.—Many Christian people rise a little higher; they conceive that even grammar and arithmetic may in some not very clear way be used for God; but the great recognition, that God the Holy Spirit is Himself, personally, the Imparterof knowledge, the Instructor of youth, the Inspirer of genius, is a conception so far lost to us that we should think it distinctly irreverent to conceive of the divine teaching as co-operating with ours in a child's arithmetic lesson, for example. But the Florentine mind of the Middle Ages went further than this: it believed, not only that the seven Liberal Arts were fully under the direct outpouring of the Holy Ghost, but that every fruitful idea, every original conception, whether in Euclid, or grammar, or music, was a direct inspiration from the Holy Spirit, without any thought at all as to whether the person so inspired named himself by the name of God, or recognised whence his inspiration came. All of these seven figures are those of persons whom we should roughly class as pagans, and whom we might be lightly inclined to consider as outside the pale of the divine inspiration. It is truly difficult to grasp the amazing boldness of this scheme of the education of the world which Florence accepted in simple faith.

Knowledge, like Virtue, Divine.—But we must not accept even an inspiring idea blindly. Were these people of the Middle Ages right in this plan and conception of theirs? Plato hints at some such thought in his contention that knowledge and virtue are fundamentally identical, and that if virtue be divine in its origin, so must knowledge be also. Ancient Egypt, too, was not in the dark in this matter. 'Pharaoh said unto his servants, can we find such a one as this, a man in whom the Spirit of God is?' Practical discernment and knowledge of everyday matters, and of how to deal with emergencies, were not held by this king of Egypt to be teachings unworthy of the Spirit of God. 'The Spirit

of God came upon him and he prophesied among
them,' we are told of Saul, and we may believe that
this is the history of every great invention and every
great discovery of the secrets of Nature. 'Then
David gave to Solomon his son . . . . the pattern of
all that he had by the spirit, of the courts of the house
of the Lord.' We have here a suggestion of the
source of every conception of beauty to be expressed
in forms of art.

Science, Art and Poetry 'by the Spirit.'—But
it is not only with high themes of science, art and
poetry that the divine Spirit concerns Himself. It
sometimes occurs to one to wonder who invented, in
the first place, the way of using the most elemental
necessaries of life. Who first discovered the means
of producing fire, of joining wood, of smelting ores,
of sowing seed, of grinding corn?

Ideas of Common Things.—We cannot think
of ourselves as living without knowing these things;
and yet each one must have been a great idea when
it first made a stir in the mind of the man who conceived it. Where did he get his first idea? Happily,
we are told, in a case so typical that it is a key to all
the rest:—

'Doth the plowman plow all day to sow? doth
he open and break the clods of his ground? When
he hath made plain the face thereof, doth he not
cast abroad the fitches and scatter the cummin, and
cast in the principal wheat and the appointed barley
and the rie in their place? For his God doth instruct
him to discretion, and doth teach him. For the
fitches are not threshed with a threshing instrument,
neither is a cart wheel turned about upon the
cummin; but the fitches are beaten out with a staff,

and the cummin with a rod. Bread corn is bruised; because he will not ever be threshing it, nor break it with the wheel of his cart, nor bruise it with his horsemen. This also cometh forth from the Lord of Hosts, which is wonderful in counsel, and excellent in working.'—Isa xxviii. 24, etc.

'God doth Instruct.'—In the things of science, in the things of art, in the things of practical everyday life, his God doth instruct him and doth teach him, her God doth instruct her and doth teach her. Let this be the mother's key to the whole of the education of each boy and each girl; not of her *children*; the divine Spirit does not work with nouns of multitude, but with each single child. Because He is infinite, the whole world is not too great a school for this indefatigable Teacher, and because He is infinite, He is able to give the whole of his infinite attention for the whole time to each one of his multitudinous pupils. We do not sufficiently rejoice in the wealth that the infinite nature of our God brings to each of us.

Subjects Divinely Taught.—And what subjects are under the direction of this Divine Teacher? The child's faith and hope and charity—that we already knew; his temperance, justice, prudence and fortitude —that we might have guessed; his grammar, rhetoric, logic, music, astronomy, geometry, arithmetic—this we might have forgotten, if these Florentine teachers had not reminded us; his practical skill in the use of tools and instruments, from a knife and fork to a microscope, and in the sensible management of all the affairs of life—these also come from the Lord, which is wonderful in counsel and excellent in working. His God doth instruct him and doth teach him. Let the mother visualise the thought as an illuminated scroll about her newborn child, and let her never contemplate any kind of instruction for her child, except under the sense of the divine co-operation. But we must remember that here as everywhere the infinite and almighty Spirit of God works under limitations.

Our Co-operation Indispensable.—Our co-operation appears to be the indispensable condition of all the divine workings. We recognise this in what we call spiritual things, meaning the things that have to do more especially with our approaches to God; but the new thing to us is, that grammar, for example, may be taught in such a way as to invite and obtain the co-operation of the Divine Teacher, or in such a way as to exclude His illuminating presence from the schoolroom. We do not mean that spiritual virtues may be exhibited by the teacher, and encouraged in the child in the course of a grammar lesson; this is no doubt true, and is to be remembered; but perhaps the immediate point is that the teaching of grammar by its guiding ideas and simple principles, the true, direct, and humble teaching of grammar, without pedantry and without verbiage, is, we may venture to believe, accompanied by the illuminating power of the Holy Spirit, of whom is all knowledge.

Teaching that Invites and that Repels Divine Co-operation.—The contrary is equally true. Such teaching as enwraps a child's mind in folds of many words that his thought is unable to penetrate, which gives him rules and definitions, and tables, in lieu of ideas—this is teaching which excludes and renders impossible the divine co-operation.

Discord in our Lives Resolved.—This great recognition resolves that discord in our lives of which most of us are, more or less, aware. The things of sense we are willing to subordinate to the things of spirit; at any rate we are willing to endeavour ourselves in this direction. We mourn over our failures and try again, and recognise that here lies the Armageddon for every soul of man. But there is a debateable land. Is it not a fact that the spiritual life is exigeant, demands our sole interest and concentrated energies? Yet the claims of intellect— mind, of the aesthetic sense—taste, press upon us urgently. We must think, we must know, we must rejoice in and create the beautiful. And if all the burning thoughts that stir in the minds of men, all the beautiful conceptions they give birth to, are things apart from God, then we too must have a separate life, a life apart from God, a division of ourselves into secular and religious—discord and unrest. We believe that this is the fertile source of the unfaith of the day, especially in young and ardent minds. The claims of intellect are urgent; the intellectual life is a necessity not to be foregone at any hazard. It is impossible for these to recognise in themselves a dual nature; a dual spirituality, so to speak; and, if there are claims which definitely oppose themselves to the claims of intellect, those other claims must go to the wall; and the young man or woman, full of promise and power, becomes a free-thinker, an agnostic, what you will. But once the intimate relation, the relation of Teacher and taught in all things of the mind and spirit, be fully recognised, our feet are set in a large room; there is space for free development in all directions, and this free and joyous development, whether of intellect or heart, is recognised as a Godward movement.

We are Safeguarded from Intellectual as from Moral Sin.—Various activities, with unity of aim, bring harmony and peace into our lives; more, this perception of the intimate dealings of the divine Spirit with our spirit in the things of the intellect, as well as in those of the moral nature, makes us as keenly alive in the one case as in the other to the insidious promptings of the spirit of evil; we become aware of the possibility of intellectual sin as of moral sin; we perceive that in the region of pure reason, also, it behoves us to see that we enter not into temptation. We rejoice in the expansion of intellect and the expansion of heart and the ease and freedom of him who is al ways in touch with the inspiring Teacher, with whom are infinite stores of learning, wisdom, and virtue, graciously placed at our disposal.

Harmony in our Efforts.—Such a recognition of the work of the Holy Spirit as the Educator of mankind, in things intellectual as well as in things moral and spiritual, gives us 'new thoughts of God, new hopes of Heaven,' a sense of harmony in our efforts and of acceptance of all that we are. What stands between us and the realisation of this more blessed life? This; that we do not realise ourselves as spiritual beings invested with bodies, living, emotional, a snare to us and a joy to us, but which are, after all, the mere organs and interpreters of our spiritual intention. Once we see that we are dealing spirit with spirit with the friend at whose side we are sitting, with the people who attend to our needs, we shall be able to realise how incessant is the commerce between the divine Spirit and our human spirit. It will be to us as when one stops one's talk and one's thoughts in the spring-time, to find the world full of bird-music unheard the instant before. In like manner we shall learn to make pause in our thoughts, and shall hear in our intellectual perplexities, as well as in our moral, the clear, sweet, cheering and inspiring tones of our spiritual Guide. We are not speaking here of what is commonly called the religious life, or of our definite approaches to God in prayer and praise; these things all Christian people comprehend more or less fully; we are speaking only of the intellectual life, the development of which in children is the aim of our subjects and methods of instruction.

Conditions of Divine Co-operation.—Supposing we are willing to make this great recognition, to engage ourselves to accept and invite the daily, hourly, incessant co-operation of the divine Spirit, in, to put it definitely and plainly, the schoolroom work of our children, how must we shape our own conduct to make this co-operation active, or even possible? We are told that the Spirit is life; therefore, that which is dead, dry as dust, mere bare bones, can have no affinity with Him, can do no other than smother and deaden his vitalising influences. A first condition of this vitalising teaching is that all the thought we offer to our children shall be *living* thought; no mere dry summaries of facts will do; given the vitalising idea, children will readily hang the mere facts upon the idea as upon a peg capable of sustaining all that it is needful to retain. We begin by believing in the children as spiritual beings of unmeasured powers—intellectual, moral, spiritual—capable of receiving and constantly enjoying intuitions from the intimate converse of the Divine Spirit.

Teaching must be Fresh and Living.—With this thought of a child to begin with, we shall perceive that whatever is stale and flat and dull to us must needs be stale and flat and dull to him, and also that there is no subject which has not a fresh and living way of approach. Are we teaching geography? The child discovers with the explorer, journeys with the traveller, receives impressions new and vivid from some other mind which is immediately receiving these impressions; not after they have been made stale and dull by a process of filtering through many intermediate minds, and have found at last their way into a little text-book. Is he learning history? His concern is not with strings of names and of dates, nor with nice little reading-made-easy stories, brought down, as we mistakenly say, to the level of his comprehension; we recognise that his power of comprehension is at least equal to our own, and that it is only his ignorance of the attendant circumstances we have to deal with as luminously as we can.

Books must be Living.—We recognise that history for him is, to live in the lives of those strong personalities which at any given time impress themselves most upon their age and country. This is not the sort of thing to be got out of nice little history books for children, whether 'Little Arthur's,' or somebody's 'Outlines.' We take the child to the living sources of history—a child of seven is fully able to comprehend *Plutarch*, in Plutarch's own words (translated), without any diluting and with little explanation. Give him living thought in this kind, and you make possible the co-operation of the living Teacher. The child's progress is by leaps and bounds, and you wonder why. In teaching music, again, let him once perceive the beautiful laws of harmony, the personality, so to speak, of Music, looking out upon him from among the queer little black notes, and the piano lesson has ceased to be drudgery.

No Neat System is of Use.—It is unnecessary to go further into details; every subject has its living way, with what Coleridge calls 'its guiding idea' at the head, and it is only as we discover this living way in each case that a subject of instruction makes for the education of a child. No neat system is of any use; it is the very nature of a system to grow stale in the using; every subject, every division of a subject, every lesson, in fact, must be brought up for examination before it is offered to the child as to whether it is living, vital, of a nature to invite the living Intellect of the universe.

Children must have the Best Books.—One more thing is of vital importance; children must have books, living books; the best are not too good for them; anything less than the best is not good enough; and if it is needful to exercise economy, let go everything that belongs to soft and luxurious living before letting go the duty of supplying the books, and the frequent changes of books, which are necessary for the constant stimulation of the child's intellectual life. We need not say one word about the necessity for living thought in the teacher; it is only so far as he is intellectually alive that he can be effective in the wonderful process which we glibly call 'education.'

CHAPTER XXVI

THE ETERNAL CHILD

The Highest Counsel of Perfection to Parents

'The Waits!
Slowly they play, poor careful souls,
With wistful thoughts of Christmas cheer,
Unwitting how their music rolls
Away the burden of the year.
And with the charm, the homely rune,
Our thoughts like childhood's thoughts are given,
When all our pulses beat in tune
With all the stars of heaven,'

—JOHN DAVIDSON.

Children necessary to Christmas Joy.—In these levelling days we like to think that everybody has quite equal opportunities in some direction; but Christmas joy, for example, is not for every one in like measure. It is not only that those who are in need, sorrow, or any other adversity do not sit down to the Christmas feast of joy and thanksgiving; for, indeed, a Benjamin's portion is often served to the sorrowful. But it takes the presence of children to help us to realise the idea of the Eternal Child. The Dayspring is with the children, and we think their thoughts and are glad in their joy; and every mother knows out of her own heart's fulness what the Birth at Bethlehem means. Those of us who have not children catch echoes. We hear the wondrous story read in church, the waits chant the tale, the church-bells echo it, the years that are no more come back to us, and our hearts are meek and mild, glad and gay, loving and tender, as those of little children; but, alas, only for the little while occupied by the passing thought. Too soon the dreariness of daily living settles down upon us again, and we become a little impatient, do we not, of the Christmas demand of joyousness.

But it is not so where there are children. The old, old story has all its first freshness as we tell it to the eager listeners; as we listen to it ourselves with their vivid interest it becomes as real and fresh to us as it is to them. Hard thoughts drop away like scales from our eyes; we are young once more with the children's young life, which, we are mysteriously made aware, is the life eternal. What a mystery it is! Does not every mother, made wise unto salvation, who holds a babe in her arms, feel with tremulous awe that, that deep saying is true for her also, 'The same is my mother'?

Every Babe bears an Evangel.—For the little child is the true St Christopher: in him is the light and life of Christ; and every birth is a message of salvation, and a reminder that we, too, must humble ourselves and become as little children. This is, perhaps, the real secret of the world's progress—that every babe comes into the world with an evangel, which witnesses of necessity to his parents' hearts. That we, too, are children, the children of God, that He would have us be as children, is the message that the newborn child never fails to bear, however little we heed, or however soon we forget. It is well that parents should ponder these things, for the child's estate is a holy one, and it is given to his parents to safeguard the little heir of blessedness.

A Child is Humble.—It is not possible to enter fully into so large a subject, but it may be worth while to characterise two or three of the landmarks of this child's estate; for how shall we safeguard that which we do not recognise, and how recognise that to which we have failed to give deliberate attention? The note of childhood is, before all things, humility. What we call innocence is probably resolvable into this grace-repellent to the nature of man until he shall embrace it, and then disclosing itself to him as divine. An old and saintly writer has a luminous thought on this subject of humility.

'There never was nor ever will be, but one humility in the whole world, and that is the one humility of Christ, which never any man, since the fall of Adam, had the least degree of but from Christ. Humility is one, in the same sense and truth as Christ is one, the Mediator is one, Redemption is one. There are not two Lambs of God that take away the sins of the world. But if there was any humility besides that of Christ, there would be something else besides Him that could take away the sins of the world.'[1] Now, if there be but one humility in the whole world, and that humility be the humility of Christ, and if our Lord pronounces the little child also to be humble, is it not because of the indwelling divinity, the glory in the child, which we call innocence?

[1] William Law.

Humility not Relative, but Absolute.—Our common notion of humility is inaccurate. We regard it as a relative quality. We humble ourselves to this one and that, bow to the prince and lord it over the peasant. This is why the grace of humility does not commend itself even to ourselves in our most sincere moods. We feel that this relative humility is hardly consistent with self-respect and due independence of character. We have been taught to recognise humility as a Christian grace, and therefore do not utter our protest; but this misconception confuses our thought on an important subject. For humility is absolute, not relative. It is by no means a taking of our place among our fellows according to a given scale, some being above us by many grades and others as far below. There is no reference to above or below in the humble soul, which is equally humble before an infant, a primrose, a worm, a beggar, a prince.

This, if we think of it, is the state natural to children. Every person and thing commands their interest; but the person or thing in action is deeply interesting. 'May I go and make mud-pies with the boy in the gutter?' prays the little prince, discerning no difference at all; and the little boy in the gutter would meet him with equal frankness.

Children do not make Self-depreciatory Remarks.—What is the secret of this absolute humility, humble alike towards higher or lower, and unaware of distinctions? Our notion of a humble person is one who thinks rather slightingly of himself, who says, deprecatingly, 'Oh, I can't do this or that, you know, I'm not clever'; 'I'm not cut out for public work of any sort, I've no power or influence'; 'Ah!

well, I hope he'll be a better man than his father, I
don't think much of myself anyway'; 'Your children
have great advantages; I wish mine had such a
mother, but I'm not a bit wise.' Such things are
often said, in all sincerity, without the least *soupcon*
of the 'Uriah Heep' sentiment. The thing we
quarrel with is, that the speakers are apt to feel that
they have, anyway, the saving grace of humility. It
is worth while to reflect that there are no such self-
depreciatory utterances ascribed to the Example of
that 'great humility' which we are bound to follow;
and if there is not the slightest evidence of humility
in this kind in the divine life, which was all humility,
we must re-cast our notions. Children, too, never
make self-depreciatory remarks; that is because they
are humble, and with the divine Example before us,
and the example of our children, we may receive it
that humility does not consist in thinking little of
ourselves. It is a higher principle, a blessed state,
only now and then attained by us elders, but in which
the children perpetually dwell, and in which it is the
will of God that we should keep them.

Humility Unconscious of Self.—Humility does
not think much or little of itself; it does not think
of itself at all. It is a negative rather than a
positive quality, being an absence of self-consciousness
rather than the presence of any distinctive virtue. The
person who is unaware of himself is capable of all
lowly service, of all suffering for others, of bright
cheerfulness under all the small crosses and worries
of everyday life. This is the quality that makes
heroes, and this is the quality that makes saints. We
are able to pray, but we are hardly able to worship
or to praise, to say, '*My* soul doth magnify the

Lord,' so long as in the innermost chamber of our hearts we are self-occupied.

The Christian Religion Objective.—The Christian religion is, in its very nature, objective. It offers for our worship, reverence, service, adoration and delight, a Divine Person, the Desire of the world. Simplicity, happiness and expansion come from the outpouring of a human heart upon that which is altogether worthy. But we mistake our own needs, are occupied with our own falls and our own repentances, our manifold states of consciousness. Our religion is subjective first, and after that, so far as we are able, objective. The order should rather be objective first and after that, so far as we have any time or care to think about ourselves, subjective.

Children are Objective in Tendency.—Now, the tendency of children is to be altogether objective, not at all subjective, and perhaps that is why they are said to be first in the kingdom of heaven. This philosophic distinction is not one which we can put aside as having no bearing on everyday life. It strikes the keynote for the training of children. In proportion as our training tends to develop the subjective principle, it tends to place our children on a lower level of purpose, character, and usefulness throughout their lives; while so far as we develop the objective principle, with which the children are born, we make them capable of love, service, heroism, worship.

Every Function may have its Subjective or Objective Development.—It is curious to observe how every function of our most complex nature may have its subjective or its objective development. The child may eat and drink and rest with most absolute disregard of what he is about, his parents taking care that these things are happily arranged for him, but taking equal care that his attention shall not be turned to the pleasures of appetite. But this is a point that we hardly need to dwell upon, as thoughtful parents are agreed that children's meals should be so regularly pleasant and various that the child naturally eats with satisfaction and thinks little or nothing of what he is eating; that is, parents are careful that, in the matter of food, children shall not be self-regardful.

Fortitude.—Perhaps parents are less fully awake to the importance of regulating a child's sensations. We still kiss the place to make it well, make an *obvious* fuss if a string is uncomfortable or a crumpled rose-leaf is irritating the child's tender skin. We have forgotten the seven Christian virtues and the seven deadly sins of earlier ages, and do not much consider in the bringing up of our children whether the grace of fortitude is developing under our training. Now fortitude has its higher and its lower offices. It concerns itself with things of the mind and with things of the body, and, perhaps, it is safe to argue that fortitude on the higher plane is only possible when it has become the habit of the nature on the lower. A baby may be trained in fortitude, and is much the happier for such training. A child should be taught that it is beneath him to take any notice of cold or heat, pain or discomfort. We do not perceive the sensations to which we do not attend, and it is quite possible to forget even a bad toothache in some new and vivid interest. Health and happiness depend largely upon the disregard of sensations, and the child who is encouraged to say, 'I am so cold,' 'I am so tired,' 'My vest pricks me,' and so on, is likely to develop into the hysterical girl or the hypochondriac man; for it is an immutable law, that, as with our appetites, so with our sensations, in proportion as we attend to them will they dominate us until a single sensation of slight pain or discomfort may occupy our whole field of vision, making us unaware that there is any joy in living, any beauty in the earth.

The Self-regardful Child no longer Humble.— But these are the least of the reasons why a child should be trained to put up with little discomforts and take no notice. The child who has been allowed to become self-regardful in the matter of sensations, as of appetites, has lost his child's estate, he is no longer humble; he is in the condition of thinking about himself, instead of that infinitely blessed condition of not being aware of himself at all. Nor must we permit ourselves to make an exception to this rule in the case of the poor little invalid. For him, far more than for the healthy child, it is important that he should be trained to take no account of his sensations; and many a brave little hero suffers anguish without conscious thought, and therefore, of course, suffers infinitely less than if he had been induced to dwell upon his pains. We say, induced, because, though a child may cry with sudden distress, he does not really think about his aches and pains unless his thoughts be turned to his ailments by those about him.

No Spartan Regimen.—I am not advising any Spartan regimen. It is not permitted to us to inflict hardness in order that the children may learn to endure. Our care is simply to direct their consciousness from their own sensations. The well-known

anecdote of the man who, before the days of chloro-
form, had his leg cut off without any conscious sensations of pain, because he determinedly kept his mind
occupied with other things, is an extreme but instructive instance of what may be done in this direction.
At the same time, though the child himself be taught
to disregard them, his sensations should be carefully
watched by his elders, for they must consider and act
upon the danger signals which the child himself must
be taught to disregard. But it is usually possible to
attend to a child's sensations without letting him
know they have been observed.

The Altruistic or Egoistic Direction.—This, of
the sensations, is only one example of the altruistic
or egoistic direction which the various operations of
a child's complex nature may receive. His affections,
again, are capable of receiving a subjective or objective
direction, according to the suggestions which reach
him from without. Every child comes into the world
richly endowed with a well of love, a fountain of
justice; but whether the stream of love shall flow to
the right or the left, whether it shall be egoistic or
altruistic, depends on the child's earliest training.
A child who is taught from the first the delights of
giving and sharing, of loving and bearing, will always
spend himself freely on others, will love and serve,
seeking for nothing again; but the child who recognises
that he is the object of constant attention, consideration, love and service, becomes self-regardful, self-
seeking, selfish, almost without his fault, so strongly
is he influenced by the direction his thoughts receive
from those about him. So, too, of that other fountain,
of justice, with which every child is born. There,
again, the stream may flow forth in either, but not in

both, of the channels, the egoistic or the altruistic. The child's demand for justice may be all for himself, or, from the very first, the rights of others may be kept before his eyes.

'It's not Fair!'—He may be taught to occupy himself with *his own rights and other people's duties,* and, if he is, his state of mind is easily discernible by the catchwords often on his lips, 'It's a shame!' 'It's not fair!' or he may, on the other hand, be so filled with the notion of *his own duties and other people's rights*, that the claims of self slip quietly into the background. This kind cometh forth only by prayer, but it is well to clear our thoughts and know definitely what we desire for our children, because only so can we work intelligently towards the fulfilment of our desire. It is sad to pray, and frustrate the answer by our own action; but this is, alas, too possible.

During each coming festival of the Eternal Child, may parents ponder how best to keep their own children in the blessed child-estate, recollecting that the humility which Christ commends in the children is what may be described, philosophically, as the objective principle as opposed to the subjective, and that, in proportion as a child becomes self-regardful in any function of his being, he loses the grace of humility. This is the broad principle; the practical application will need constant watchfulness and constant efforts, especially in holiday seasons, to keep friends and visitors from showing their love for the children in any way that shall tend to develop self-consciousness.

Humility the Highest Counsel of Perfection.— This, of humility, is not only a counsel of perfection, but is, perhaps, the highest counsel of perfection; and when we put it to parents, we offer it to those for whom no endeavour is too difficult, no aim too lofty; to those who are doing the most to advance the Kingdom of Christ.

Appendix

CHAPTER I

THE FAMILY

1. How and to what did Rousseau succeed in awaking parents?

2. In what respects is the family a commune?

3. Why, and in what ways, must the family be social?

4. Show some ways in which the family must serve poorer neighbours.

5. In what way is it open to the family to serve the nation?

6. What is the divine order for the family as regards other nations?

7. Mention ways of securing fellowship with other nations.

8. What is meant by the phrase 'the restoration of the family'?

9. Add hints from your own experience on each of the points taken up in this chapter.

CHAPTER II

PARENTS AS RULERS

1. In what respects is the family an absolute monarchy?

2. Show that the rule of parents cannot be deputed.

3. Give some causes which lead to the abdication of parents.

4. In what does the majesty of parents consist?

5. Show that children are a public trust and a divine trust.

6. Define the scope and state the limitation of parental authority.

7. Comment and enlarge upon any of the above points from your knowledge and experience.

CHAPTER III

PARENTS AS INSPIRERS

Children must be born again to the Life of Intelligence

1. Explain and verify the statement that parents owe a second birth to their children.

2. Show exactly how science supports this contention.

3. What are the processes and methods of this second birth?

4. Summarise Dr Maudsley's views on heredity.

5. Distinguish between disposition and character.

6. What does Dr Maudsley say regarding the structural effects of 'particular life experiences'?

7. Enumerate the articles of the educational charter which our age may be said to have acquired.

8. Make further comments on any of the above points.

CHAPTER IV

PARENTS AS INSPIRERS

The Life of the Mind grows upon Ideas

1. Summarise the preceding chapter.

2. Why are not the educational conceptions of the past necessarily valid now?

3. Explain and illustrate Pestalozzi's theory.

4. And Froebel's theory.

5. In what way is the kindergarten a vital conception?

6. But science is changing front How does this fact affect educational thought?

7. What bearing has 'heredity' upon education?

8. Is education formative? Discuss the question.

9. Prove that the individual is not at the mercy of empirics. Is this a gain?

10. Why is 'education' an inadequate word?

11. What is the force of 'bringing up'?

12. Give an adequate definition, and show why it is adequate.

13. Show the importance of method as a way to an end.

14. Illustrate the fact that the life of the mind grows upon ideas.

15. What is an idea?

16. Trace the rise and progress of an idea.

17. Illustrate the genesis of an idea.

18. An idea may exist as an 'appetency.' Give examples.

19. Show that a child draws inspiration from the casual life around him.

20. Describe and illustrate the order and progress of definite ideas.

21. What is the Platonic doctrine of ideas?

22. Show that ideas only are important in education.

23. How should the educational formula run?

24. The 'infallible reason'—what is it?

CHAPTER V

PARENTS AS INSPIRERS

The Things of the Spirit

1. Show that parents are necessarily the revealers of God to their children.

2. Show that they must fortify children against doubt.

3. In what three ways may this be attempted?

4. Why is the first unfair?

5. Show that 'evidences' are not proofs.

6. How does their outlook upon current thought affect young people?

7. Show that children have a right to 'freewill' in thought.

8. What may be done in the way of preparation?

9. In what ways should children be taught to wait upon science?

10. Knowledge is progressive. How should this affect our mental attitude?

11. Show that children should learn some laws of thought.

12. Should look at thoughts as they come.

13. Upon what does the appeal of the children rest?

14. Show that children should have the thought of God as a 'hiding-place.'

15. Prove and illustrate from your own experience that the mind of the child is good ground.

16. Is it true that children suffer from a deep-seated discontent? If so, why? Illustrate.

CHAPTER VI

PARENTS AS INSPIRERS

Primal Ideas derived from Parents

1. What is the chief thing we have to do in the world?

2. Name two ideas of God specially fit for children.

3. 'We ought to move slowly up through the human side.' Why not?

4. Distinguish between logical certainty and moral right.

5. How might the Crucifixion have appeared to a conscientious Jew? How, to a patriotic Jew?

6. Show what primal ideas children get from their parents.

7. What have you to say as to the first approaches to God made by a little child?

8. Discuss the question of archaic forms in children's prayers.

9. Show how fit for a child is 'the shout of a King.'

10. Also the notion of the 'fight for Christ against the devil.'

11. "How very hard it is to be a Christian." Is this a child's experience?

CHAPTER VII

THE PARENT AS SCHOOLMASTER

1. What is a schoolmaster supposed to do for a boy?

2. For what various reasons is this task left to the schoolmaster?

3. With what class of children does he succeed?

4. Why does not the discipline of school always affect the life?

5. Discuss 'Edward Waverley' as an example of mental 'sprawling.'

6. Show that we are not meant to grow up in a state of Nature.

7. Prove that the first function of the parent is that of discipline.

8. Show that education is a discipline.

9. Distinguish between discipline and punishment.

10. How are disciples lured?

11. Show that discipline means steady progress on a careful plan.

CHAPTER VIII

THE CULTURE OF CHARACTER

Parents as Trainers

1. How far does *heredity* count?

2. Show the value of opportunity to children.

3. Describe a curious experiment in education.

4. Show that character is an achievement.

5. What two ways have we of preserving sanity?

6. Show that the development of character is the chief work of education.

7. Give some plausible reasons for doing nothing towards character training.

8. How does the advance of science affect the question?

9. What is a parent's duty towards a lovely family trait?

10. Towards distinctive qualities?

11. What are the four conditions of culture?

12. Exemplify in the case of a child with an inherited turn for languages.

13. Show that work and waste of brain tissue are necessary.

14. Point out the danger of eccentricity.

15. Name some causes of oddity in children.

16. How shall we save our 'splendid failures'?

CHAPTER IX

THE CULTURE OF CHARACTER

The Treatment of Defects

1. What is the ultimate object of education?

2. How are parents concerned with 'the defects of their qualities' in their children?

3. Give some cases of children thus 'defective.'

4. Indicate the special treatment in each case.

5. Show that moral ailments need prompt attention.

6. Show that 'one custom overcometh another' is a gospel for parents.

7. In what way is there a material register of educational efforts?

8. Prove that mother-love is not sufficient in itself for child-training.

CHAPTER X

BIBLE LESSONS

Parents as Instructors in Religion

1. Why are Sunday Schools necessary?

2. Show that parents should instruct their own children in religion.

3. Describe an Australian outcome of the Parents' Union.

4. What is the gist of the report of the Committee on the Religious Education of the Upper and Middle Classes?

5. Give a few of the reasons why parents fail to instruct their children in religion.

6. Discuss the discredit thrown upon the Bible.

7. Discuss, 'miracles do not happen.'

8. Show that our conception of God depends upon miracles.

9. Discuss miracles as contrary to natural law.

10. Show how fitting are the miracles of Christ.

CHAPTER XI

FAITH AND DUTY

Parents as Teachers of Morals

1. What does Mr Huxley consider to be the sole practical outcome of education?

2. Have we an infallible sense of 'ought'?

3. Show the educational value of the Bible as a classic literature.

4. How should a mother's diary be useful?

6. Of fables.

7. Of Bible stories.

8. Why should the language of the Bible be used in teaching?

9. Should the stories of miracles be used in moral instruction?

10. Should the whole Bible be put into the hands of a child?

11. Give some moral rules to be gleaned from the Pentateuch.

12. Show the value of the 'Odyssey' and the 'Iliad' in moral teaching.

13. What is the initial weakness of 'secular' morality?

14. What is to be said in favour of lessons on duty?

15. Show the moral value of manual training.

16. Show the danger of slipshod moral teaching.

17. Show the importance of methodical ethical instruction.

CHAPTER XII

FAITH AND DUTY

Claims of Philosophy as an Instrument of Education

1. Show that English educational thought tends towards naturalism.

2. What is Madame de Stael's verdict upon 'Locke'?

3. Show that our educational efforts lack aim.

4. That we are on the verge of chaos.

5. But also on the verge of an educational revolution.

6. Is our system of education to be the issue of naturalism or idealism?

7. What is to be said of the ethical view of education?

8. Show that no attempt has been made to unify education.

9. What are the claims of philosophy as an educational agent?

10. Show that a nation should be educated for its proper functions.

11. How do the minor moralities become easy?

12. How is a habit initiated?

13. Can spirit act upon matter?

14. How is the individuality of children safeguarded?

CHAPTER XIII

FAITH AND DUTY

Man lives by Faith, Godward and Manward

1. Show that 'sacred' and 'secular' is an irreligious classification.

2. How is all intercourse of thought maintained?

3. Why is it obvious and natural that the Father of spirits should deal with the spirits of men?

4. Why is easy tolerance mischievous?

5. Show that man lives by faith in his fellows and in God.

6. Describe faith in God.

7. Show that faith is natural.

8. Is not a self-originated impulse.

9. What have you to say of the worship of faith?

10. How is 'righteousness' defined by the author in question?

CHAPTER XIV

THE HEROIC IMPULSE

Parents are concerned to give this impulse

1. Of what value is heroic poetry in education?

2. Show that Beowulf is our English Ulysses.

3. Show that he represents the English ideal.

4. Illustrate the gentleness of our forefathers

5. Can you give any old English riddles?

CHAPTER XV

IS IT POSSIBLE?

The Attitude of Parents towards Social Questions

1. Show that we are facing a moral crisis.
2. How does this crisis show that we love our brother?
3. How does the 'idol of size' affect us?
4. *Cui bono*? Show the paralysing effect of.
5. Can character be changed?
6. What is the question of the age?
7. What is the essential miracle?
8. Why should hope fail for the vicious by inheritance?
9. For the vicious by inveterate habit?
10. For the vicious in thought?
11. What hope is there in the received doctrine of heredity?
12. Show that education is stronger than nature.
13. That there is *natural* preparation for salvation.
14. That 'conversion' is no miracle.
15. That 'conversion' is not contrary to natural law.
16. That there may be many 'conversions' in a lifetime.
17. Under what conditions is an idea potent?
18. Show the potency and fitness of the ideas included in Christianity.
19. Why is curative *treatment* necessary?
20. Show that a strong organisation may afford relief.
21. Show that work and fresh air are powerful agents.

CHAPTER XVI

DISCIPLINE

A Consideration for Parents

1. What do people commonly mean by discipline?
2. Distinguish between a method and a system.

3. What is to be said for a 'wise passiveness'?

4. Discuss the question of punishment by consequences.

5. Show that children may rather enjoy punishment.

6. Show that wrongdoing is necessarily followed by penalties.

7. Is punishment reformative?

8. What are the best disciplinarians?

9. Comment on the mother who is 'always telling' her children to do so and so.

10. Give nine practical counsels for a parent who wishes to deal seriously with a bad habit.

11. How would you treat an inquisitive child, for instance?

CHAPTER XVII

SENSATIONS AND FEELINGS

Sensations Educable by Parents

1. Show that 'common sense' has usually scientific opinion for its basis.

2. What is the origin of sensations?

3. Show that sensations should be treated as interesting on account of the thing perceived, not of the person who perceives.

4. Why are object-lessons in disfavour?

5. Show that a baby works at object-lessons.

6. What is the effect of Nature's early teaching?

7. What two points must we bear in mind in the education of the senses?

8. Show that object-lessons, to be of value, should be incidental.

9. What advantages has the home in this sort of teaching?

10. How should children be taught care in the use of positive and comparative terms?

11. How would you correct the indiscriminate use of epithets?

12. How would you teach children to form judgments as to weight?

13. As to size?

14. To discriminate sounds?

15. To discriminate odours?

16. To discriminate flavours?

17. Can you suggest some sensory gymnastics?

18. Some sensory games?

CHAPTER XVIII

SENSATIONS AND FEELINGS

Feelings Educable by Parents

1. What do you understand by reflected sensations?

2. Show that we have here a reason why open-air memories should be stored.

3. Show that delightful *memories* are a source of bodily well-being.

4. And of mental restoration.

5. Distinguish between sensations and feelings.

6. Show that feelings should be objective, not subjective.

7. Show what the feelings are and are not.

8. Show that every feeling has its positive and its negative mode.

9. Are the feelings moral or immoral?

10. Show the connection between unremembered feelings and acts.

11. Certain trifling acts may be 'the best portion of a good man's life.' Why so?

12. Is perception of character a feeling?

13. Show its delicacy and importance.

14. Show how feelings influence conduct.

15. Discuss enthusiasm.

16. Give the genesis of our activities.

17. Show that in educating the feelings we modify the character.

18. What is to be said of the sixth sense of *tact*?

19. Why must we beware of words?

20. How is a feeling communicated?

21. What feelings especially differentiate persons?

22. Show that to deal with the feelings of the young is a delicate task.

CHAPTER XIX

WHAT IS TRUTH?

Moral Discrimination required by Parents

1. Show that, as a nation, we are both losing and gaining in truthfulness.

2. What two theories are held with regard to lying?

3. Is lying an elemental or a secondary symptom?

4. How would you treat 'pseudophobia'?

5. 'The lie heroic.'

6. 'Truth for friends, lies for enemies.'

7. 'Lies inspired by selfishness.'

8. 'The deceptions of imagination and play.'

9. 'Pseudomania.'

10. How must children be trained to truthfulness?

CHAPTER XX

SHOW CAUSE WHY

Parents Responsible for Competitive Examinations

1. Mention some points we have gained by asking 'Why?'

2. Why does Tom go to school?

3. Show that the same impulse carries him through school and university.

4. What is the tendency of 'grind'?

5. Show that the tyranny of competitive examinations is supported by parents.

6. Are examinations themselves an evil?

7. Under what conditions should they be held?

8. What are the primary desires?

9. Are they virtuous or vicious?

10. What end do they serve?

11. Show that throughout the schoolboy's life one natural desire takes the place which properly belongs to another.

12. Why does he no longer want to know?

13. How is this a loss to the boy?

14. Show that emulation is an easier spring to work than curiosity.

15. Show that an examination-ridden empire would be a calamity.

CHAPTER XXI

A THEORY OF EDUCATION PROPOSED TO PARENTS

1. How far should the ideal of education be a class ideal?

2. What difference is there between the children of educated and those of ignorant parents as regards vocabulary, imagination, etc.?

3. When is the development of 'faculties' an important part of education, and when is it not so?

4. What are the chief things the educator has to do?

5. Show that it is necessary to recognise the material and spiritual principles of human nature.

6. How does this lead us to recognise the supreme Educator?

7. By what test may the value of studies be judged?

8. Show that 'Nature' knowledge educates a child.

9. What is to be said for the use of good books in education?

10. Discuss the question of 'child-nature'.

11. Why are we tenacious of the individuality of children?

12. Why must we consider proportion in our scheme of education?

13. Show that children have a right to knowledge.

CHAPTER XXII

A CATECHISM OF EDUCATIONAL THEORY

1. Show that character is an achievement.

2. What gives rise to conduct?

3. What means have we of modifying disposition?

4. Give the history of a habit.

5. How may a bad habit be corrected?

6. Show that our conduct is generally directed by unconscious, or sub-conscious cerebration.

7. How far do the habits of a 'well-brought-up' person make life easy for him?

8. Why does the forming of a habit demand time?

9. Trace the logical development of a notion.

10. Show that reason is not an infallible guide to conduct.

11. Show how confusion as to logical and moral right works in the history of the world.

12. Why, then, should a child know what he is as a human being?

13. Show how far such knowledge is a safeguard.

14. What is the part of the will in the reception of ideas?

15. How are ideas conveyed?

16. What may we believe is the part of the divine Educator in things natural and spiritual?

17. What part do lessons play in education?

18. What principle as regards a curriculum do we find in a child's natural aptitude for knowledge?

CHAPTER XXIII

WHENCE AND WHITHER

A Question for Parents. Whence?

1. What was the leading thought about children in the past generation?

2. What intellectual labour does a child go through in his first year?

3. Remark on the intelligence of children.

4. Show that they are highly endowed but ignorant.

5. Choose between 'happy and good' and 'good and happy' as an educational maxim.

6. By what test would you try various systems of education?

7. Show the duty of advancing with the tide.

CHAPTER XXIV

WHENCE AND WHITHER

A Question for Parents. Whither?

1. How are children great?

2. What is wisdom?

3. Show that children grow in wisdom rather than in intelligence.

4. Show that all possibilities are present in a child.

5. Show that we all live for the advancement of the race.

6. Show that we find our '*whence*' in the potency of the child.

7. Our '*whither*' in the thought of the day.

8. How should the thought of the day affect education with regard to science?

9. With regard to art?

10. With regard to books?

11. How should the idea of the *solidarity* of the race affect education?

12. How may we teach children that to serve is promotion?

13. How shall we guard them from considerations of expediency?

CHAPTER XXV

THE GREAT RECOGNITION REQUIRED OF PARENTS

1. Show that education is not religious and secular.

2. Show that knowledge, like virtue, is from above.

3. Have we any authority for thinking that science, art and poetry are 'by the Spirit'?

4. Have we any teaching as to the origin of the first ideas of common things?

5. Show that divine teaching waits upon our co-operation.

6. What manner of teaching invites and what repels divine co-operation?

7. Show that this 'recognition' resolves certain discords in our lives.

8. How does it safeguard us from intellectual sin?

9. How does it lead to harmony in our efforts?

10. Why must teaching be fresh and living?

11. Why must books be living?

12. Why can we not get rid of our responsibility by using some neat system?

13. Why must children read the best books?

CHAPTER XXVI

THE ETERNAL CHILD

The Highest Counsel of Perfection for Parents

1. Show that every babe bears an evangel.

2. Show that a child is humble.

3. That humility is not relative but absolute.

4. Show that the Christian religion is objective.

5. That children are objective in tendency.

6. Show that our care must be to give every function an objective and not a subjective employment.

7. What part should fortitude play in education?

8. Show that the self-regardful child is no longer humble.

9. Show that the tendencies of children may receive an altruistic or an egoistic direction.

10. How does this apply to the cry,—'It's not fair'?

11. Show that humility is the highest counsel of perfection.

Index